Selling Your Private Company

The **Value Enhancement Framework**™ for Business Owners

Howard E. Johnson
MBA, FCMA, CA, CBV, CPA, CFA, ASA

Library and Archives Canada Cataloguing in Publication

Johnson, Howard E.
Selling your private company : the value enhancement framework for business owners / Howard E. Johnson.

ISBN 1-55385-164-1

1. Sale of business enterprises—Canada. 2. Private companies—Canada. I. Canadian Institute of Chartered Accountants II. Title.

HD1393.4.C3J63 2005 658.1'64'0971 C2005-903022-4

Veracap Corporate Finance Limited
34 St. Patrick Street, Suite 400
Toronto, Ontario M5T 1V1

www.veracap.com

Printed and bound in Canada.

Preface

It takes a special kind of individual to build a successful private company. Over the past many years, I have had the privilege of working with some of Canada's foremost business owners, and I have learned a great deal from these experiences.

These business owners take pride in what they accomplish, and so they should. They make considerable sacrifices to build strong companies. For many, the company becomes an integral part of their being. As with a son or daughter who they raise and nurture, in building the company they experience growing pains and misadventures, as well as breakthroughs and successes. Not surprisingly, selling their company is often an emotionally charged process. Not only is it difficult to let go, but also for the majority of business owners, the transaction represents the single largest monetary event of their lifetime.

Despite the impact it will have on their lives, many business owners do not prepare for the eventuality of succession. As a result, they often fail to realize full value for their company. Often this is because the owner does not recognize that the sale of a privately held company is a complex and time-consuming endeavour. Accordingly, business owners need to engage trusted, experienced advisors who can help them navigate the challenges and implications of the selling process.

When addressing the succession issue, business owners are faced with a host of fundamental questions such as:

- When is a good time to sell my company?
- What should I do to prepare for the sale?
- What is my company worth?
- Who are the most likely buyers?
- What information about my company should I provide to buyers?
- Should I sell the shares or the net assets of my company?

- What negotiating strategies should I use to get the best deal?
- How do I ensure that the transaction proceeds smoothly?

This book provides straightforward, practical guidance on these and other important issues. Central to this book is the *Value Enhancement Framework™*, which is designed to help business owners understand what they can do at each stage of the private company sale process in order to maximize the value ultimately realized upon the sale.

Value enhancement is more than just a set of isolated initiatives. It represents a fundamental business philosophy. Importantly, many of the value enhancement initiatives contained in this book can be carried out independent of the sale process. For those business owners who are not currently thinking about selling, it is still important for them to understand what steps they can take today to increase the value of their company and prepare themselves for an unsolicited offer or a sudden change in their personal circumstances that lead to a sale.

Value is a subjective concept, and value enhancement creation and realization involves more than just increasing the purchase price for a company. The economic terms of the deal, including when, how, and under what conditions payment is received, have a significant impact on value. In addition, the intangible aspects of the deal must be considered, such as the provisions in a management contract and non-competition agreement, as well as other terms and conditions of the deal that impact the business owner's feeling of self-fulfillment. When a transaction is completed the business owner must be satisfied that it has been done on the best terms possible and that they have achieved their personal and financial goals. Helping business owners to realize their goals is the underlying objective of this book.

Howard E. Johnson
April 18, 2005

Acknowledgements

I would like to thank the following individuals who contributed to the development of this book:

- Ian Campbell, founder of Campbell Valuation Partners Limited, for his advice in preparing this book and for his guidance over the years, which has helped me in expanding my knowledge and abilities in the field of business valuation;
- Dennis Roberts, Chairman of The McLean Group, LLC for his advice, input and support, which has helped me in formalizing many of the concepts set out in this book;
- my colleagues, Andrew Pigott and Chris Polson for their editorial comments;
- Peter Hoult, Maggie Tyson, Tracey Jones, Susan Smith and Sheri Allen of the Canadian Institute of Chartered Accountants for their support in producing and launching this book;
- Donna Henhoeffer and Brenda Makela for their administrative assistance; and
- my colleagues, Chris Nobes, Tom Tsiokos, Dennis Leung and Lynn Smith for their support.

Howard E. Johnson

Dedication

To my wonderful family – my Mother, the late Lorraine Johnson, my Father, Howard Senior, my wife Julie and our four precious children, Veronica, Michael, Laura and Russell. May I never become so preoccupied in my work that I forget what is truly important in my life.

About the Author

Howard E. Johnson, MBA, FCMA, CA, CBV, CPA, CFA, ASA

Howard is President of Veracap Corporate Finance Limited (www.veracap.com), which specializes in shareholder value enhancement. Veracap is an affiliate of Campbell Valuation Partners Limited, Canada's longest established independent business valuation firm. Howard has advised numerous business owners throughout Canada and beyond on matters dealing with business valuation, and has helped them in enhancing shareholder value in the sale of their privately held company.

Howard is co-author of *The Valuation of Business Interests* (Canadian Institute of Chartered Accountants, 2001), co-editor of *Canada Valuation Service* (Thomson-Carswell, periodical) and is a frequent speaker at conferences held throughout North America on the subjects of business valuation, acquisitions and divestitures.

Howard holds a Bachelor of Commerce Degree from Concordia University (Governor General's Award, 1988), a Graduate Diploma in Public Accountancy from McGill University (Kenneth F. Byrd Prize, 1989) and a Masters Degree in Business Administration from McMaster University (D.M. Heddon Gold Medal, 1992). He is a Fellow of the Society of Management Accountants of Canada and a member of the Canadian Institute of Chartered Accountants, the Canadian Institute of Chartered Business Valuators, the American Institute of Certified Public Accountants, the Chartered Financial Analysts Institute and the American Society of Appraisers.

Howard is an avid hockey player. He currently resides in Oakville, Ontario with his wife, Julie, and their four children, Veronica, Michael, Laura and Russell.

Table of Contents

Disclaimer

The Private Company Sale Process

Section I

SECTION I

The Private Company Sale Process

Overview of this Book

The purpose of this book is to provide business owners with a straightforward and practical guide to the stages involved in the private company sale process and what they can do when planning for and executing the sale to better achieve their personal and financial objectives. The discussion in this book revolves around the *Value Enhancement Framework™*. In brief, the *Value Enhancement Framework™* is a synthesis of the keys to value enhancement in each stage of the private company sale process that business owners should focus on in order to increase the value that ultimately is realized. In this context, value encompasses not only the stated purchase price, but also the terms of the deal, which influence both economic value and the intangible aspects of value that are unique to every business owner.

This section provides an overview of the eight stages in the private company sale process (sometimes simply referred to as the "sale process") and the components that make up each of those stages. The general time frame of the private company sale process and an overview of value enhancement within that process are also addressed. Section II provides a detailed discussion of value enhancement and introduces the *Value Enhancement Framework™*. In Section III, Stages 1 through 8 examine value enhancement initiatives within each of the eight stages of the private company sale process. Finally, Section IV recaps the concepts presented throughout this book and discusses some of the mistakes commonly made by business owners when selling a privately held company.

While this book is intended to provide business owners with a sound understanding of the stages involved in the private company sale process and value enhancement initiatives, it is by no means exhaustive. Every transaction is unique. Therefore, it is essential that appropriate legal, income tax and other professional advice be obtained in each case.

The principles, practices and value enhancement initiatives described in this book apply to almost any type of business, from manufacturers to service companies, and from old economy to new. That said, the discussion in this book is geared toward owners of mid-size Canadian privately held companies. While there is no strict definition of what constitutes a mid-size privately held company in Canada, it generally is regarded as an established company generating annual revenues in the range of $5 million to $200 million.

While much of what is presented in this book could apply to small businesses (for example, convenience stores, dry cleaners and small consulting firms), the practical dynamics of transactions involving small businesses frequently are different. This is due, in part, to the fact that many small businesses are "lifestyle" companies, where the buyer often is an individual who is to some degree "buying a job", as opposed to making an economic investment. In addition, some of the value enhancement initiatives described in this book may not be cost-beneficial on a smaller scale.

Transactions involving the sale of publicly held companies also differ in some respects, mainly due to public equity market regulations. Again, while much of what is set out herein can be applied to public companies, important differences necessitate additional considerations that are not addressed in this book.

This book is written based on the following underlying assumptions about the company being sold (referred to throughout this book as the "company"):

- it will be marketed for sale to one or more third party buyers, as opposed to a pre-arranged family or management buyout or a transaction among existing or related shareholders, where external parties are excluded from the competitive bidding process. While much of the discussion in this book can apply to "internal sales", there normally are other important considerations that must be addressed in such transactions;

- it operates as a "going concern". That is, the buyer believes that the company will generate positive cash flows and remain a viable operating entity over the longer term, as contrasted to a company whose assets will be liquidated on a piecemeal basis;
- it is being sold *en bloc* (i.e., all shareholders are willing to sell their respective interests) or a majority of the voting shares are being sold. This is in contrast to a sale of a minority share interest (or "non-controlling interest") in the company. Depending on the circumstances, the sale of a minority interest in a privately held company may be subject to a substantial discount from its pro-rata portion of *en bloc* value to reflect lack of control and/or illiquidity; and
- it is a privately held Canadian company, although the buyer may be located in Canada, the U.S. or overseas. This assumption does not impact on the private company sale process itself, but rather on some of the discussions surrounding income taxation and certain value enhancement initiatives.

Stages of the Private Company Sale Process

As illustrated in Exhibit I-1, there are eight stages involved in selling a privately held company. Each of these stages is comprised of three components, as discussed below.

Exhibit I-1

THE PRIVATE COMPANY SALE PROCESS

STAGE	COMPONENTS
1. Deciding When to Sell	(i) The Owner's Personal Situation (ii) Economic and Industry Conditions (iii) Company Performance and Prospects
2. Preparing for the Sale	(i) Operational and Financial Structuring (ii) Income Tax and Estate Planning (iii) Transaction Advisors
3. Estimating Value and Price	(i) Cash Flows and Valuation Methodologies (ii) Rates of Return and Valuation Multiples (iii) The Company's Financial Position
4. The Search for Buyers	(i) Identifying Prospective Buyers (ii) Qualifying Prospective Buyers (iii) Initial Buyer Contact
5. Preliminary Due Diligence	(i) The Confidential Information Memorandum (ii) Initial Buyer Meetings (iii) Other Information and Procedures
6. Deal Structuring	(i) Shares vs. Net Assets (ii) Forms and Terms of Payment (iii) The Management Contract
7. Negotiations	(i) Preparing for Negotiations (ii) Negotiating Strategies and Tactics (iii) The Letter of Intent
8. Closing	(i) Detailed Due Diligence (ii) The Purchase Agreement (iii) Final Closing

While the stages and components summarized above and discussed throughout this book usually are encountered when selling a privately held company, every transaction is unique. A set formula for selling a privately held company does not exist. The various stages and components may be bypassed, combined, extended or changed, depending on the circumstances. Business owners and their team of advisors need to approach the transaction with flexibility in order to remain in control of the sale process and thereby improve the likelihood of maximizing the value realized.

Stage 1 — Deciding When to Sell

As a first step, the business owner must decide if they want to sell their company, and when is the appropriate time to do so. The decision of whether and when to sell can arise from a lengthy and well-structured planning process, or it can result from an unexpected event, such as failing health or an unsolicited purchase offer.

Where the decision has been made to sell to a third party, aside from pressing circumstances that dictate otherwise, the business owner must consider the timing of the sale. As discussed later in Stage 1, the three factors influencing this decision are the:

(i) owner's personal situation and circumstances, including their personal interests, health, family situation, financial resources and other pertinent factors. Business owners who are active in the company should consider how long they are prepared to remain active, and in what capacity, following the sale. This may influence the price that a buyer will pay for the company and the terms of the deal;
(ii) current and forecast economic and industry conditions, which influence the number of potential buyers at any given time, their ability to transact and the prices they are willing to pay; and
(iii) company's recent and prospective operating and financial performance. Companies tend to be more readily saleable where they have demonstrated strong operational and financial performance in the years immediately prior to sale and where the outlook for future performance is favourable.

Stage 2 — Preparing for the Sale

After the decision to sell has been made, the preparation process begins. As discussed later in Stage 2, the three major elements for the business owner to consider when preparing for the sale of their company are:

(i) changes to the operating and financial structure of the company in order to make it more attractive to prospective buyers;
(ii) personal income tax and estate planning for the owner and their family. These initiatives can generate considerable income tax savings for the owner upon the sale of the company. Pre-sale planning may also improve

the owner's flexibility when structuring a deal with buyers, which in turn may increase the price that a buyer is willing to pay and/or improve the terms of a deal; and

(iii) engaging a team of advisors who will assist in the sale process. This usually includes a lawyer, income tax expert, transaction intermediary and possibly other professionals.

A great deal of effort should go into preparing for the sale of the company, as it creates the foundation on which value enhancement can be achieved. Ideally, preparations should begin one to three years prior to the time that prospective buyers are actively solicited. However, as a practical matter, critical initiatives often are left too late, particularly where the decision to sell arises suddenly due to health issues or an unsolicited purchase offer. It is advisable for business owners to be proactive in terms of personal income tax and estate planning and business structuring, even if they do not anticipate selling their company in the foreseeable future. Such advance planning initiatives allow business owners to be prepared for situations and opportunities that may arise unexpectedly.

Stage 3 — Estimating Value and Price

After the business owner has decided when to sell, and in many cases as part of that decision process, they normally want to know what their company is worth. Unfortunately, it is not possible to accurately predict what price a company might fetch in the open market. This is because the price paid is influenced by numerous factors that are unknown at the outset of the sale process. Such factors include the number and quality of prospective buyers, the negotiating strength and abilities of the buyer, seller and their respective representatives, the terms of the deal and other factors that are unique to each transaction.

Furthermore, there may be a significant difference between the "intrinsic" value of the company and the price paid for the company in the open market. The company's intrinsic value represents the value of its existing operations as a stand-alone entity, viewed independently of whether or not a sale takes place. The price actually paid for the company in the open market may reflect some amount of post-acquisition synergies that a buyer expects to realize by combining the company with its existing operations. The ability for a business owner to realize a "premium" over the intrinsic value of the company in respect of synergies is, to a large extent, a function of how effectively the company is marketed for sale, how much is known about the operations and strategy of prospective buyers, recent open market transactions involving similar businesses, each party's negotiating strength and abilities, and the structure of the deal. Depending on these things, the "premium for synergies" could represent a small component or a large component of the actual purchase price.

It usually is helpful for a business owner to obtain advice as to the likely range of the company's intrinsic equity value (i.e., the value of the company's shares or net assets) and the price they can expect to receive prior to exposing the company for sale in the open market. When conducted at a sufficiently early stage in the sale process, an independent valuation can assist the business owner in understanding the key "value drivers", which may allow them to take action to proactively increase the intrinsic equity value of the company. As discussed later in Stage 3, from a technical standpoint, the determinants of the equity value for a company that operates as a going concern is a function of the:

(i) cash flow the company is expected to generate in the future;
(ii) rate of return (or its reciprocal, which is referred to as a 'valuation multiple') applied to the expected cash flow, which is influenced by the perceived risk level, growth prospects and debt capacity of the company; and
(iii) company's financial position, which reflects the amount of debt used to finance its operations, the adequacy of its net operating assets and other assets that may exist.

Stage 4 — The Search for Buyers

Once preparations for the sale have been completed and the business owner has an indication of the company's intrinsic equity value and the price that might be obtained, the next stage is to search for prospective buyers. At this point, the process of actively marketing the company for sale begins and the business owner transitions from being an operator of the company (either passively or actively) to a seller. As discussed later in Stage 4, the search for buyers consists of:

(i) identifying prospective buyers, which may include competitors, customers, suppliers, organizations with complementary products and services and possibly organizations from outside of the industry in which the company operates. Financial buyers also are gaining more of a presence as acquirers of mid-size privately held companies in Canada;

(ii) research to determine which of the buyers that have been identified represent quality prospects. This involves developing an initial indication as to why each buyer might be interested in the company, the synergies it might perceive to exist and its ability to consummate a transaction that would be acceptable to the seller; and

(iii) making initial contact with prospective buyers. Initial contact must be done in a way that captures the interest of qualified prospects. Buyers that are interested in receiving more information about the company are asked to execute a non-disclosure agreement (NDA).

Stage 5 — Preliminary Due Diligence

Buyers who execute a satisfactory non-disclosure agreement are given the opportunity to conduct preliminary due diligence on the company. As discussed later in Stage 5, preliminary due diligence consists of:

(i) a confidential information memorandum prepared by the seller (or more likely the seller's intermediary), which contains summary information regarding the company in terms of its operations, financial position, competitive advantages, and so on;

(ii) initial meetings between the seller and prospective buyers to discuss the operations, risks, prospects and financial results of the company in greater detail. As a general comment, the discussion at the initial meetings should focus on the operations of the company as opposed to valuation, pricing and deal structuring; and

(iii) other documentation and procedures, including more detailed financial and operational information as well as summary information regarding the company's major contracts, customers, technology and so on. Preliminary due diligence may also involve plant tours and other procedures that offer prospective buyers a better understanding of the company's operations.

Preliminary due diligence should be done in a piecemeal fashion, whereby the seller initially releases general information about the company and more sensitive information is released as discussions with a particular buyer move forward. This mitigates against highly sensitive information (such as details of customer pricing strategies) being released prematurely, in circumstances where such information may be harmful to the company in the event that a transaction with that particular buyer does not proceed.

During the preliminary due diligence stage, the seller should be performing due diligence on the buyer in order to better understand the buyer's motivations and the price it might be willing to pay. This includes analysis of public information and any non-public information regarding the buyer's operations and financial position that can be obtained during the initial buyer meetings or that the buyer otherwise provides to the seller.

Stage 6 — Deal Structuring

The terms of any deal are just as important, and perhaps even more important, as the stated purchase price for the company. The manner in which a deal is structured will dictate if and when the proceeds of the sale are received and the income tax implications to the seller. The structure of the deal can also affect the intangible aspects of value that are important to the business owner, such as the length of time they must remain actively involved with the company following the sale.

Deal structuring can be complex, and it often requires the assistance of lawyers, income tax experts and other advisors. As discussed later in Stage 6, deal structuring revolves around three major areas, being:

(i) whether the shares or the net assets of the company are sold. As a general rule, buyers prefer to buy assets because of the benefits available in terms of income tax savings and reduced liability. However, sellers generally prefer to sell shares, as it usually results in a reduced tax burden on the sale. Therefore, parties to a transaction usually will negotiate a different purchase price depending on whether the shares or the net assets of the company are sold;

(ii) the forms and terms of payment. Seldom is the stated purchase price for a privately held company entirely paid in cash at closing. The forms and terms of payment can vary widely and might include hold-backs, seller take-backs, share exchanges, earnouts, and other non-cash forms of consideration. The forms and terms of payment dictate the amount that will (or may) be paid to the seller, the timing of payment, the conditions for payment and the risks of non-payment, all of which have a significant impact on the value that ultimately is received; and

(iii) the management contract. Most buyers of privately held companies want the seller (where that person was actively involved in the company prior to the sale) to remain with the company for a period of time following the transaction to ensure a smooth transition. However, the time frame, nature and extent of the seller's post-divestiture involvement can vary substantially. In addition, the compensation and incentives paid to the seller as part of the post-transaction management contract effectively may incorporate a portion of the purchase price for the company. It is important that the seller be satisfied with the post-transaction arrangements in terms of the time period involved, their responsibilities and the basis of compensation, as these things influence both the economic and intangible aspects of value in the transaction.

Stage 7 — Negotiations

While rigorous analysis is needed to determine what a company might be worth, the price and the terms of the deal are ultimately derived through negotiation. As discussed later in Stage 7, there are three key components to the negotiation stage:

(i) preparing for negotiations. This includes research and analysis to understand the buyer's business, the reasons for its interest and the price that it might be willing to pay. Preparation also involves deciding who should be involved in the negotiations from the seller's side, what information should and should not be provided, and an objective assessment of the relative negotiating strength of the buyer and seller;

(ii) formulating the strategies and tactics that will be adopted during the course of the negotiations. The negotiating strategies and tactics adopted are, to a large extent, a function of the seller's perceived negotiating strength relative to that of the buyer; and

(iii) drafting the letter of intent (LOI). The LOI sets out the framework of the offer with respect to price, forms and terms of payment and other significant parameters of the proposed deal. While the LOI is not legally binding, it is critical in that it establishes expectations and sets the tone for subsequent negotiations. Once the seller agrees to the LOI, the buyer usually is granted the opportunity to conduct detailed due diligence and to negotiate a purchase agreement with the seller on an exclusive basis for an agreed period of time.

Stage 8 — Closing

Following the execution of an LOI, the transaction moves to closing. As discussed later in Stage 8, closing consists of:

(i) detailed due diligence. This involves a comprehensive review of the operational, financial, and other aspects of the company so that the buyer can determine whether the proposed deal as set out in the LOI is satisfactory in light of all the pertinent facts. Detailed due diligence normally involves such things as the inspection of customer contracts, an analysis of employee payroll, discussions with key employees and other procedures that the buyer considers necessary in order to satisfy itself that its assumptions about the company are valid and to detect if there are any issues or risks that previously had not been identified;

(ii) the purchase agreement. This represents the legally binding contract for the sale of the company. The purchase agreement is a comprehensive document that addresses all aspects of the deal. It includes representations and warranties of both the buyer and the seller, which in and of themselves can have a material impact on the value received by the seller. Other agreements are drafted concurrently, such as the non-competition agreement. The negotiation of the purchase agreement and related agreements is affected by the buyer's findings in its detailed due diligence investigation and by the perceived relative negotiating position of the buyer and seller at that time; and

(iii) the final closing. This usually takes place at an attorney's office in the weeks following the execution of the purchase agreement. While the final closing normally is a formality, unexpected challenges and last-minute negotiations sometimes do occur that can affect the terms of the deal, or even if the deal closes at all. Following the closing date, a final audit of the company's financial statements is completed, which may result in adjustments to the purchase price.

Time Line of the Private Company Sale Process

The process of selling a private company is time-consuming and complex. Most transactions take between six months to a year (or longer) from the time that prospective buyers are identified and contacted to the time that the deal is closed. In addition, prior to exposing their company for sale in the open market, many business owners spend months or years deciding when to sell and in preparing for the sale.

The time line for the sale of a privately held company can be divided into two broad phases: the planning phase and the execution phase. A general guideline for the timing of the private company sale process is depicted in Exhibit I-2.

Exhibit I-2

TIMELINE FOR THE PRIVATE COMPANY SALE PROCESS

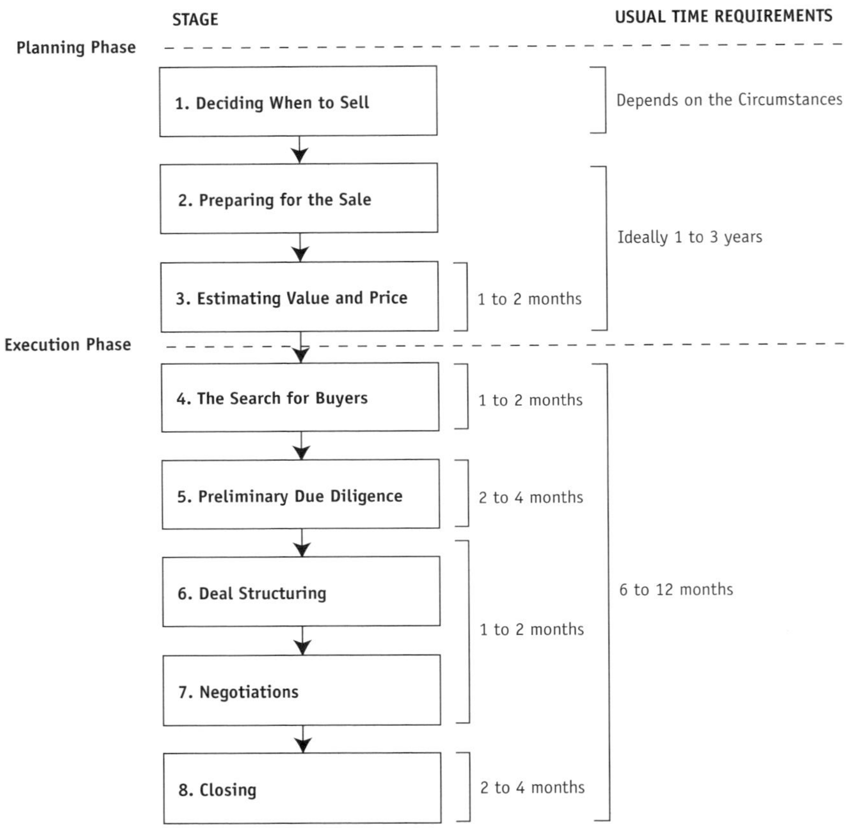

The planning phase involves those stages undertaken prior to the time that the company is exposed for sale in the open market. This includes deciding when to sell, preparing for the sale and estimating value and price. The time horizon of the planning phase can vary significantly, depending on the specific circumstances. The time that a business owner spends in deciding when to sell can range from a few days to a few years. Preparing for the sale normally should take one to three years to complete. Concurrent with presale preparation, the business owner should engage an independent business valuation expert or request their intermediary to estimate the value of the company and the price it might fetch in the open market. The valuation stage normally takes around one to two months to complete. During that time, prospective buyers are identified and information is gathered that will be needed for the confidential information memorandum and preliminary due diligence. Therefore, some degree of overlap between the stages of the private company sale process does exist.

The execution phase begins when the seller and their intermediary actively begin searching for buyers. The time line for the execution phase tends to be more defined than the planning phase. The formal buyer search, including initial contact and securing NDA's with buyers, normally takes around one to two months to complete. Preliminary due diligence usually is completed in the two to four months that follow. The time line for deal structuring and negotiations, which go hand in hand, generally is shorter. These stages together normally take about one to two months and ideally result in the consummation of an agreed LOI. Closing of the deal, including detailed due diligence, negotiating and drafting the purchase agreement and final closing, normally occurs within two to four months after an agreed LOI. Therefore, in aggregate, the execution phase of the private company sale process normally takes between six months to a year to complete.

While some deals may transpire more quickly than the time line set out above, the business owner must be satisfied that they are not rushing into a transaction and hence compromising the value that is received. Conversely, companies that are actively marketed for sale for significantly longer than a year often face challenges due to changing business and industry conditions, which can make such transactions more difficult to close. This does not suggest that a company must be sold within a year, but rather that the seller and their intermediary must keep the sale process moving forward in order to realize value enhancement.

An Integrated Process

While this book examines the private company sale process as a series of distinct stages and components, it is important to recognize that these stages and components overlap, and each stage must be viewed in the context of the entire process. This concept is illustrated in Exhibit I-3.

Exhibit I-3

THE PRIVATE COMPANY SALE PROCESS: AN INTEGRATED VIEWPOINT

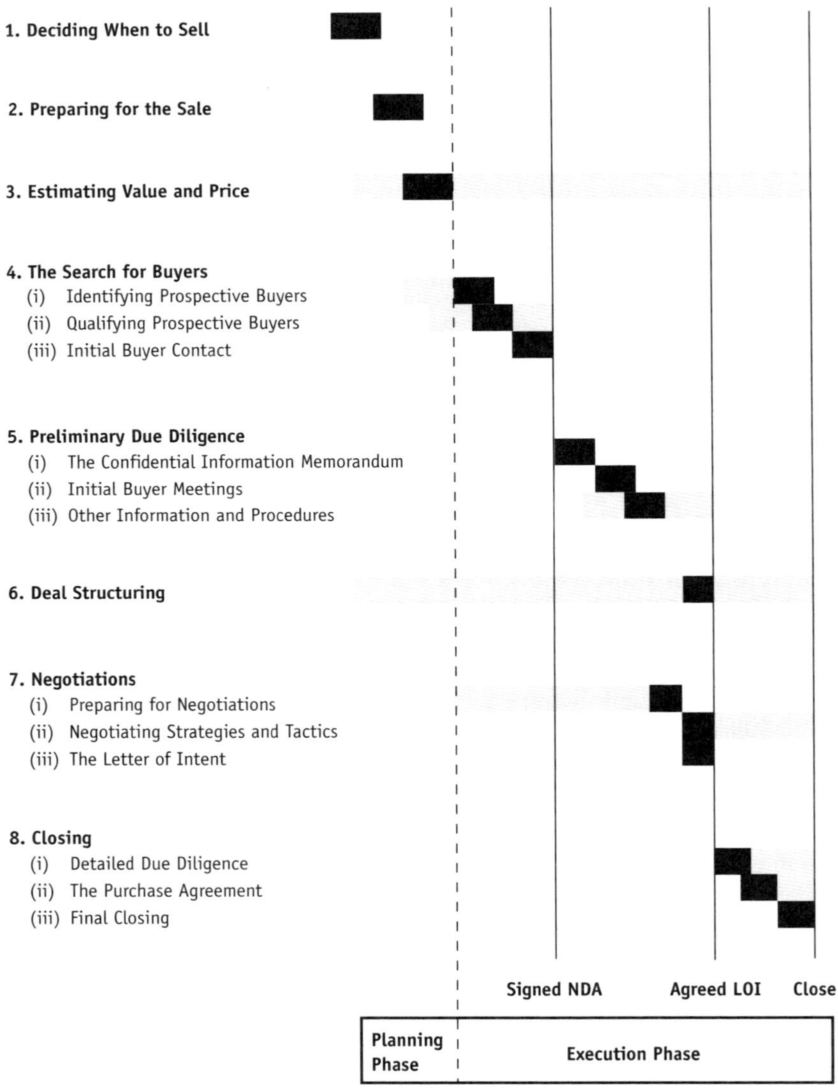

The first two stages, deciding when to sell and preparing for the sale, usually are sequential. While estimating value and price normally is done concurrently with preparing for the sale, the essence of that stage and the underlying value drivers are evident throughout the entire sale process. The business owner often obtains an estimate of value and price when determining if and when to sell their company. Furthermore, estimates of value and price constantly are being considered and revisited throughout the execution phase, from the time that prospective buyers are sought to the time that the deal is closed.

The components of the search for buyers stage, which include identifying prospective buyers, qualifying prospective buyers and initial buyer contact, are relatively sequential in and of themselves. That said, the identification of prospective buyers normally has its roots in the planning phase, when preparing for the sale and estimating value and price. Furthermore, much of the process of identifying and qualifying prospective buyers is done concurrently.

Following the receipt of an NDA, the process moves to the preliminary due diligence stage. Sending a confidential information memorandum to prospective buyers is the first component of that stage, which usually is followed by initial buyer meetings. Other documentation provided and procedures undertaken during the preliminary due diligence stage normally occurs in conjunction with (or sometimes even prior to) initial buyer meetings. Other documentation and procedures extends through the negotiation stage, as the seller provides additional information to buyers with whom an LOI is being negotiated.

While the deal structuring stage formally occurs in conjunction with negotiations, as a practical matter it extends across the entire sale process. Deal structuring considerations should commence in the planning phase, as the business owner contemplates what forms of consideration and deal terms would be acceptable to them. It extends through the early stages of the execution phase, as the seller and their intermediary gain a better understanding of marketplace demand during the search for buyers and a buyer's expectations in the preliminary due diligence stage. Finally, deal structuring considerations remain a top-of-mind issue when negotiating the purchase agreement through to final closing.

While the negotiations stage formally follows preliminary due diligence, preparation for negotiations are made well before that time. Specifically, preparations for negotiations begin when prospective buyers are first being identified, qualified and contacted in terms of understanding their needs and interests. Preparation for negotiations also occurs during the preliminary due diligence stage as the seller gathers additional information on each buyer's needs, interests and relative negotiating position. Negotiation strategies and tactics are used when negotiating the LOI with buyers. While the signing of an agreed LOI represents a definitive milestone, the use of negotiation strategies and tactics carries through to the negotiation of the purchase agreement and final closing.

The first component of the closing stage is the buyer's detailed due diligence investigation. However, the seller should recognize that the buyer's detailed due diligence normally continues all the way through to the final closing. The purchase agreement normally is negotiated and drafted concurrent with detailed due diligence, although there may be modifications to that agreement leading up to the final closing.

It is important for the business owner and their advisors to understand the integrated nature of the private company sale process, to ensure that opportunities for striking a good deal are capitalized on, and to modify the process as required in order to meet the fact-specific circumstances that prevail in any given transaction.

Value Enhancement Within the Private Company Sale Process

The shares or underlying assets of a company that operates as a going concern have an intrinsic economic value. However, the determination of both intrinsic value and the possible sale price is subjective. Both are a function of economic variables that are subject to varying underlying assumptions. In addition, there are non-quantifiable elements that every business owner should consider when entering into a transaction. These things, which are unique to each individual, have an impact on the intangible value received by the business owner.

Value (and by extension, value enhancement) refers to more than just the stated purchase price for a company. It also is a function of the terms on which the deal is struck. As noted earlier in this Section and as discussed in detail in Stage 6, deal structuring involves whether the shares or the net assets of the company are sold, the forms and terms of payment and the terms of the post-transaction management contract and related agreements between the seller and the buyer. Therefore, the structure of a deal has implications on both the economic aspects and the intangible aspects of value to the seller.

Maximizing value from the sale of a private company requires that the business owner and their team of advisors undertake both initiatives that set the foundation for value enhancement creation and initiatives that serve to achieve value enhancement realization. The ability to create and realize value enhancement within the private company sale process lies in the adequacy of planning for the sale and the effectiveness with which the sale of the company is executed. These issues are addressed in the next section.

Summary

The process of selling a privately held company can be lengthy and complex. Ideally, planning for the sale should begin at least one to three years prior to the time the company is exposed for sale in the open market. This should allow sufficient time for the business owner to decide if and when to sell, prepare for the sale and obtain an objective assessment of value and price.

When considering the timing of the sale, the business owner should reflect on their own personal situation, economic and industry conditions and the company's recent performance and future prospects. Adequate preparation for the sale in terms of operational and financial structuring as well as the owner's personal income tax and estate planning is instrumental to creating an attractive organization and structuring a tax-efficient transaction. The business owner should retain competent, objective advisors to help guide them through the private company sale process. Estimating the value and price that the shares or net assets of the company might fetch is a function of its prospective cash flows, the rate of return (or valuation multiple) applied to those cash flows and its current financial position.

The execution phase of the private company sale process normally takes between six months and a year (or longer) to complete. This includes the search for buyers, preliminary due diligence, deal structuring, negotiations and closing.

The search for buyers involves identifying prospective buyers, qualifying those prospects and making initial contact. Buyers that execute an NDA are afforded the opportunity to conduct preliminary due diligence on the company, which consists of the confidential information memorandum, initial meetings between the seller and buyer and other documentation and procedures. Structuring the deal must take into account whether the shares or assets of the company are sold, the forms and terms of payment and the terms of a post-transaction management contract. The efforts involved in preparing for negotiations, the negotiation strategy and the implementation of that strategy and tactics are fundamental to the price and terms of the deal that ultimately accrue to the seller. The negotiations should culminate in an agreed LOI between the seller and a particular buyer. Closing the deal involves the buyer's detailed due diligence investigation, negotiating the purchase agreement (and related agreements) and, ultimately, the final closing.

Value enhancement within the private company sale process refers to more than just the stated purchase price. It also incorporates the economic terms of the deal and intangible aspects that are unique to each individual. It is important for the seller and their advisors to control the sale process and that they be prepared to adjust the stages, components and time lines to accommodate the unique circumstances of each transaction in order to maximize value enhancement in the eyes of the business owner.

The Foundations of Value Enhancement

Section II

SECTION II

The Foundations of Value Enhancement

Introduction

The goal of every business owner should be to realize the highest value possible upon the sale of their company. From an economic standpoint, the value of the equity in a company is a function of the cash flows that it is expected to generate, the rate of return (or valuation multiple) applied to those cash flows and its underlying financial position. However, in the context of selling a privately held company, value refers to more than just the stated purchase price. The terms of the deal affect the economic value received. In addition, there are intangible aspects of value that are unique to each individual business owner that must be considered. The intangible aspects of the deal include things such as the impact on the livelihood of the owner caused by restrictions on what they can or cannot do for a period of time following the sale. Consequently value and, by extension, value enhancement, must be considered within the parameters of the personal value system of the business owner. The three elements of value that business owners should consider when selling their privately held company are depicted in Exhibit II-1.

Exhibit II-1

THE ELEMENTS OF VALUE TO THE BUSINESS OWNER

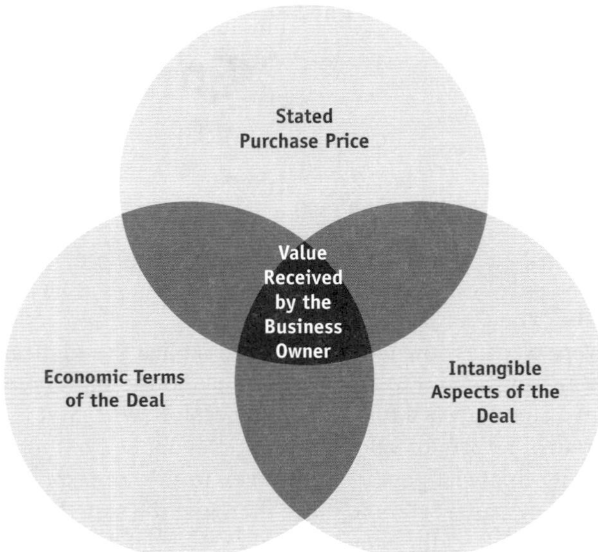

The foundation for creating value enhancement lies in the planning phase of the private company sale process. This includes timing the sale to coincide with favourable personal and business conditions, structuring the affairs of the company to increase its attractiveness to buyers, and identifying and undertaking initiatives that increase the intrinsic and strategic equity value of the company.

With a strong foundation in place, the momentum for value enhancement realization builds through the execution phase of the private company sale process through the ability of the seller and their intermediary to create an effective auction. The platform for the effective auction is established by attracting a sufficient number of qualified buyers. The seller should control the flow of information to increase the perceived value of the company among those buyers. Proposals that are received should be evaluated based on their risk-reward parameters and income tax efficiency. The apex of value enhancement rests on securing a comprehensive letter of intent (LOI) that offers the best value to the business owner in terms of the stated purchase price, economic terms of the deal and intangible aspects of the deal. The seller must retain their negotiating position through the closing stage in order to crystallize the value that has been created throughout the sale process. Collectively, the underlying foundation for value enhancement and the ability to build value enhancement through the planning and execution phases of the private company sale process is referred to as the *Value Enhancement Framework™*.

The Determinants of Economic Value

Value vs. Price

There is a fundamental difference between the value of a company, often referred to as its "fair market value", established using generally accepted business valuation methodologies, and the price that is paid for that company in the open market. When determining fair market value, certain underlying assumptions normally are made, such as:

- an open marketplace exists in which no prospective buyer is excluded or restricted from transacting;
- both the seller and the buyer have equal knowledge of the company and equal negotiating position and abilities;
- both the seller and the buyer are prudent and neither is compelled to transact; and
- the transaction price is entirely represented by cash on closing.

These assumptions seldom hold true in the open market. This is because:

- no organized market exists for the sale of privately held companies in Canada. Therefore, the extent to which prospective buyers are aware that a particular company is for sale is a function of the effectiveness of the marketing efforts by the seller and their intermediary. Further, while a prospective buyer may want to transact, that buyer may be constrained from doing so due to financial, regulatory or other reasons;
- sellers and buyers have a different set of knowledge on which they base their valuation and pricing decisions. The seller better understands the prospective cash flow, risks, growth prospects and financial position of their company. The buyer better understands the synergies and strategic advantages that it expects to realize following the transaction. These things influence the negotiating position and negotiating abilities of the buyer and seller and their respective advisors;

- sellers and buyers are not always prudent. Furthermore, business owners sometimes are compelled to sell in pressing circumstances, such as failing health or a sudden change in their financial situation. Buyers may feel compelled to transact due to competitive pressures or to meet market expectations; and
- apart from cash on closing, private company divestitures frequently include other forms of consideration, such as seller take-backs, share exchanges, earnouts and other arrangements. The terms and conditions of non-cash consideration can have a significant impact on the value received by the seller.

The reasons for the difference between fair market value and open market price are summarized in Exhibit II-2. Consequently, the price paid for a privately held company in the open market may be greater than, or less than, its estimated fair market value. As a practical matter, the price that a company ultimately will fetch cannot be determined with any degree of certainty prior to the time that a deal is consummated.

Exhibit II-2

FAIR MARKET VALUE VS. OPEN MARKET PRICE

Fair Market Value	Open Market Price
An open marketplace exists in which no prospective buyer is excluded or restricted from transacting	Restrictions may exist where prospective buyers are not aware of the opportunity or where interested buyers are unable to transact
The seller and buyer have equal knowledge of the company and have an equal negotiating position and negotiation abilities	The seller and buyer have differing knowledge about the company and post-transaction synergy expectations, and have differing negotiating abilities
The seller and buyer are prudent and neither is compelled to transact	Either the seller, the buyer or both may be imprudent or compelled to transact
The transaction is consummated entirely in the form of cash on closing	Other forms of consideration may be used, including seller take-backs, share exchanges, earnout agreements and other arrangements

The Components of Value and Price

Most generally accepted business valuation methodologies establish the aggregate equity value of a company as being the value of all of its issued and outstanding share capital or its underlying net assets. From a buyer's perspective, that aggregate equity value can be segregated into five underlying components: (1) the net operating assets of a company; (2) the financial liabilities of a company; (3) the company's intangible value; (4) redundant assets owned by a company; and (5) the value of buyer-perceived synergies. This concept is illustrated in Exhibit II-3.

Exhibit II-3

COMPONENTS OF EQUITY VALUE AND PRICE

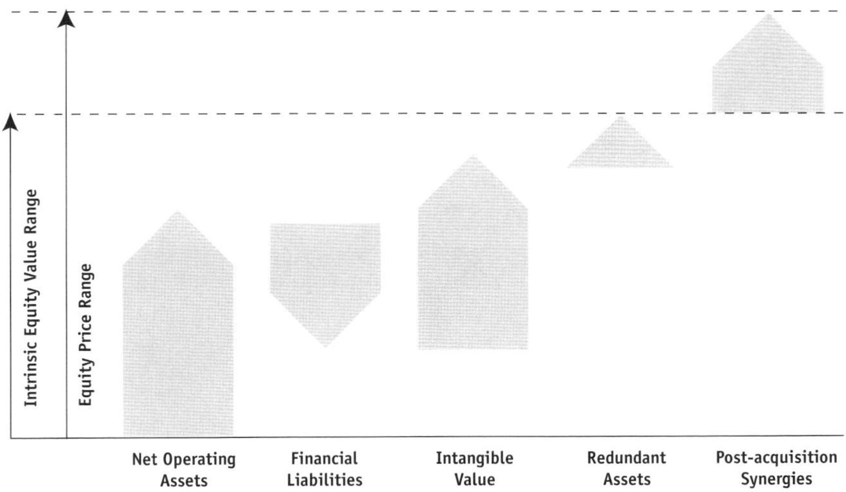

Net operating assets

"Net operating assets" refer to the value of a company's tangible assets that are used in its ongoing operations, less the economic value of its operating liabilities. Net operating assets includes such things as accounts receivable, inventories and fixed assets, but excludes the intangible assets of a company such as deferred costs (which has no separately identifiable value) and patents and other identifiable intangibles that are accounted for separately. The "operating liabilities" of a company refer to the debts that it incurs as part of its ordinary operations, such as accounts payable and accrued liabilities. Operating liabilities exclude financial liabilities (e.g., bank loans), which are discussed below.

A company's balance sheet reflects the historical cost of its assets and liabilities in accordance with generally accepted accounting principles. A buyer may restate the value of a company's net operating assets to their estimated market values (e.g., to reflect the replacement cost of a company's fixed assets) as opposed to their book values. While such an estimate is subjective, it does provide the buyer with an indication of the cost to replace the net operating assets of a company which, depending on the nature of the business, may be viewed as an alternative to acquisition. As a general rule, the greater the value of the underlying net operating assets of a company (i.e., the stronger its balance sheet), the greater the value of that company.

A point of clarification should be made. The term "net operating assets" is not the same as "net assets". As noted above, net operating assets refer to the tangible operating assets of a company less its operating liabilities. The net assets of a company on the other hand include its net operating assets as well as its intangible assets and redundant assets, less its financial liabilities. The net assets of a company so derived are comparable to the share value of a company (either of which represents the company's intrinsic equity value). To summarize:

	Tangible operating assets
–	operating liabilities
=	Net operating assets
–	financial liabilities
+	intangible assets
+	redundant assets
=	Net assets or share value (also referred to as intrinsic equity value)

Financial liabilities

"Financial liabilities" refer to interest-bearing debts, such as bank operating loans, mortgages and term loans. Financial liabilities also include obligations that are similar in substance to bank loans, such as advances from shareholders and related parties, whether or not these debts are interest-bearing. Financial liabilities do not include accounts payable, accrued liabilities or other obligations that arise in the ordinary course of business and which are considered to be operating liabilities, as discussed above. Financial liabilities serve to reduce the portion of the purchase price that is paid to the business owner in their capacity as a shareholder of the company.

Intangible value

The next component of value lies in the intangible assets of a company. Intangible assets refer to such things as a company's established customer base, its brand names, proprietary technology and general "goodwill" that a company enjoys. In this regard, in order for goodwill to have value in the open market, it must attach to the company itself or be transferable from the existing owner over a relatively short period of time, and not attach solely to the owner of the company in their personal capacity. Buyers will not pay for the "personal goodwill" of the business owner in terms of their contacts, personal reputation and so on, where such things cannot be transferred from the seller to the buyer in a relatively short time frame.

In most cases, a company's financial statements do not fully reflect the economic value of its intangible assets due to limitations in conventional accounting. Furthermore, most intangible assets cannot be segregated from the company itself. Consequently, the value of intangible assets usually is derived by determining the company's *en bloc* equity value and then adding back financial obligations and deducting the value of net operating assets and redundant assets. To summarize:

  En bloc equity value
\+ financial obligations outstanding
\- value of net operating assets
\- redundant assets
____
= Value of intangible assets

Redundant assets

"Redundant assets" (or "non-operating assets") are those that are not required in the ongoing operations of a company and that can be withdrawn from the company without impairing its ability to generate prospective cash flows or change its risk profile. As a practical matter, business owners normally withdraw redundant assets from their company prior to sale since buyers usually are not interested in purchasing redundant assets. Where sold with a company, the value of redundant assets is reflected in a higher purchase price for the equity of the company. When withdrawn prior to the sale, the value of redundant assets remains with the business owner who is free to realize on their value separately from the company.

As indicated in Exhibit II-3, the net operating assets less financial liabilities plus intangible value and redundant assets (if any) represents the "intrinsic value" (or "stand-alone" value) of a company's equity. That is, the value of a company's shares or net assets to its current owner or operated on its own.

Post-acquisition synergies

Many buyers perceive that upon acquiring a company they will be able to realize synergies that cause the company to be worth more to the buyer than to the seller. Examples of synergies include cost savings through economies of scale, incremental revenue opportunities and other strategic advantages that a buyer perceives it can realize by combining the company with its existing operations. Synergies are unique to every buyer and the extent to which buyers are prepared to pay a premium over the intrinsic equity value of a company for those synergies is, to a large extent, influenced by the effectiveness to which the company is marketed for sale, the negotiating position of the buyer and seller and the structure of the transaction.

To summarize, the price that a buyer may be willing to pay for the shares or net assets of a company is influenced by its subjective assessment of the intrinsic equity value of the company, the quantum of synergies that it expects to realize and what it believes it must offer in order to consummate a transaction. As previously noted the price that is paid for the equity (i.e., the shares or net assets) of a company in the open market may be greater than or less than its intrinsic fair market value.

Understanding the components of equity value and price are important in creating and realizing value enhancement. These things help the business owner to convey the benefits associated with their company to prospective buyers that may not be evident on the surface. Such understanding also helps the business owner in identifying and implementing initiatives during the planning phase of the private company sale process that facilitate value enhancement realization in the execution phase. This might include initiatives that serve to increase the perceived value of their company's intangible assets, or that cause a buyer to believe that greater synergies are achievable.

Enterprise Value vs. Equity Value

An important distinction must be made between the value of a company itself (referred to as its "enterprise value") and the value of the equity in a company as represented by its overlying shares or underlying net assets.

When establishing value and price, buyers typically first determine the enterprise value of a company, which represents what the operations of the company are worth, regardless of how those operations are financed. Stated another way, the enterprise value of a company does not depend on whether the owner has financed its operations through bank loans or through their own personal capital. The equity value of a company, on the other hand, represents the portion of the enterprise value that accrues to the benefit of the business owner. That is, the value attributable to the shares or net assets of a company represents the residual amount of its enterprise value after the obligations to financial debtors (such as the bank and other lenders) have been satisfied.

As an example of the difference between enterprise value and equity value, consider the example of two identical houses that each sell for $400,000. House A has a mortgage of $300,000 against it, while House B has no mortgage. The value of each house (i.e., their "enterprise value") is $400,000. The value of each house is not affected by the size or existence of a mortgage. However, the proceeds to each homeowner (i.e., their "equity value") differ. In the case of House A, the bank receives the first $300,000 to settle the mortgage, so the homeowner retains $100,000 of the gross proceeds. In the case of House B where there is no mortgage, the homeowner retains the entire $400,000.

Therefore, when discussing value and price, it is important for the business owner to understand whether reference is being made to the value of the company (i.e., its enterprise value) or the value of the equity in the company (i.e., its shares or net assets), the difference between the two being represented by the amount of financial liabilities settled upon the closing of the transaction and, in some cases, other adjustments to account for excess or deficient net operating assets or redundant assets of the company. These concepts are discussed below.

From the standpoint of the business owner, the equity value is of primary concern since it represents the value that the business owner will receive for their interest in the company. Therefore, value enhancement initiatives should focus on the determinants of equity value, either directly or through increasing the enterprise value of the company and realizing some or all of that increase through higher equity value participation.

While business valuation methodologies are discussed at some length in Stage 3 (see Section III), an initial discussion at this point is helpful to understand how value enhancement is created and realized. Importantly, enhancing intrinsic equity value can be done independently of the private company sale process. Even if a business owner is not ready to sell, proactively enhancing the intrinsic equity value of their company will generate rewards to the business owner in terms of greater cash flows and/or a reduction in business risk. A proactive approach to value enhancement also is important in the event that the business owner is presented with an unsolicited offer, or where a sudden change in circumstances (e.g., rapidly deteriorating health) necessitates the divestiture of their company sooner than expected.

The Determinants of Enterprise Value

The enterprise value of a company is a function of the cash flow that it is expected to generate in the future and the risks (expressed in the form of a rate of return) associated with that cash flow. As a simplistic example, if Company A is expected to generate after-tax cash flow of $1 million each year and a 10% after-tax rate of return is considered appropriate, then the enterprise value of Company A is $10 million (calculated as *$1 million / 0.1*). However, it is important to understand what is meant by cash flow and what factors influence the rate of return applied thereto.

Cash flow

From both a valuation and pricing perspective, the enterprise value and equity value of a company ultimately are a function of its prospective after-tax "discretionary cash flow". Discretionary cash flow represents the cash that a company generates which can be withdrawn by the owner in the form of a dividend, remuneration above market rates or by other means, without impairing the economic stability of the company. Alternatively, rather than withdrawing discretionary cash flow from the company, that money can be retained in the company in the form of a redundant asset or reinvested into incremental growth opportunities. In such cases, the business owner is forgoing an immediate cash withdrawal in favour of the likelihood of increasing the value of the company to be realized at a later date. Whichever the case, discretionary cash flow represents the return on investment to the business owner or to a buyer of the company.

Discretionary cash flow is calculated as a company's revenues less cash operating costs required to operate the company, capital expenditure requirements, incremental working capital requirements and cash income taxes. However, when determining discretionary cash flow, no deduction is made for debt servicing costs, such as interest expense or principal repayment on loans outstanding. This is because a company's enterprise value is determined independently of the way its operations are financed. While the details of calculating discretionary cash flow will be introduced in Stage 3 (see Section III), at this point, the key things to remember are that:

- the economic value of a company is a function of its discretionary cash flow, not its accounting profits;
- the discretionary cash flow generated by a company not only takes into account its revenues and cash operating costs, but also its capital expenditure requirements, the incremental working capital required to support projected growth and income taxes; and
- economic value is based on the discretionary cash flow a company is expected to generate in the future, and not what it has generated historically. That said, historical discretionary cash flow typically is considered when projecting what will be generated in the future.

When considering how to enhance the enterprise value (and equity value) of a company through increasing discretionary cash flow, the business owner must fully understand the economic implications of the initiatives being contemplated. For example, a business owner might try to increase revenues by offering more favourable credit terms to customers. However, this initiative might not translate into incremental discretionary cash flow where the costs of additional bad debt expense and delays in collecting accounts receivable outweigh the benefits of higher revenues and gross profits.

Rates of return

The other key determinant of enterprise value is the rate of return applied to the prospective discretionary cash flow of a company. The rate of return adopted when determining enterprise value is a function of the perceived likelihood that the discretionary cash flow that a company is expected to generate will be achieved, given the risks and growth opportunities facing the company and the perceived debt capacity of the company. Risk is influenced by such factors as economic and industry conditions, the stability of a company's revenue stream, its operating cost structure and other variables. In this context, growth opportunities refer to growth in excess of what has been accounted for in the expected discretionary cash flow of a company. To the extent that growth is incorporated in the discretionary cash flow projections, it should not be double-counted when determining the rate of return. The ability to finance a company with debt is based on an assessment of its underlying financial position and cash flow expectations, independent of whether and to what extent debt actually is used by a company to finance its operations. A more extensive explanation of risk, growth, debt capacity and rates of return is provided in Stage 3 (see Section III).

It is important to recognize that discretionary cash flows and the rates of return applied thereto are inter-related. Therefore, in order to enhance the enterprise value (and equity value) of a company, these variables must be considered together and not in isolation. Consequently, while a business owner might consider ways to increase the discretionary cash flow generated by their company (such as reducing operating costs, improving working capital management and so on), it is important for the business owner to assess whether or not such initiatives would negatively impact the perceived risk level of the company, thereby negating the benefits achieved.

Returning to the previous example, recall that the enterprise value of Company A was calculated as $10 million, based on $1 million in annual discretionary cash flow divided by a 10% rate of return. Now assume that the owner of Company A is considering an initiative that is expected to increase the company's annual discretionary cash flow to $1.5 million. However, assume the contemplated initiative is perceived to be risky, and therefore the required rate of return for Company A increases to 15%. Consequently, the enterprise value of Company A remains unchanged at $10 million (now represented by $1.5 million divided by 15%). In this example, while the prospective discretionary cash flow to Company A has increased, no incremental value is created.

The Determinants of Equity Value

As previously mentioned, the equity value of a company is calculated as its enterprise value less outstanding financial liabilities and, where necessary, other adjustments to reflect excess or deficient net operating assets and any redundant assets. Collectively, these things are reflected in the financial position of the company at a given date.

As discussed earlier in this Section, financial liabilities refer to the interest-bearing debt of a company, such as bank operating loans, mortgages and term loans, as well as debts with similar substance such as shareholder advances, regardless of whether or not these debts are interest bearing. The rationale is that when a buyer acquires a company, it must settle the financial liabilities on closing, or make arrangements to assume those obligations. However, financial liabilities do not include accounts payable and accrued liabilities incurred in the ordinary course of business, where such obligations provide a continuing source of interest-free financing for the company.

Other adjustments that are made when deriving equity value from enterprise value are those required to compensate for excessive or deficient net operating assets of the company and the redundant assets of the company, if any. Recall that net operating assets refer to the tangible assets of the company that are used in its ongoing operations (such as accounts receivable, inventories and fixed assets), less its operating liabilities (such as accounts payable and accrued liabilities). If, for example, a buyer perceives that a company's net working capital (the amount by which its current assets exceed its current liabilities) is inadequate to support its ongoing operations, that buyer will make a downward adjustment to the price that it will pay for the equity of that company. This is done to reflect the fact that the buyer anticipates that it will have to invest additional capital in the company following the acquisition in order to compensate for the perceived net working capital deficiency. In addition, as previously illustrated in Exhibit II-3, where redundant assets are sold with a company, the agreed purchase price of those assets is added to the equity value of the company otherwise determined.

Returning to the example of Company A, assume that its enterprise value is $10 million based on annual discretionary cash flow of $1 million and a 10% rate of return. Further assume that Company A has $3 million of financial liabilities outstanding and that it has redundant assets worth $1 million. Finally, assume that Company A's net operating assets including its net working capital position are considered adequate, given the nature of its business and cash flow expectations. In this case, the equity value of Company A would be calculated as follows:

	Enterprise value	$10,000,000
–	financial liabilities outstanding	$(3,000,000)
+ / –	adjustments to net operating assets	nil
+	redundant assets	$ 1,000,000
=	Equity value	$ 8,000,000

To summarize, equity value is a function of the enterprise value of a company, adjusted for financial liabilities outstanding and other adjustments where necessary, to reflect excess or deficient net operating assets or the existence of redundant assets. Enhancing the equity value of a company requires that all these things be considered collectively as opposed to in isolation.

Value Expectations of the Business Owner

Business owners sometimes have inflated expectations as to the economic worth of their company. Some business owners are disappointed when they receive an offer from a prospective buyer that falls well below their expectations. Where this occurs, common reasons are that business owners:

- may not understand the determinants of value and price in the open market. Consequently, they fail to take the initiatives in the years prior to sale that contribute to a buyer's positive perception of the company's cash flow-generating ability and its perceived risks and opportunities;
- sometimes confuse the concept of "sweat equity" with economic value. The amount of physical and mental effort that an owner invests in their company is meaningless to a buyer unless it translates into realized or expected operating results. Therefore, the key to realizing value enhancement is for business owners to ensure that their efforts likely will result in an increase in the maintainable prospective discretionary cash flow of the company and/or a reduction in business risk over the longer term;
- believe that price earnings multiples of publicly traded companies that operate in their industry can be applied to the operating results of their company. Public equity market multiples reflect a fundamentally different valuation dynamic compared to the purchase and sale of a privately held company. Most notably, public company multiples reflect trading in small lots of marketable securities with varying degrees of liquidity, buyer/seller knowledge, investment strategy and expected hold period. The purchase and sale of a privately held company generally is different in terms of its degree of liquidity, risk parameters, buyer strategy and expected hold periods. In addition, there is the prospect of post-acquisition synergies that a buyer might anticipate through the purchase of a privately held company, which is not reflected in the ordinary course of public stock trading of public company share prices. This is not to suggest that public equity market multiples have no relevance to private company values whatsoever, but rather to highlight the fact that a direct comparison cannot be made;

- cause the company to be overly dependent on their personal involvement. Buyers of privately held companies are wary of the risk of losing key employees, major customers and so on, once the business owner is no longer directly involved. Buyers usually reduce the price they are willing to pay, or change the terms of the deal, to reflect this perceived risk. Therefore, a key to enhancing value is for business owners to ensure that the company has a strong infrastructure in place. In this way, the employees who remain following the sale will be able to ensure that the company's customer base, trade secrets and other intangible elements of value are retained; and
- fail to objectively assess both the strengths and weaknesses of their company. Business owners sometimes believe that the strengths of their company are greater than they really are, or that weaknesses and threats are not as material as might be perceived from an outsider's perspective. Therefore, a key to enhancing value is to obtain an objective assessment of the company's strengths and weaknesses and the opportunities and threats that it faces early in the sale process, so that these things can be addressed and improved prior to exposing the company for sale in the open market.

Finally, it is not uncommon for business owners to make an inconsistent comparison between the offer price for the equity value of their company and their remuneration from the company prior to sale. Consider the example of Company B that generates $1 million each year before taxes and remuneration to its owner, Mr. Bee. Mr. Bee's practice is to withdraw the entire $1 million each year as a salary to himself. If Mr. Bee receives an offer of $5 million for the shares of Company B, he may think to himself "if I invest this money in government bonds that yield 5%, I'll only earn $250,000 a year, which is a lot less than what I am drawing from the company now".

There are several flaws in Mr. Bee's thinking. First of all, Mr. Bee is comparing a low-risk investment (such as government bonds) with a much riskier stream of cash flows from Company B. Second, assuming that Mr. Bee was active in Company B, he has not segregated the return on physical capital (i.e., his employment efforts) from the return on economic capital. For example, if following the sale Mr. Bee could get a senior management position in another company and earn $200,000 per year, Mr. Bee's annual economic return on his investment in Company B is only $800,000. Finally there is the issue of taxation. The $1 million paid in remuneration is fully taxable to Mr. Bee. Conversely, substantial income tax savings may be achievable on the proceeds of sale for the shares of Company B, depending on the structure of the transaction and pre-sale planning initiatives undertaken in respect of Mr. Bee's personal affairs.

This is not to suggest that business owners never receive what they believe their company is worth. In some cases, owners are pleasantly surprised at the offers they receive for their company. Rather, it is to say that the comparison of the price offered for the equity of a company and the owner's earnings prior to sale can be a complicated task, and professional advice usually is required. In some cases, it may indeed be preferable for the owner to operate the company for a few more years rather than selling at the present time, depending on expected developments from an industry and macro-economic perspective.

Intangible Aspects of Value

Business owners typically seek a feeling of self-fulfilment and personal satisfaction from the sale of their company. While the price paid for the equity of the company goes a long way toward establishing that sentiment, the intangible aspects of the deal can also play an important role. Common issues in terms of the intangible aspects of the deal include:

- What will become of the company's employees following the sale, including members of the owner's family that are actively employed by the company?
- Will the name of the company continue, or will its identity be lost after the sale?
- What will be the owner's involvement following the sale in terms of their responsibilities, authority levels and so on, as set out in the management contract?
- Will the business owner be free, and when, to pursue other opportunities within the industry, unencumbered by the terms of a non-competition agreement?

In many cases, there is a trade-off between economic value and the intangible aspects of a deal. For example, a business owner who is actively involved with the company but who is not prepared to remain with the company for any period of time following the sale for personal reasons may have to accept a lower purchase price or not consummate a transaction at all.

The intangible aspects of value are a function of the business owner's personal value system, so they are highly subjective. Consequently, an in-depth discussion of the intangible aspects of value and how these things may be affected by the terms of a transaction is not meaningful. However, it is important for business owners to reflect on the personal values that are important to them, and what they are prepared to give up, prior to the time their company is exposed for sale in the open market. In order to realize the intangible elements of value enhancement, business owners must establish what value means to them in the first place. A fundamental change in the owner's stated interests at a late stage in the sale process can compromise their negotiating position and can diminish the owner's ability to realize value enhancement.

Value Enhancement Planning and Execution

Planning for Value Enhancement

The foundation for creating value enhancement opportunities in the private company sale process revolves around the extent and quality of planning that is done prior to the time that the company is exposed for sale in the open market. This includes timing the sale to coincide with favourable personal and business conditions, structuring the affairs of the company to increase its attractiveness to buyers and identifying and undertaking initiatives to increase the intrinsic and strategic equity value of the company. Each of these components is explained below. As depicted in Exhibit II-4, deciding when to sell, preparing for the sale and estimating (and increasing) value and price are inter-related, and these things should be considered in unison to develop the foundation for value enhancement creation.

Exhibit II-4

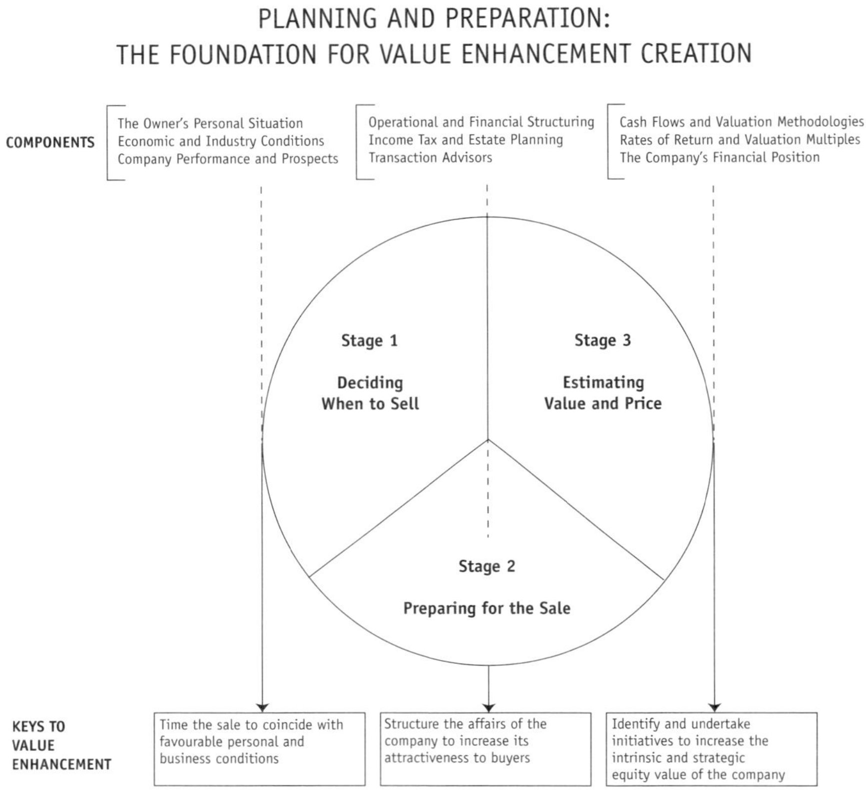

Stage 1 — Deciding When to Sell

As further explained in Stage 1 (see Section III), in deciding when to sell their company, the business owner should consider their own personal situation, economic and industry conditions, and the company's recent and prospective operating performance. Value enhancement opportunities are created where the timing of the sale coincides with favourable personal and business conditions.

The owner's personal situation refers to such things as their health, financial situation and level of interest in remaining with the company following the sale. In some cases, the business owner is compelled to sell their company before they may otherwise want to, due to failing health, age or other circumstances. While the timing of a compelled sale may or may not be ideal from the perspective of economic and industry conditions and the company's recent and prospective operating performance, value enhancement opportunities may still be available in such circumstances through creating an effective auction and by offering flexibility to prospective buyers to the extent possible. In deciding when to sell, the business owner should take into account that, depending on the nature of the company and the particular buyer, a buyer might want the owner to remain actively involved in the company for a period of time following the sale. An owner who is unwilling to make such a commitment may have to compromise on other elements of value. The nature and extent of post-transaction involvement has a bearing on the intangible aspects of value in the eyes of the business owner.

With respect to economic and industry conditions, not surprisingly, the private company sale process is facilitated, and business values generally are higher, where such conditions are favourable. Strong economic and industry conditions positively influence a buyer's expectations of the company's prospective discretionary cash flow and growth potential, and reduce its risk perceptions. In particular, where an industry is going through a period of heightened merger and acquisition activity, that phenomenon tends to increase liquidity and contributes to higher prices being paid for companies that operate in that industry than may have otherwise been the case.

The company's recent and prospective operating performance has a significant influence on the number of prospective buyers that may be interested in the company and the prices they are prepared to pay. Attempting to sell a company after it has experienced a relatively bad year in terms of operating results is fraught with challenges. Buyers usually are skeptical of a business owner's attempt to justify why things went wrong and how they will change for the better. Conversely, where a company has experienced one or more years of good operating results prior to the time that it is exposed for sale and its prospects in that regard appear favourable, the business owner can more easily justify the expectations of strong prospective cash flow, growth opportunities and reduced risk.

Stage 2 — Preparing for the Sale

As discussed in detail in Stage 2 (see Section III), preparing for the sale encompasses operational and financial structuring of the company, organizing the owner's income tax and estate planning affairs and engaging transaction advisors. The key to creating value enhancement opportunities when preparing for the sale is to structure the affairs of the company to increase its attractiveness to buyers. Ideally, preparations for the sale should begin at least one to three years prior to the time prospective buyers are solicited.

When preparing the company for sale, emphasis should be placed on those operational and financial structuring initiatives that will cause buyers to perceive that the company has a sustainable competitive advantage in terms of its products, services, technology, business processes or other areas. Creating the perception of a sustainable competitive advantage supports the expectation of higher prospective cash flows and/or reduced business risk, which in turn increase the equity value of the company. It also is important that the affairs of the company be structured such that buyers perceive a smooth transition following the transaction and the ability to realize post-acquisition synergies on a cost-efficient basis.

When preparing for the sale, the affairs of the business owner (and their family) should be organized so that the owner can offer greater flexibility to the buyer in terms of alternatives for structuring a deal with favourable risk-reward parameters, and in a way that serves to reduce the owner's income tax burden upon the sale.

Finally, business owners need to engage the right advisors who will guide them through the sale process. This includes lawyers, tax experts, transaction intermediaries and other advisors. The business owner should appoint one of these advisors (normally the transaction intermediary) to coordinate the private company sale process. However, it is important that the all advisors who are involved are not only competent, but that they will provide objective advice to the business owner and they have experience in transactions involving the sale of privately held Canadian companies. Advisors should be actively involved throughout the planning phase in order to assist the business owner and to ensure a smooth transition from the planning phase to the execution phase of the private company sale process.

Stage 3 — Estimating Value and Price

As discussed earlier in this chapter, and as described more fully in Stage 3 (see Section III), the enterprise value of a company is determined based on the discretionary cash flow it is expected to generate and the rate of return applied to that cash flow. The equity value of a company is derived as its enterprise value less the amount of financial liabilities outstanding and, where required, other adjustments to reflect excess or deficient net operating assets or redundant assets.

Enterprise value is enhanced where the business owner focuses on those initiatives that increase the company's discretionary cash flow and the growth prospects thereof and/or reduce the perception of business risk. Translating increased enterprise value into increased equity value is a function of how debt is used to finance the operations of the company and how effectively the company's net operating assets are managed.

It is important for the business owner to have an understanding of the key determinants of equity value on an ongoing basis so that appropriate initiatives can be implemented, and their success demonstrated, prior to the time the company is exposed for sale. It generally is easier for the business owner to convey, and to receive value for, proven initiatives rather than those that are just being contemplated or planned. Furthermore, the business owner will be rewarded for initiatives that enhance the economic value of their company even if it is not put up for sale.

Executing Value Enhancement Realization

While adequate planning sets the foundation for value enhancement creation, the realization of enhanced value depends on the ability of the business owner and their team of advisors to create an effective auction when selling the company. At this stage, the business owner transitions from being an operator of the company (either actively or passively) to being a seller.

As depicted in Exhibit II-5, the platform for creating an effective auction begins with attracting a sufficient number of qualified buyers. The seller should control the flow of information to increase the perceived value of the company among those buyers. Proposals that are received should be evaluated based on their risk-reward parameters and income tax efficiency. The essence of an effective auction occurs where the seller and their intermediary develop a competitive bidding environment to secure a comprehensive LOI that offers the best value to the business owner. The seller must then maintain their negotiating position through the closing stage to crystallize the value that has been created throughout the sale process.

Exhibit II-5

THE EFFECTIVE AUCTION:
THE FOUNDATION FOR VALUE ENHANCEMENT REALIZATION

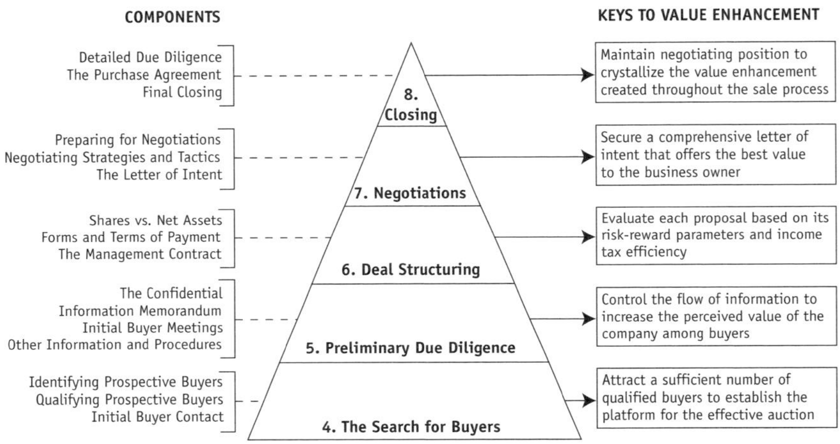

Building deal momentum and the effective auction

Before discussing the components of each stage within the execution phase it is important to address how to build momentum in a deal. The ability to create and realize value enhancement rests to a large degree in the ability of the business owner and their team of advisors to build momentum throughout the course of the private company sale process. The three stages in the planning phase, being the decision of when to sell, preparing for the sale and estimating value and price, serve as the foundation upon which value enhancement is built in the execution phase. The business owner and their intermediary should work to increase momentum as the sale process moves through the search for buyers, preliminary due diligence, deal structuring and negotiations. Ideally, deal momentum should peak in the negotiation stage through the development of a competitive bidding environment that culminates in an agreed LOI that reflects the best value to the business owner. Thereafter, it is important that deal momentum be sustained through the closing stage in order to crystallize the value enhancement generated throughout the sale process. The concept of setting the foundation for value enhancement in the planning phase and increasing value enhancement by building momentum throughout the execution phase is illustrated in Exhibit II-6.

Exhibit II-6

BUILDING MOMENTUM THROUGHOUT THE PRIVATE COMPANY SALE PROCESS

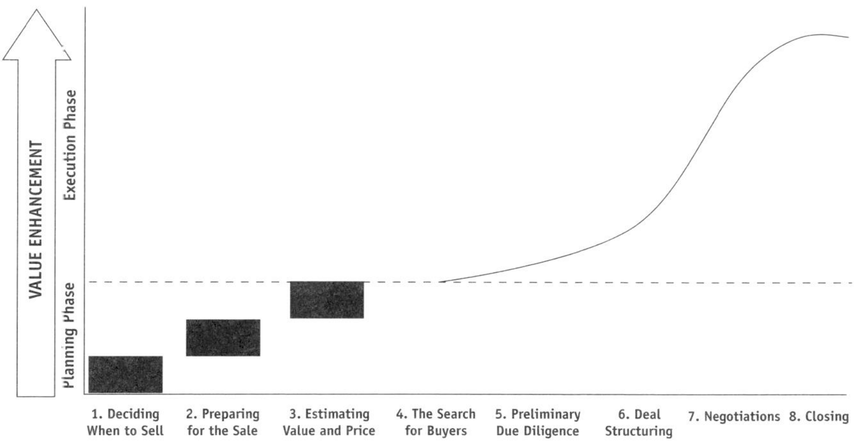

Building momentum in the execution phase of the private company sale process is facilitated through the creation of an effective auction. An effective auction is created where attractive alternative offers become available concurrently through a competitive bidding process. In Section I it was noted that the timeline of the private company sale process shortens as it moves from preliminary due diligence to deal structuring and negotiations. Prospective buyers may be at different points of the sale process at any given time. An effective intermediary will be able to speed up some buyers and slow down others in order to get buyers to submit proposals within a relatively short time frame of one another. This allows the seller to leverage buyers against one another, thereby improving the seller's alternatives and hence value enhancement opportunities. The ability to create an effective auction by aligning buyers without irritating those that are caused to speed up, or without causing those to slow down to lose interest in the deal, is an important part of the art of successful business sale negotiation.

In most cases the number of prospective buyers declines as the auction process unfolds. This is to be expected since there will be some buyers at the outset of the sale process that become disinterested in pursuing further discussions, or that are not perceived by the seller to be satisfactory prospects as the process moves forward. The key element from the seller's perspective is to ensure that the buyers that remain in the later stages of the sale process represent quality prospects who perceive considerable value in the company and who are prepared to consummate a transaction on terms that are attractive to the seller. Ideally, the seller will agree to an LOI with the one buyer that offers them the best value and the deal will close with that buyer on those terms.

An effective auction can be created either through a formal auction or an informal auction. The private company sale process outlined in Section I describes an informal auction. That is, the seller does not establish strict dates or deadlines at the outset of the sale process as to when buyers must provide a formal indication of interest, an LOI and so on. Rather, the seller and their intermediary work tactfully to create an auction among prospective buyers, thereby augmenting the value realized by the seller.

This is in contrast to a formal auction, which generally entails the same steps as the informal auction except that it is common practice in a formal auction to establish specific deadlines with prospective buyers. It is also common in a formal auction for the seller to ask buyers to submit an initial "expression of interest" early on in the process. That is, based on limited information (such as only what is disclosed in the confidential information memorandum), prospective buyers are asked to disclose in a non-binding letter the range of what they believe the company is worth and the terms of a possible transaction. The seller then selects the prospective buyers who have submitted the most attractive expressions of interest and restricts its dealings to those buyers. The formal auction process then continues to the stages of initial meetings with buyers through to the LOI and ultimately closing with one of those buyers, just as in an informal auction. Again, the only modification is the establishment of deadlines and other formalities as dictated by the seller.

The formal auction sometimes appears preferable because it allows the seller to clearly establish the "rules of the game" at the outset and facilitates the creation of a competitive bidding environment. The seller's hope is that the expression of interest requirement will cause prospective buyers to submit attractive proposals in order to "stay in the game", and that those initial non-binding proposals will provide the seller with an advantage in the negotiations. However, a formal auction can backfire if it is not well managed. Credibility can quickly be lost where the seller allows deadlines to lapse or where prospective buyers artificially inflate their initial value propositions expecting that they will subsequently uncover information that negatively affects the company and that will allow a buyer to justify the re-evaluation of its initial submission.

In Canada, most privately held companies are sold by way of an informal auction because of the flexibility afforded to the seller, which is fundamental to maintaining control of the sale process. The formal auction tends to be restricted to divestitures involving divisions of public companies where only a few logical buyers exist, or under the conditions of a forced or publicly announced sale. In the end, either approach is valid, so long as the seller maintains control of the sale process and creates an effective auction that ultimately enhances the value received.

Stage 4 — The Search for Buyers

As discussed in Stage 4 (see Section III), the search for buyers includes identifying prospective buyers, qualifying those prospects through initial research and initial contact with buyers. The key to value enhancement in the search for buyers stage rests in the seller's ability to attract a sufficient number of qualified buyers to create the platform for an effective auction.

The identification of prospective buyers requires a comprehensive analysis of the marketplace to determine who might be interested in acquiring the company. This usually entails searching for prospects outside of the company's immediate industry segment to identify buyers who operate in other segments or complementary industries. Fundamental to identifying prospective buyers is a sound understanding of the benefits that the company might convey to buyers in other industry segments, or different industries altogether, in terms of the company's products and services, its customer base, business processes, proprietary technology, market presence and so on.

Preliminary research on each prospective buyer that has been identified is important to establishing whether a prospective buyer is a qualified candidate and in tailoring the initial contact message to that buyer, thereby increasing the likelihood of capturing its interest. Preliminary research also is important in terms of building a base of knowledge that can be used in discussions with buyers who proceed to preliminary due diligence and negotiations.

Liquidity, defined as the number of qualified buyers that are interested in the company, is fundamental to realizing value enhancement. Therefore, the message that is conveyed and the manner in which it is conveyed when initially contacting buyers must generate sufficient interest among qualified prospects. Qualified buyers that are interested in the company are asked to sign a non-disclosure agreement.

Stage 5 — Preliminary Due Diligence

After qualified buyers have executed a satisfactory non-disclosure agreement, the seller builds momentum for value enhancement realization by increasing the perceived value of the company among those buyers. As discussed in Stage 5 (see Section III), this is accomplished by controlling the flow of information conveyed to the buyer through the confidential information memorandum, initial meetings and other documentation and procedures.

The confidential information memorandum should highlight the positive aspects of the company and serve to increase the buyer's initial perception of the company. As the first piece of non-public information that the buyer will review, the confidential information memorandum should convey an attractive acquisition opportunity and motivate prospective buyers to move relatively quickly to seize that opportunity.

Initial meetings between the seller and prospective buyers are critical in generating value enhancement momentum. Careful consideration should go into what information should be provided during those meetings and how, so that buyers perceive the company in a positive sense. It also is important to consider how best to deal with any issues or concerns that a buyer might have about the company and to address these things up front. This helps to prevent buyers from retracting their stated position on value, price and deal terms where previously undisclosed issues become known at a later date. Furthermore, during the initial meetings with prospective buyers, the seller should gather important information about each buyer, such as the specific reason(s) for its interest in the company and its plans for the company if a transaction does take place. Such information can be extremely valuable when structuring and negotiating the deal.

In most cases, as part of its preliminary due diligence investigation, a buyer may ask to review other documentation and information not included in the confidential information memorandum. Buyers may also ask for a tour of the company's facilities or to conduct other procedures (such as a technical evaluation of the company's proprietary software). It is important for the seller to control the flow of information and to create a "give and take" atmosphere with the buyer. The seller should be cautious about providing highly sensitive information to a particular buyer too early in the preliminary due diligence stage in the event that a transaction with that buyer does not proceed. Further, upon providing a prospective buyer with additional information about the company, the seller should request some feedback regarding what influence that information has on the buyer's perception of value, deal structure, its continued interest level and so on. Such feedback allows the seller to better understand the buyer's position and to modify the process with that buyer and other buyers in order to continue building momentum toward value enhancement realization.

Stage 6 — Deal Structuring

As discussed in Stage 6 (see Section III), deal structuring involves whether the shares or the net assets of the company are sold, the forms and terms of payment, and the terms of the management contract. The important thing for business owners to remember is that the terms of the deal are just as important (and perhaps more important) as the stated purchase price for their company. The creation and realization of value enhancement, both from an economic standpoint and from the perspective of the business owner's personal value system, ultimately depends on the structure of the deal. In this regard, value enhancement can be realized where proposals are evaluated based on their risk-reward parameters and their income tax efficiency to the seller.

Owners of privately held companies normally prefer to sell shares to receive more favourable income tax treatment. Conversely, buyers normally prefer to buy assets due to the tax advantages that will accrue to them and to avoid undisclosed liabilities. When comparing offers that are received for the shares of their company as opposed to its net assets, the seller must consider the after-tax proceeds that would be realized under either scenario. In this regard, reorganization of the owner's personal affairs and estate planning that was done when preparing for the sale set the foundation for tax minimization and value enhancement realization at the deal structuring stage.

With respect to the forms and terms of payment, the price that is paid for a privately held company seldom is entirely represented by cash on closing. It is not uncommon for buyers to use other forms of consideration, such as holdbacks, seller take-backs, earnout arrangements and other forms of payment that contain an element of risk to the seller. Therefore, it is important for the seller to understand that an increase in the stated purchase price does not necessarily translate into an increase in the value received upon the sale. When evaluating an offer for their company, the seller should consider not only the stated purchase price, but the timing of payment, the conditions for payment, and the risks of non-payment. Any portion of the purchase price that is not received in the form of cash at the closing date of the transaction is subject to the risk of not being realized. The seller should be satisfied that the potential rewards from a non-cash deal structure offset the risks that they assume.

Finally, the terms of the post-transaction management contract and related non-competition agreement and other agreements must be carefully considered. With respect to the management contract, the seller must be satisfied with their responsibilities, basis of compensation, and the duration of the agreement. With respect to the non-competition agreement, the seller must be satisfied with the nature and geographic scope of prohibited activities and the duration of those restrictions. These agreements can have a bearing on both the economic value of the deal as well as the intangible aspects of value that are important to the business owner.

Stage 7 — Negotiations

The ability of the seller to realize value enhancement is largely dependent upon their negotiating position and the negotiating skills of their intermediary. As discussed in Stage 7 (see Section III), preparations undertaken by the seller and their team of advisors prior to negotiations and the negotiating strategies and tactics that are used, are fundamental in this regard. Ultimately, the negotiations should culminate in an agreed LOI between the buyer and seller. The key to the value enhancement realization in the negotiations stage is to secure an LOI that offers the best value to the business owner. As previously illustrated in Exhibit II-1, value to the business owner is a combination of the stated purchase price, the economic terms of the deal and the intangible aspects of the deal.

Extensive preparation is essential prior to entering into negotiations. This includes research and analysis on each buyer with whom negotiations will take place, the reasons for their interest in the company and an objective assessment of the relative negotiating position of the buyer and seller. The better the information base of the seller and their team of advisors, the greater the ability to employ a negotiating strategy and tactics that will generate enhanced value for the seller. For this reason, it is essential that information regarding each prospective buyer be gathered throughout the sale process, including during the search for buyers and when buyers are conducting their preliminary due diligence on the company.

The negotiating strategies and tactics used by the seller and their intermediary are a function of the perceived negotiating position and negotiating strength of the seller relative to the buyer. Negotiating position and strength are in turn a function of the alternatives available to each party. Therefore, the ability to create and realize value enhancement rests in the ability of the seller and their intermediary to develop and maintain attractive alternatives in terms of the number of qualified prospective buyers, and to understand each buyer's negotiating position and expectations.

Interested buyers will prepare an LOI for the seller's consideration, and request that the seller sign back the LOI to indicate their agreement. This affords the buyer a specified period of time to conduct detailed due diligence and to negotiate the purchase agreement with the seller on an exclusive basis. The seller should carefully consider the content of an LOI received from a prospective buyer prior to agreeing to same. Negotiating the LOI can be very intense. Value enhancement is created where the seller and their intermediary can orchestrate a competitive bidding environment to receive letters of intent from two or more buyers around the same time. This allows the seller to leverage buyers against each other. To realize value enhancement, sellers should ensure that any LOI agreed to with a buyer addresses all significant aspects of the deal in a clear and unambiguous manner. This reduces the ability of the buyer to renegotiate significant terms of the deal after it has been granted a period of exclusivity.

Stage 8 — Closing

As explained in Stage 8 (see Section III), closing the deal consists of the buyer's detailed due diligence, negotiating the final price and terms as reflected in the purchase agreement (and related agreements) and the final closing. In the closing stage, the seller's emphasis shifts from value enhancement creation to value enhancement retention. Ideally, all of the value enhancement elements of the deal will be reflected in the agreed LOI. Buyers often attempt to use the detailed due diligence process in order to negotiate downward price and value adjustments to what had previously been proposed to the seller in the agreed LOI. The key to value enhancement in the closing stage is for the seller to maintain their negotiating position in order to crystallize the value enhancement created throughout the sale process.

The seller should be satisfied that the buyer will not uncover any new information in its detailed due diligence review that will justify any modifications to the proposed terms of the transaction. The seller should consider and prepare for the buyer's due diligence expectations beforehand to help ensure that the process is conducted efficiently and with minimal disruption to the company's ongoing operations. A shorter detailed due diligence period normally is preferred since it reduces the likelihood of an adverse event within the company, the industry or the economy in general, that may complicate the process or result in the transaction not closing.

The seller should work to ensure that the negotiations of the purchase agreement and related agreements proceed smoothly by maintaining some degree of flexibility in order to meet the buyer's concerns following the findings of its detailed due diligence. The seller should be wary of representations and warranties in the purchase agreement that may fundamentally increase the risk to the seller and hence diminish the value that is received.

The seller should strive for a smooth closing and avoid any issues that would provide the buyer with grounds for last-minute renegotiations. In this regard, the seller should continue to operate the company as usual throughout the closing period, subject to any restrictions imposed in the agreed LOI. Maintaining a strong, attractive company diminishes the likelihood that a deal will not close on the agreed terms and puts the seller in a better negotiating position should unforeseen issues arise at closing. Further, the seller should be satisfied that the financial statements of their company at the closing date are fairly stated so as to avoid a reduction in the purchase price pursuant to post-closing audit adjustments.

The *Value Enhancement Framework™*

The *Value Enhancement Framework™*, depicted in Exhibit II-7, illustrates the keys to value enhancement in each stage of the private company sale process.

Exhibit II-7

THE *VALUE ENHANCEMENT FRAMEWORK™*

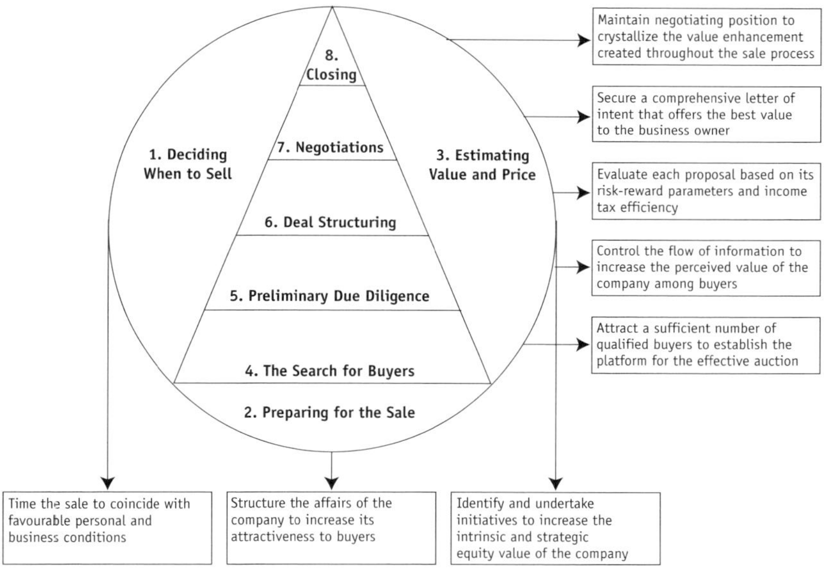

As indicated in Exhibit II-7, there are two distinct facets to creating and realizing value enhancement. The outer layer of the framework encompasses the planning phase of the private company sale process. This includes deciding when to sell, preparing for the sale and estimating value and price. These things are inter-related. As discussed earlier in this chapter, the equity value of a company is a function of its prospective discretionary cash flow, the rate of return applied thereto and its financial position. A company's equity value fluctuates over time based on economic and industry conditions. Further, adequate pre-sale preparation can increase a buyer's perception of a company's prospective cash flow, growth prospects and so on, and therefore have an impact on the price that a buyer is willing to pay.

The inner pyramid of the framework incorporates the stages of the execution phase of selling a privately held company. Through creating an effective auction, the seller and their intermediary build momentum for value enhancement through the search for buyers, preliminary due diligence, deal structuring and negotiations, and crystallize that value on closing.

Value creation and realization during the execution phase is facilitated where adequate planning has been conducted in terms of timing of the sale, structuring the affairs of the company and undertaking initiatives to increase the company's equity value. However, while the stages of the planning phase may be completed, value enhancement will be achieved only if the seller and their intermediary are successful in creating an effective auction when executing the sale of the company. Creating the effective auction requires that the seller generate liquidity for the company by controlling the sale process and developing a competitive bidding environment, while maintaining the flexibility needed in order to react to issues and opportunities as they arise. Therefore, creating and realizing value enhancement is a function of both adequate planning and effective execution.

A more detailed discussion of how value enhancement is created and realized within each stage of the private company sale process is provided in the following Stages in Section III.

Summary

The price that is paid for a company in the open market may be substantially different from a determination of its fair market value for many reasons, including the knowledge base of the buyer and seller, the structure of the deal and other reasons. The aggregate equity value of a company can be segregated between its net operating assets, financial liabilities, intangible value, redundant assets and the synergies that a buyer anticipates following a transaction.

The enterprise value of a company is a function of its prospective discretionary cash flow and the rate of return applied thereto. Discretionary cash flow is calculated as revenues less cash operating costs, capital expenditure requirements, incremental working capital, and cash income taxes, but before financing costs. The rate of return is a function of a company's perceived risks, growth prospects and debt capacity. The equity value of a company is determined as its enterprise value less the amount of its outstanding financial liabilities. Further adjustments are made where necessary, to reflect excess or deficient net operating assets and redundant assets.

Business owners should understand the determinants of equity value in order to assess how and where it can be increased prior to the time their company is exposed for sale in the open market. Understanding the determinants of equity value also helps to dispel misconceptions that business owners sometimes have about the economic worth of their company. In addition, business owners should reflect on their own personal value system prior to the sale in order to ensure that these things are not compromised when finalizing the transaction.

In the context of selling a privately held company, the value received by the owner is a function of the stated purchase price, the economic terms of the deal and the intangible aspects of the deal. The *Value Enhancement Framework™* illustrates that value enhancement is achieved through a combination of adequate planning and effective execution. Value enhancement is created in the planning phase of the private company sale process through timing the sale to coincide with favourable personal and business conditions, structuring the affairs of the company to increase its attractiveness to buyers and by identifying and undertaking initiatives to increase the intrinsic and strategic equity value of the company.

Value enhancement is realized in the execution phase of the private company sale process where the seller builds momentum through the creation of an effective auction. The platform for an effective auction is established by attracting a sufficient number of qualified buyers. Value enhancement momentum is gained through controlling the flow of information to increase the perceived value of the company among buyers. Proposals that are received should be evaluated based on their risk-reward parameters and income tax efficiency. The essence of value enhancement realization occurs where the seller and their intermediary develop a competitive bidding environment to secure a comprehensive LOI that offers the best value to the business owner. Thereafter, it is important for the seller to maintain their negotiating position through the closing stage to crystallize the value enhancement that has been created throughout the sale process.

Stages of the Private Company Sale Process

Section III

SECTION III

Stages of the Private Company Sale Process

Stage 1 Deciding When to Sell

Introduction

Every business owner must face the reality that someday, in some manner, they and their company must part ways. Despite the prevalence of this ultimate succession issue, many business owners often don't consider it until they are forced to do so.

The decision as to when to sell a privately held company can arise either over a lengthy time frame or as a reaction to circumstances or opportunities. In either case, the business owner should consider the factors that are important to them both from an economic and a personal standpoint prior to entering into discussions with prospective buyers.

As an alternative to sale, business owners sometimes seek to find one or more individuals who will operate their company without taking an ownership interest. As a practical matter, this strategy is difficult to execute, particularly where an able operator is not readily available. In any event, it is an interim solution since every business owner must ultimately divest of their company at some point.

In some cases, a company is liquidated rather than sold, whereby the assets are sold in a piecemeal manner and the residual proceeds are distributed to the owner. Liquidating a company generally is less favourable than selling it because the proceeds of liquidation usually are much lower than the proceeds which the business owner would receive if their company were sold as a going concern. This is particularly true where severance payments to employees and other costs of winding up the company offset the value of its remaining assets. However, when faced with a very low offer price for their company, the owner might consider voluntary liquidation as an alternative. That said, liquidation, other than forced liquidation pursuant to receivership, is seldom a viable economic alternative. Accordingly, the discussion in this book assumes the company is sold as a going concern.

There are at least five basic avenues of succession for the owner of a privately held company that operates as a going concern: (1) sell or gift to family members; (2) sell to management or employees; (3) sell to other existing non-family third party shareholders (where there are two or more arm's length shareholders in the company); (4) sell to an arm's length third party buyer; or (5) pursue an initial public offering. While the focus of this book is a sale to an arm's length third party buyer, many of the principles and processes apply to the other avenues as well.

The optimal time to sell a privately held company can never be determined with certainty. However, value enhancement opportunities are created where the business owner times the sale to coincide with favourable personal and business conditions. These conditions include the owner's personal situation, economic and industry conditions, and the company's recent and prospective operating results.

The intangible aspects of value are more readily attainable where the business owner aligns the transition of the company with their personal interests. From a pricing and deal structuring perspective, it is not surprising that value enhancement is more readily achievable where economic and industry conditions are favourable and where the company has demonstrated strong recent operating results and its outlook is promising. Deciding when to sell within the context of the *Value Enhancement Framework™* is depicted in Exhibit III-1-1.

Exhibit III-1-1

DECIDING WHEN TO SELL WITHIN
THE *VALUE ENHANCEMENT FRAMEWORK*™

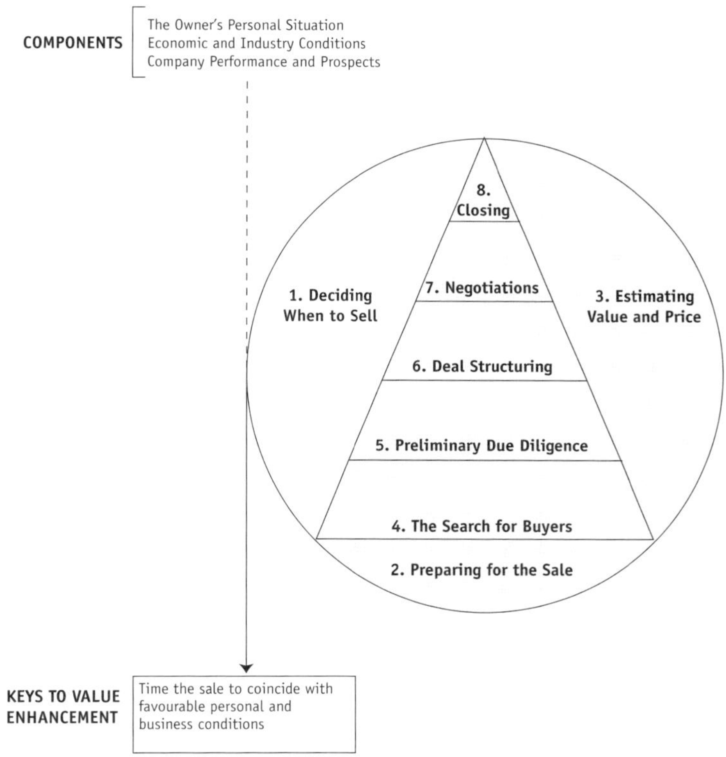

(i) The Owner's Personal Situation

Circumstances Leading to Sale

Compulsion to sell

The decision to sell a privately held company can arise either due to circumstances or opportunity. Business owners can be compelled to sell under certain circumstances, such as death, disability, failing health or the death of a key business partner. Having to sell a privately held company when compelled to do so is undesirable, since the business owner (or their estate) may be placed at a disadvantage when negotiating with prospective buyers. Therefore, ongoing estate planning is important, even if the business owner has no intention of selling their company in the foreseeable future. In this regard, adequate death and disability insurance can provide a means to allow the business owner or their estate to more effectively prepare for and execute the sale in such circumstances. This helps ensure that opportunities to realize value enhancement are not compromised by the need to act hastily.

The growing company dilemma

In some cases, business owners would prefer not to sell, but feel compelled to do so because they lack the resources (financial or otherwise) needed to realize their company's full potential. It is not unusual, for example, that a company experiencing a high rate of growth will be cash-poor. This is because a growing company may require significant cash outlays for capital expenditures, working capital and other expenses to realize its growth opportunities. Once a company and its owner have reached their borrowing capacity, the owner must decide how to raise additional capital. While a private equity investment sometimes can be obtained, this is not always possible or desirable. Alternatively, owners of rapidly growing companies may seek out a buyer willing to pay a premium for its inherent growth opportunities.

Where the business owner feels compelled to sell but believes that their company's growth prospects are strong, they may be able to realize on that growth potential by structuring the sale on an earnout or similar basis. This can afford significant value enhancement over the medium to longer term. Deal structuring is discussed in Stage 6.

Owners of rapidly growing companies must be careful not to compromise their negotiating position by causing their company to have excessive amounts of debt leading up to the sale. Given the time that it takes to complete a deal, the business owner must ensure that by the time negotiations with buyers are underway, the company has not found itself in a position of excessive debt caused by the need to finance growth. Such a circumstance can cause the business owner to be more compelled to act, thereby weakening their negotiating position. In addition, a company with excessive debt may be an undesirable acquisition target for certain buyers. Therefore, it is particularly important for the owner of a rapidly growing company to actively monitor and manage its cash flow to ensure that its financial stability is retained.

Voluntary retirement or change of interests

Other circumstances leading to a sale include the owner's loss of interest in their company or voluntary retirement. Such circumstances should be most accommodating to proper pre-sale planning. However, many business owners make the mistake of waiting until they are ready to retire before beginning the sale process.

Business owners should recognize that buyers of mid-size privately held companies typically want the owner to remain active in the company following the sale to facilitate the transition. Owners who are not prepared to make themselves available must be prepared to accept a lower price (or less favourable terms) for their company, assuming that the buyer will enter into a deal at all. The degree to which a buyer demands that the owner remain with the company following the sale is a function of the buyer's perception of the owner's importance to the ongoing operations in terms of their knowledge, contacts, expertise and so on. These things reinforce the importance of having a proper management and operational structure in place prior to the sale, which are discussed in Stage 2.

In any event, business owners often choose to remain with the company after the transaction where a significant component of the purchase price is contingent upon the future operating results of the company. Not surprisingly, most business owners do not feel comfortable in relinquishing total control of their company to the buyer during an earnout period. Business owners often want to remain involved in some capacity to comfort themselves that the company is being run properly following the sale. Furthermore, they may want to ensure that the company's profits are not eroded as a result of unreasonable cost allocations from the buyer, which reduce the contingency payments received by the business owner.

The nature and duration of the owner's involvement in the company following the sale can have a significant impact on both the economic and the intangible elements of value enhancement. Business owners should carefully consider the extent and conditions under which they are prepared to be involved after the transaction and their degree of flexibility on this issue, long before their company is exposed for sale in the open market. An owner's negotiating position may be compromised where they initially state a willingness to enter into a management contract and subsequently change that position.

Unsolicited offers

In some cases, a business owner receives an unsolicited approach from a buyer that is interested in discussing the possibility of a transaction. Unsolicited offers can represent attractive opportunities for business owners, but the process must be carefully managed to ensure that the ability to realize value enhancement is not compromised. Since the possibility of an unsolicited offer always exists, business owners should regularly review their corporate and personal affairs to ensure that they can react quickly to such opportunities.

As a starting point, any business owner receiving an unsolicited inquiry from an intermediary should insist on knowing the identity of the ultimate buyer. In addition, it is important for the business owner to ensure that a satisfactory non-disclosure agreement is obtained prior to disclosing any confidential information about their company.

Some business owners make the mistake of acting too hastily upon receiving an unsolicited offer. They are eager to get the process going and to find out what a buyer might be willing to pay for their company. A tactic used by some buyers is to exert pressure on the business owner to consummate a transaction following an unsolicited offer. This sometimes is done where the buyer suggests that it only has adequate funds for one or two transactions and that it will go elsewhere if the owner does not respond quickly. While this might be true, the business owner should remember that they have something that the buyer wants, and that negotiating with a buyer whose sole interest is buying companies at a bargain price will undermine the inherent value of their company.

It usually is best for the business owner who receives an unsolicited offer to play the role of the 'coy seller' and to demand more information from the prospective buyer at the outset of the discussions. The business owner should enquire, for example, what specifically attracted the buyer to their company. This will provide some insight into important value drivers that the buyer perceives. The business owner also should try to ascertain whether the buyer is broadly soliciting the market for acquisition opportunities or whether it is being selective. There is a good chance that if the owner's company is one of a number that meet broad criteria set by a buyer, the buyer may just be "bargain hunting".

When approached with an unsolicited offer, the sale process is somewhat simplified in that the search for buyers is not conducted. Rather, the sale process normally proceeds from providing preliminary due diligence information through to deal structuring, negotiations and closing. While on the surface this simplification may be attractive to the business owner, value enhancement normally is best realized through a competitive bidding process. When making an unsolicited approach, the buyer is trying to secure the exclusive opportunity to conduct due diligence and negotiate a purchase agreement without having to bid against other possible buyers. It is in the buyer's interest to place a tight deadline in an unsolicited offer scenario so that the business owner has limited or no opportunity to shop around for other prospective buyers.

It is important for the business owner to remain in control of the sale process even when the buyer makes the first approach. This often means that the business owner should slow down the process while they obtain professional advice. If a buyer truly is interested in the company, the buyer will not walk away just because the business owner wants to be cautious.

Business owners sometimes get so caught up in the high-pressure sales tactics used by a buyer that they fall into the trap of dealing with a single buyer. This generally should be avoided. As discussed in Stage 7, negotiating strength is a function of the alternatives available to the buyer and the seller, which normally stems from building momentum throughout the sale process and the creation of a competitive bidding environment. Where an unsolicited offer is received, so long as other alternatives remain available (e.g., finding another buyer or not selling at all), the business owner's negotiating position need not be compromised. Value enhancement can be created and realized in circumstances of an unsolicited offer where the business owner remains in control of the process and at least creates the perception that other viable alternatives exist.

Considerations Prior to Sale

The sale of a privately held company usually has a profound impact on the life of the owner and their family. This is particularly the case where one or more members of the owner's family are actively involved in the company. Many business owners fail to fully consider these consequences prior to the sale. Business owners should carefully reflect on their personal values and thoroughly consider what their lives, and the lives of their families, will be like following the sale. Reflecting on personal values prior to the sale also helps the business owner in structuring a deal that meets with their unique interests and circumstances. Mental preparation for a fundamental life transition is important to ensure that the intangible aspects of value enhancement are realized.

The transition sometimes is facilitated where the business owner remove themselves from the company gradually over the course of a few years by working fewer hours, taking longer vacations and affording greater responsibility and authority to arm's length managers and employees. In addition, a graduated exit from the company is viewed favourably by potential buyers, as it will cause them to perceive that the continued involvement of the owner is not essential to the long-term viability of the company. However, a graduated exit is not always possible or desirable.

An issue that frequently arises is the difficulty that some business owners have in making the transition from owner to employee where they are retained under a management contract for a period of time following the sale. As previously discussed, most buyers of privately held companies expect that the business owner will remain with the company in some capacity for some period of time following the sale to facilitate the transition. It is not uncommon for buyers of privately held companies to expect the business owner to remain for a period of six months to three years to ensure that customers, employees, suppliers and other key parties are comfortable with the buyer. The role and responsibilities of the former owner are subject to negotiation, but might range from a part-time consulting position to full-time employment. Therefore, prior to selling the company, owners must consider the scope of relationship which they are willing to enter into with a buyer, both in terms of their responsibilities as well as the duration of such an arrangement. Prior to selling their company, owners should also consider what they would like to do following the sale and any post-sale employment period. This will influence the parameters of any management contract and non-competition agreement that they are willing to enter into.

Business owners who are uncertain about whether or not to sell will sometimes hire a third party general manager to run their company. While this might be an ideal scenario for some business owners, it does present practical problems. First and foremost is the difficulty in finding a capable general manager where one does not already exist within the company. Even if a capable manager is found, that individual often expects to become a shareholder in the company, which can create a new set of challenges. Sometimes this issue can be resolved by offering the manager a lucrative bonus with a special incentive if the company is sold. Alternatively, the manager could have a right of first refusal on the purchase of the company, so long as that right is structured in such a way so as not to impede the competitive bidding process.

Another fundamental consideration for business owners prior to sale is whether to sell (or transfer) their company to family, sell to management or employees or to find a third party buyer. Deciding whether or not to sell or transfer the company to family members is a function of the owner's belief in their family's level of interest in the company and their ability to operate it. Unfortunately, difficulties often arise because owners sometimes cannot or do not objectively assess the ability of their family members to achieve a smooth transition and successfully run the company over the long term.

The advantage of selling to existing management is that the sale process is somewhat simplified, which can reduce the time and cost involved. However, this avenue prevents the owner from using the sale process to create an auction to realize added value. Furthermore, company managers often are subject to financial constraints, which limits the price that they are able to pay, or causes the terms of sale to be less favourable to the business owner. Finally, as internal buyers, managers typically cannot realize synergies which further reduces the attractiveness of the management (or employee) buyout option.

While selling to a strategic buyer normally results in a higher price being paid, there are other issues that business owners must consider. Some owners are sensitive to what will become of their company and its employees following the sale. Where such concerns do exist, business owners are best to address them with prospective buyers up front so that expectations are made clear near the outset of the sale process. Where a buyer is restricted in its ability to operate the company following the sale, it usually results in a reduction in the purchase price or a change in deal structure, if a deal can be consummated at all.

Finally, business owners should clearly understand their personal financial situation and cash needs prior to a sale. To the extent that the owner does not require cash on the closing of the transaction and can offer prospective buyers deferred or contingent payments for a portion of the purchase price, that flexibility may attract a greater number of interested buyers, thereby increasing liquidity and placing the business owner in a position to realize greater value enhancement over time. However, even if the business owner does not require a cash deal, such a deal may be desirable if they are not comfortable with taking on the risk associated with non-cash forms of consideration.

The factors that business owners should consider prior to the sale are summarized in Exhibit III-1-2. Each of these things has an impact on the intangible aspects of value that is realized by the business owner upon the sale.

Exhibit III-1-2

KEY CONSIDERATIONS PRIOR TO SALE

Personal Impact on Owner and Family	Who Should Buy the Company
Family members that are actively involved Feasibility of a graduated exit Transition from owner to employee	Employees/family/third party buyer Price and terms these parties can afford Ability to effect the transition
Plans Following the Sale	**Personal Financial Situation**
Terms and duration of a management contract Provisions of a non-competition agreement	Ability to accept non-cash forms of payment Willingness to accept risk in proceeds

(ii) Economic and Industry Conditions

Economic Conditions

The sale of privately held companies tends to be more prevalent when economic conditions are favourable. The underlying reasons for this include:

- strong economic conditions generally make it easier for buyers to raise capital in order to effect transactions;
- when interest rates are low or declining, buyers are able to reduce their cost of capital, which increases the price they are willing to pay to acquire attractive acquisition targets;
- where public equity markets are trading at high valuations, publicly held companies are more willing to use their own stock as currency in order to effect a share-exchange transaction; and
- favourable economic conditions often result in companies having cash surpluses, which can be used for acquisitions.

Favourable economic conditions generally increase the number of interested buyers, which improves the liquidity of the market for corporate acquisitions and therefore increases the prices (and values) that are paid. Liquidity is an underlying driver of value. While it is not possible to anticipate when ideal economic conditions will occur, business owners should be aware of general economic indicators that provide some perspective on whether conditions are likely to improve or deteriorate.

"Economic conditions" refers to more than just statistical macro-economic indicators such as gross domestic product. It also refers to changing geo-political and global business infrastructure conditions that impact the demand for companies operating within certain industry sectors. Examples in recent years include the impact of the Internet and e-commerce on businesses, the growing influence of imported goods from Asia and significant fluctuations in the Canadian dollar against the US dollar. Each of these things has a differing impact on the overall competitiveness of Canadian companies and the general interest levels that buyers have for companies that operate within certain industry sectors. Business owners should be cognizant of changing global factors and carefully consider how those factors will influence their operating results and the level of interest that buyers might have in their company.

Ideally, business owners should be prepared to react on a timely basis when economic conditions seem right to do so. That said, the market for the purchase and sale of privately held companies in Canada exists through good times and bad. While not ideal, business owners can still attain significant value enhancement under weak or declining economic conditions where the sale is adequately planned and effectively executed.

Industry Conditions

Not surprisingly, the conditions of a particular industry influence the number of transactions and the prices that are paid for companies operating within that industry. Companies operating in growth industries tend to fetch higher prices than those operating in mature or declining industries. This is because companies operating in industries characterized by growing demand for their products and services do not need to take market share away from their competitors in order to continue growing. In addition, pricing pressures tend to be less in growing industries than in mature industries. The ability of a company to grow its revenues and maintain or increase its profit margins will increase its prospective discretionary cash flow which, as discussed previously in Section II, is a key determinant in business valuation and pricing.

Many industries go through cycles, which often are related to general economic cycles. Where practical, it usually is preferable for business owners to time the sale of their company to capitalize on favourable industry conditions characterized by an upswing in the industry cycle for many of the same reasons as timing the sale to coincide with favourable economic conditions. Once again, while ideal timing with respect to industry conditions can never be known with certainty, business owners should be aware of leading indicators that suggest prospective growth or decline within their industry and be prepared to react in a timely manner. This includes the impact that developments have on certain industries, and the resultant influence on the level of interest that buyers might have for companies operating in those industries.

Industry consolidation

Many industries experience periodic phases of consolidation, where one or more buyers set out to purchase companies within an industry sector in order to achieve rapid growth. This is sometimes done due to macro-market forces that compel large corporate buyers to believe that "bigger is better", or because certain parties foresee an opportunity to "roll up" companies within a given industry. In the case of a roll-up strategy, it is not uncommon for a single buyer to acquire several privately held companies in the same industry, merge them together, and float an initial public offering. The rewards of such a strategy can be very lucrative if everything goes according to plan (which often proves not to be the case). Consolidations also are spurred where the general sentiment among many companies within a given industry is that they must combine their resources in order to survive and prosper, given current and foreseeable economic conditions (e.g., to alleviate long-term industry overcapacity or to realize economies of scale in order to compete more effectively against one or more large industry players).

"Liquidity", defined as the number of qualified prospective buyers at a given point in time, has a significant influence on business pricing and deal structuring. Since liquidity is greater during periods of industry consolidation, the prices that are paid for privately held companies during that time normally are higher than they otherwise might be.

A common mistake that business owners make when trying to time the sale of their company is missing out on the premiums paid during a period of industry consolidation. Business owners operating in an industry that is going through a consolidation phase sometimes believe that the highest prices will go to those who hold out until the end, however, this generally is not the case. Industry consolidation cycles tend to last in the order of one to three years. Business values (as represented by applicable valuation multiples) generally are at their highest levels around the middle of the cycle because, in the early stages of a consolidation phase, many buyers may be slow to react, and not realize that a consolidation is underway due to the time delay in acquisition announcements. During the last part of a consolidation phase, buyers often are too busy digesting what they have acquired, and so their appetite for new acquisitions is diminished. Therefore, business owners who are considering selling into a consolidation phase generally should be wary of waiting too long and thereby compromising their ability to realize value enhancement.

(iii) Company Performance and Prospects

The price and terms of sale for a privately held company are influenced to a large extent by its recent and prospective operating results and other performance indicators. As a practical matter, privately held companies tend to attract a greater number of interested buyers, and therefore sell for higher prices, following one or more years of strong financial results, as opposed to being exposed to the market following one or more years of poor results. As explained in Section II, privately held companies are valued based on the cash flow they are expected to generate in the future. It generally is easier for business owners to convince buyers that the outlook for their company's future cash flow is favourable where strong cash flow has been generated in the recent past. Conversely, it usually is more difficult to convince buyers that better times lie ahead following a year of weak financial results, unless there is a compelling explanation for why a change will occur.

Further, rightly or wrongly, transaction prices often are influenced by a valuation multiple that buyers are willing to pay based on a company's trailing operating results, such as a multiple of earnings before interest, taxes, depreciation and amortization (i.e., a multiple of "EBITDA" – which is described in Stage 3). The business owner's prospects for increasing the price paid and the terms of the deal generally improve where the company has reported strong financial results in recent years. Therefore, it usually is advisable for business owners to undertake initiatives that have the best chance of resulting in a strong, growing cash flow and profitability in the years leading up to the sale of their company.

In addition to strong historical results, business owners can generate incremental value by illustrating to buyers in a tangible way that the operating results of their company will continue to improve for the foreseeable future. For example, a growing order backlog, new customer contracts or recent cost reduction initiatives might serve to convey a plausible argument to prospective buyers that stronger operating results can be expected in the coming years. Buyers consider the prospective operating results of a company when determining its value and the price they are willing to pay.

Company performance and prospects also entail the issue of "critical mass". While a specific indicator does not exist, a company generally is considered to have achieved critical mass where it has a meaningfully established market presence and its production and service volume are at or approaching levels that can justify its operational and managerial infrastructure. In contrast to small businesses, companies that have attained critical mass in their operations tend to be attractive to a wider array of prospective buyers because of their established market presence, infrastructure and other advantages. As a general statement, bigger companies tend to be of greater interest to a larger number of qualified buyers, which positively influences liquidity and therefore the value that can be realized by the business owner. So, in some cases, business owners might be advised to defer the sale of their company until such time as it is perceived to have attained critical mass.

While it is advantageous to sell a company after it has experienced a good year, business owners should not allow themselves to get caught in the trap of becoming overly optimistic about what their company might be worth following one or more years of strong operating results. The price that a buyer will pay for a company might be higher where its growth prospects are strong, rather than after near-term growth has been realized and the outlook for longer-term growth is more modest.

Consider the following example. Mrs. Sea is the sole owner of Company C. She learns that private companies in her industry are selling today for 7x earnings before interest, taxes, depreciation and amortization (EBITDA). Mrs. Sea determines that Company C's EBITDA last year was $5 million. Then Mrs. Sea thinks to herself, "Today my company is worth $35 million, but this upcoming year should be a good one. If EBITDA grows by 40%, to $7 million, using the same multiple, my company will be worth $49 million." In the following year, Company C does grow, but not to the extent anticipated. EBITDA increases by 20% to $6 million. Mrs. Sea is dismayed to learn that the EBIT-

DA multiple her company will fetch has declined to 5x, translating into a value of $30 million. Hence, by waiting one more year, Mrs. Sea experienced a loss in value of $5 million.

As discussed later in Stage 3, valuation multiples (and rates of return) reflect the growth expectations of a company. Where growth expectations diminish, so do the valuation multiples, which impact business value. Therefore, when determining the ideal time to sell, business owners must consider both the historical and prospective cash flows of their company. This will influence the rates of return and valuation multiples that buyers adopt when determining economic value and price.

Summary

The decision of when to sell a privately held company can result from various circumstances, some of which are more compelling than others. To ensure that opportunities for realizing value enhancement are available even where unexpected circumstances arise, business owners are advised to review their estate and their company's operations on an ongoing basis. Where business owners are approached with an unsolicited offer from a prospective buyer, they generally are well advised to proceed slowly, gather information and obtain the necessary professional advice to ensure that they control the sale process and increase the likelihood of realizing value enhancement.

Prior to selling their company, business owners should consider important factors that will influence their lives and the lives of their families, as well as factors that will affect the structure and conditions of an eventual deal. In particular, business owners should consider what role and responsibilities they are prepared to accept following the sale, as well as their personal financial needs.

It usually is easier to sell a privately held company where economic and industry conditions are favourable, and the prices fetched tend to be higher. This mainly is due to the higher level of liquidity in the marketplace during such times. Prospects for liquidity and business values are particularly favourable where an industry is going through a period of consolidation.

Privately held companies tend to attract a greater level of interest among buyers where they have attained critical mass and have demonstrated one or more years of strong operating performance in the years prior to sale. Strong recent operating results tend to improve a buyer's perception of the outlook for continued favourable results and future growth. The explanation supporting the expectation of future cash flow growth is more credible where the business owner can provide tangible evidence to that effect, such as a growing order backlog or proven cost reduction initiatives. That said, business owners should be aware that when considering the benefits of growing their company one more year, they must also consider the prospective rates of return and valuation multiples that might prevail at that time.

SECTION III

Stage 2 Preparing for the Sale

Introduction

Adequate preparation for the sale of a privately held company is essential to achieving value enhancement. The process of actively preparing for the sale ideally should begin one to three years (or more) prior to the time the company is exposed to the open market. This is because many of the initiatives involved are time-consuming to execute.

When preparing for the sale, the key to value enhancement is to structure the affairs of the company to increase its attractiveness to buyers. This requires a comprehensive review of the company's operations and finances so that initiatives can be undertaken before the sale that will cause buyers to perceive that the company has a sustainable competitive advantage that can be readily transferred following the acquisition. When preparing the company for sale, business owners should keep in mind the fundamentals of value enhancement discussed in Section II. Recall that value (from an economic standpoint) is a function of the prospective discretionary cash flow that a company is expected to generate, the rate of return applied thereto and the financial position of the company. Therefore, the initiatives that are undertaken when preparing the company for the sale should serve to positively influence these key variables over the long term. Preparing for the sale and valuation and pricing (discussed in Stage 3) go hand-in-hand.

When preparing the company for sale, the business owner and their team of advisors should consider what information buyers most likely will want to review as part of their due diligence process and begin gathering such information at that time. This will help the business owner to be better prepared when presenting the positive aspects of the company and when addressing the issues and risks facing the company.

Preparing for the sale also involves organizing the personal affairs of the business owner in a way that will afford them greater flexibility when negotiating a deal with buyers and in structuring a tax-efficient transaction. Finally, as part of pre-sale preparations, business owners should engage objective, competent advisors who will help guide them through the sale process and who will contribute to value enhancement creation and realization.

Pre-sale preparation results in what can be termed the "business sale paradox". Business owners preparing their company for sale end up doing many of the things they should have been doing all along as part of good business practices, but were just too busy to complete them. Business owners should constantly be thinking about how to enhance the value of their company (and related estate planning) simply for the purpose of reaping the benefits that are associated with enhanced value, even if they decide not to sell. Furthermore, a discipline of continuous value enhancement planning and execution is important in the event that the business owner is compelled to sell (for example, due to deteriorating health) or is approached with an unsolicited offer. Pro-active business and estate planning also allows for the costs and benefits of value enhancement opportunities to be assessed more thoroughly. Further, professional fees and other costs often are more manageable when business and estate planning initiatives are not conducted in a hasty manner.

An important issue that has to be addressed when preparing for the sale is that of confidentiality. It generally is not possible for the business owner and their team of advisors to gather the necessary information and implement value enhancement initiatives in isolation. Employees are likely to become curious and possibly concerned over the future of the company and their place in it. These concerns generally are reduced where the business owner has developed a discipline of constantly pursuing value enhancement initiatives and therefore any formal preparations for sale may not stand out as a fundamental change in business philosophy.

Preparing for the sale within the context of the *Value Enhancement Framework™* is depicted in Exhibit III-2-1.

Exhibit III-2-1

PREPARING FOR THE SALE WITHIN
THE *VALUE ENHANCEMENT FRAMEWORK*™

(i) Operational and Financial Structuring

Preparing a privately held company for sale involves a comprehensive review of its operations and its financial affairs. Value enhancement opportunities are created where the business owner is effective in structuring the affairs of the company to increase its attractiveness to prospective buyers. The attractiveness of a privately held company is increased where initiatives are undertaken that:

- establish and reinforce the company's perceived sustainable competitive advantage in the marketplace. Buyers are more willing to pay a premium for companies that offer proprietary products or services, or that have a perceived competitive advantage in terms of their established customer base, technology, market presence and so on; and
- afford flexibility in its operating structure so that buyers perceive they can more easily integrate the company with their existing business. Buyers are more willing to pay a premium for companies where they perceive they can achieve synergies such as cost reductions and increased revenues, without having to incur excessive costs or undertake a substantial restructuring of the company's affairs.

Operational Matters

Business owners should conduct a thorough and objective assessment of their company well in advance of exposing it for sale in the open market. This should include an analysis of the company's customers and the markets that it serves, its management and organizational structure and other operational and administrative matters. It often is helpful to prepare a SWOT analysis, which objectively sets out the company's key strengths and weaknesses, as well as the opportunities and threats that it faces.

Customer and market analysis

Prior to selling their privately held company, and as part of good management practice, business owners should have a sound understanding of the company's customer base, why those customers purchase products or services from the company, the growth opportunities in the markets served by the company and important competitive and technological trends and developments in the marketplace. Buyers normally will inquire about these things during their due diligence investigation. As discussed in Stage 3, revenue stability and customer concentration influence the rates of return and valuation multiples used in business valuation and pricing. Value enhancement can be created where it can be demonstrated that the company has a loyal customer base and, where possible, contracts or commitments with customers that provide some level of confidence in the company's ability to generate prospective sales.

As part of the competitive analysis process, it is useful to gather information regarding recent merger and acquisition transactions involving companies that operate in the same industry and related industries. This can help the business owner to better understand what characteristics buyers might be looking for and get an indication of the prices (and resultant valuation multiples) that are being paid for similar businesses. This can provide business owners with some insight into what their company might be worth. Keeping abreast of competitive transaction activity also is helpful in identifying when an industry might be undergoing a period of consolidation, which as noted earlier in Stage 1, can offer a unique opportunity for business owners.

Management and employees

Prior to exposing the company for sale in the open market, the owner should ensure that a management and employee team is in place that will be attractive to prospective buyers. Most buyers seek to acquire companies with strong management depth, where the company is not dependent on one or a handful of individuals. In this regard, business owners sometimes fail to effectively transfer their own knowledge, contacts and other advantages to management and consequently the company remains dependent on the owner's continued involvement. This can be a costly trap since buyers are less likely to be interested in a company where a large portion of the value rests in its owner personally. Even where a buyer remains interested despite the company's reliance on its owner, the buyer often will structure the deal such that the owner must remain with the company for an extended period of time following the sale and have a substantial portion of the purchase price contingent upon the prospective operating results of the company.

Business owners should ensure that key positions within the company are filled with competent individuals prior to soliciting prospective buyers, as it can be harmful to the owner's negotiating position where senior management roles remain vacant. However, business owners generally should try to portray that they operate a lean organization, because where a buyer perceives the company has excessive personnel to support its operations (disregarding possible headcount reductions due to post-acquisition synergies), the buyer may become concerned about the costs associated with termination and restructuring.

Many companies employ one or more individuals who are critical to its long-term prosperity. This may include key people in the area of sales, product development or other areas of the business. The business owner must determine when they will advise these key employees that the company is being marketed for sale. Where key employees are not advised of the pending sale of the company until a buyer begins its detailed due diligence investigation, the business owner runs the risk of jeopardizing their negotiating position since most buyers want to meet with key employees prior to finalizing the purchase of the company. If key employees react with concern or leave the company prior to the sale, the buyer may significantly reduce the price it is willing to pay, or even withdraw its offer altogether.

Consequently, it generally is advisable for the business owner to inform key employees of a pending sale of the company at a relatively early stage in the process (at least prior to negotiations with prospective buyers). Ideally, these key individuals should be asked to execute an employment agreement that helps to retain them over the medium to long term, and possibly limits their ability to directly compete against the company (or at least solicit customers and employees of the company) for some period of time following their departure. This generally necessitates offering some consideration to key employees in return, such as incentive payments or a "parachute clause" that provides key employees with a guaranteed lump sum payment in the event they are terminated following the sale of the company. While the costs associated with retaining key employees might reduce the price that a buyer is willing to pay, the business owner must weigh that risk against the reduction in value that might be experienced if key employees leave prior to the sale, or a buyer perceives that one or more key employees may leave shortly thereafter.

General operational matters

Ideally, business owners should strive to portray an efficient, well-run operation that enables a buyer to readily integrate the company with its existing operations. There are initiatives that business owners can undertake when preparing their company for sale, which include:

- making the facility clean and presentable. This may necessitate minor repairs, painting, and so on;
- ensuring that the equipment is in good working order. Unrepairable or unusable equipment should be removed or divested of prior to the sale to avoid the perception that the company is inefficient or disorganized;
- reviewing inventories and removing obsolete items. Inventories should be properly organized so that they appear well managed;
- ensuring that ongoing research and development projects are well documented and that the costs and benefits associated with planned developments have been duly considered;

- putting in place reporting systems to track the company's key performance indicators. Key performance indicators are those that are believed to be leading indicators of the medium to longer term success of the company. They may include both financial and non-financial measures, such as market share, capacity utilization, product returns and employee productivity. The business owner may be able to raise the buyer's perception of the company by demonstrating a favourable trend in the key performance indicators;
- inspecting real property owned by the company and obtaining an independent environmental review where appropriate. Buyers are wary about purchasing real property that has any form of environmental contamination and they often will insist on some form of environmental audit and "escrowed funding" related to environmental contamination prior to finalizing the transaction;
- updating the website to portray an attractive image of the company. The company's website is one of the first things that buyers will examine upon learning that the company is for sale. Therefore it will influence the buyer's initial perception of value and its overall interest in the company; and
- carefully considering the implications of entering into any new long-term commitments prior to sale. For example, a buyer that had planned to consolidate facilities may take a negative view of a company that enters into a 10-year lease agreement before the sale.

Administrative matters

On the administration side, business owners should ensure that the affairs of the company are in proper order prior to soliciting buyers. This includes the company's minute books and corporate records, lease contracts, policy manuals, customer and supplier contracts, banking agreements and similar types of documentation.

Organizing the administrative affairs prior to marketing the company for sale is important in several respects. First, any loose ends can be rectified before they become problematic. Second, buyers normally will want to review contracts and records during their detailed due diligence. Therefore, such documentation should be readily available in order to prevent delays and to portray an image to buyers that the organization is well run. Finally, where important contracts and information cannot be made readily available, that delay may cause a buyer to believe that no other buyers are interested in the company, which can in turn be harmful to the owner's relative negotiating position.

Summary of operational matters

The cornerstones of operational matters that should be addressed when preparing the company for sale are summarized in Exhibit III-2-2.

Exhibit III-2-2

CORNERSTONES OF OPERATIONAL MATTERS WHEN PREPARING THE COMPANY FOR SALE

Customer and Market Analysis	Management and Employees
Analysis of customer base Growth opportunities in the market Competitive trends and developments Revenue stability and predictability Transactions involving similar companies	Management depth Vacancies in key positions Ability of management to effect a transition Contracts with key employees Informing employees of the sale
General Operational Matters	**Administrative Matters**
Presentation and inspection of facilities Inventories and equipment well maintained Company website up-to-date Key performance indicators R&D projects justified and documented	Minute books and corporate records Lease agreements Customer and supplier contracts Policy manuals Banking agreements

Financial Matters

While value is future oriented, it generally is easier to sell a company based on its actual financial results than on its prospective results due to the (normally) higher level of credibility in what historically has been achieved rather than what might prospectively be achieved. Buyers tend to place considerable emphasis on the operating results of the company in the year(s) just prior to the sale. Therefore, business owners can create value enhancement opportunities by improving the financial results of their company in the years leading up to the sale. This involves work on the income statement and the balance sheet, which is addressed below.

Owners of privately held companies that normally do not have their company's financial statements audited or reviewed by a qualified accountant may wish to consider doing so in the years prior to the sale. An audit or review provides prospective buyers with some assurance that the financial statements are free of material misstatements. Furthermore, an audit or review normally is conducted effective as of the closing date of the transaction. If any accounting issues arise at that time, the business owner may be subject to unfavourable adjustments to the purchase price. If financial reporting issues can be identified and addressed beforehand, it might allow for pre-empting of issues that could give rise to an unfavourable adjustment.

The income statement

A business owner's negotiating position and prospects of realizing value enhancement usually are improved where their company has a demonstrated trend of strong revenue and profit growth in the years leading up to the sale. Incremental revenue growth might be accomplished where there is an opportunity for the business owner to accelerate the timing of selling products and services to customers. However, accounting standards governing revenue recognition must be considered. Revenue growth might also come from putting into place short-term sales initiatives so long as such initiatives are structured such that they do not entice undesirable behaviour (e.g., where the company's sales representatives are motivated to sell products at negative profit margins so as to generate a top-line oriented sales bonus).

Controlling expenses in the years leading up to the sale can have a significant impact on profitability. However, business owners should be cautioned that most buyers will be on the lookout for reductions in operating expenditures that are required to support the long-term viability and growth of the company. For example, in the years leading up to the sale, business owners sometimes reduce costs that may not offer an immediate payback, such as advertising, research and development and equipment maintenance. However, when a buyer discovers that expenses such as these have been artificially reduced, they usually adjust the purchase price accordingly.

That said, there sometimes are discretionary expenses within a privately held company that can be curtailed without impairing its operations. This is not to suggest that business owners should discontinue declaring shareholder bonuses to reduce earnings to the small business threshold or discontinue income-splitting, as such expenses normally are adjusted as part of the valuation process (see Stage 3). However, owners of privately held companies sometimes incur expenditures that are not essential to the operations of their business, and that can be reduced or eliminated with no unfavourable effect on its long-term operating results. This practice can be particularly fruitful for a business owner where the buyer expresses the purchase price as a multiple of recent historical operating results. For example, if a buyer indicated that it was prepared to pay 5x trailing EBITDA (earnings before interest, taxes, depreciation and amortization) for the company, then by legitimately reducing expenditures by $100,000 in the year prior to the sale, the business owner could increase the purchase price by $500,000.

Finally, in the years prior to the sale, business owners may want to consider capitalizing certain expenditures rather than expensing them. Most privately held companies in Canada are operated with a goal of tax minimization. Therefore, purchases of capital assets with relatively low monetary values often are expensed. However, by capitalizing and depreciating some of these items (where justified), the business owner may be able to increase the purchase price for the company, particularly where a buyer relies on a "multiple of EBITDA" as one of its primary valuation methodologies (see Stage 3).

The balance sheet

From a balance sheet perspective, financial clean-up should commence with the removal of any redundant assets that will not be sold as part of the company (redundant assets are those not required in the ongoing operations of the company). Many owners of privately held companies hold redundant assets through their company rather than personally (e.g., vacant land that was purchased on speculation and which is not required in the company's ongoing operations). Buyers normally do not want to purchase redundant assets because, in most cases, those assets would just have to be re-sold. Where buyers do acquire redundant assets, they often discount the price they are willing to pay by a considerable amount. For these reasons, redundant assets normally are removed from the company prior to sale. In most cases, the withdrawal of redundant assets can be done on a tax-deferred basis.

Working capital management is another balance sheet matter that should be addressed. A company's net working capital is defined as its current assets (such as accounts receivable, inventories and prepaid expenses) less its current liabilities (such as accounts payable and accrued liabilities).

When buyers analyze a company's financial statements, they often calculate ratios such as the number of days it takes to collect accounts receivable or to sell inventories. These calculations normally are done over a period of several years so that the buyer can detect if there is a trend or other issues. It is desirable for the business owner to demonstrate favourable trends, such as a reduction in the number of days that accounts receivable are outstanding over the period of several years, because the less the company needs to retain working capital to support its operations, the more cash can be removed from the company to provide the buyer with a return on its investment. It follows that in the years leading up to the sale, value enhancement opportunities can be created by carefully managing working capital items, thereby portraying an efficiently run company. If there is a need to take a reserve against uncollectible accounts receivable or obsolete inventories, it is better to take such a reserve several years prior to when the company is exposed for sale in the open market rather than in the year immediately preceding the sale.

Likewise, capital spending should be closely monitored in the years prior to sale. In particular, business owners should be cautious about undertaking major expansion initiatives in the years prior to the sale, as such initiatives will serve to increase the company's debt (or decrease its cash or other financial resources), while making it difficult to get paid for the benefits of the expansion. Buyers often are skeptical about a company's ability to meet the growth projections that underlie its expansion initiative.

Finally, business owners should be conscious of under-accrued liabilities in their company, such as employee vacation pay, pension obligations, post-retirement benefits and product warranties. Buyers normally closely scrutinize liabilities that will be assumed at the closing date. To the extent that liabilities exist that were not previously identified, it can serve to reduce the purchase price at closing. Further, where liabilities that exist at the closing date are identified after closing, it may also result in a subsequent negative purchase price adjustment.

Summary of financial matters

The financial matters that should be addressed when preparing the company for sale are summarized in Exhibit III-2-3. Note that these initiatives relate to the key parameters of value that were discussed in Section II.

Exhibit III-2-3

FINANCIAL MATTERS TO ADDRESS WHEN PREPARING THE COMPANY FOR SALE

Cash Flows	Rates of Return	Financial Position
Increase or accelerate product and service revenues where possible	Manage risk through increasing the perceived predictability of cash flows	Manage working capital and capital expenditure requirements
Control discretionary expenses	Demonstrate growth prospects through strong year over year performance	Ensure complete and accurate reporting of all liabilities
Capitalize expenditures where appropriate	Increase perceived debt capacity through asset and cash flow management	Remove redundant assets

Other Company Preparation Initiatives

Certain other initiatives that business owners should consider in the years prior to sale in order to enhance the value of their company include:

- raising the profile of the company. This involves doing things that will cause prospective buyers to believe that the company is a good corporate citizen and an attractive acquisition target. There are many ways this might be accomplished on a cost-efficient basis, such as media attention in the local press or a trade magazine that features innovative new products offered by the company or the company's work with local charities; and
- avoiding litigation where possible. While it is not possible for a company to avoid having lawsuits launched against it, some business owners attempt to recover prior losses by initiating a legal claim against suppliers or other parties. This tactic sometimes backfires where the company then becomes the defendant in a counter-claim. Buyers are wary about purchasing a company that is subject to a legal claim due to the uncertainty involved. As a minimum, an outstanding legal claim normally results in a portion of the purchase price being held in escrow until the matter is resolved, which could take several years.

(ii) Income Tax and Estate Planning

An important part of preparing for the sale of a privately held company involves the owner's personal affairs, particularly in terms of income tax and estate planning. Income tax and estate planning matters can be complex, and professional advice usually is needed. The business owner should seek to structure their personal affairs in such a way as to offer flexibility when negotiating with prospective buyers and to improve the likelihood of structuring a tax-efficient deal, while at the same time being cognizant of the cost-benefit tradeoff when doing so. Higher value can often be realized where the business owner is able to offer the buyer greater flexibility in terms of how their company is acquired and how the purchase price is paid. Flexibility in deal structuring generally leads to a greater number of quality alternatives becoming available to the business owner, which in turn serves to enhance the value that ultimately is realized upon the sale.

A detailed discussion of personal tax planning is beyond the scope of this book. However, a brief overview of some of the more common income tax and estate planning initiatives in effect at the date of writing is provided below. Business owners should be aware that tax laws are ever changing, and they should consult their professional advisors to determine which, if any, of these initiatives is right for them.

Holding Companies

Rather than holding the shares of a privately held company personally, it sometimes is beneficial to own the shares through a holding company. In Canada, transfers of operating company shares to holding companies usually can be done on a tax-deferred basis. Holding companies often are established when business owners crystallize their lifetime capital gains exemption (discussed below). Holding companies also can be used to hold redundant assets that are transferred out of the company prior to sale.

Dividends paid from one Canadian company to another are tax-free. Therefore, in some cases, dividends are paid out of an operating company to a holding company prior to the sale. This can result in a tax deferral opportunity for the business owner where the proceeds are retained in the holding company.

Consider the following simplified example. The shares of Company D, an operating company owned by Mr. Dee, are worth $10 million. The shares have a nominal cost base and the effective tax rate on capital gains is 25% (reflecting that only 50% of capital gains are taxable), ignoring the lifetime capital gains exemption. Therefore, if the shares of Company D were sold for $10 million, then Mr. Dee would pay capital gains taxes of $2.5 million and retain $7.5 million after tax. Now assume that prior to the sale, Mr. Dee transfers his shares in Company D to a holding company, which then becomes the direct owner of Company D. Company D then pays a $2 million (non-taxable) dividend to the holding company. The purchase price of the shares of Company D should decline to $8 million (being the $10 million original price less the $2 million dividend). The net income taxes paid on the sale would be $2 million (i.e., 25% of $8 million paid to the holding company) and Mr. Dee would retain $6 million after tax. In addition, Mr. Dee would own the shares of the holding company which holds $2 million in cash. Therefore, Mr. Dee retains $8 million in total (comprised of $6 million from the sale of shares plus $2 million from the dividend). The net benefit to Mr. Dee is $500,000. While Mr. Dee would pay tax on the cash held in the holding company if withdrawn, if that cash is not immediately required, it can be invested. In effect, Mr. Dee benefits by earning a return on money that would otherwise be paid as taxes. The other benefit of this strategy is that the purchase price for the shares of Company D has been reduced. This may help to attract a larger number of interested buyers or in structuring a more attractive deal.

Lifetime Capital Gains Exemption

Presently in Canada, each individual is entitled to a lifetime exemption on the capital gains realized on the sale of a "qualifying small business corporation" up to $500,000. Essentially, a qualifying small business corporation is a Canadian Controlled Private Corporation (as defined in the *Income Tax Act*) that meets certain defined criteria. Even owners of large-size private companies can be eligible for this tax benefit. Therefore, if the business owner's effective personal tax rate on capital gains is 25%, the tax savings realized on the $500,000 lifetime capital gains exemption is $125,000. The lifetime capital gains exemption is one of the reasons that owners of privately held Canadian companies prefer to sell the shares of their company as opposed to the underlying net assets. In some cases, the lifetime capital gains exemption can be multiplied among family members with appropriate ownership structuring or the use of family trusts.

Where possible, it usually is advisable for owners of privately held Canadian companies to crystallize their lifetime capital gains exemption prior to exposing their company for sale in the open market and even as part of ordinary course estate planning. Not only can tax laws be changed that may reduce or eliminate the benefit of the lifetime capital gains exemption, but also the owner's alternatives are improved when negotiating the sale. Specifically, as discussed in Stage 6, buyers normally prefer to buy the underlying net assets of a company due to the tax advantages of doing so, among other reasons, so buyers often are willing to pay a higher price for the net assets of a company as opposed to its shares. The lifetime capital gains exemption only applies when the shares of the company are sold and not when its net assets are sold. By crystallizing the lifetime capital gains exemption beforehand, business owners may be able to sell the underlying net assets of their company at a higher price while still reaping some available tax benefits, thereby increasing the after-tax proceeds they realize on the sale.

Corporate Income Tax Accounts

A company that qualifies as a Canadian Controlled Private Corporation (CCPC) for income tax purposes has special corporate income tax accounts, including a Capital Dividend Account (CDA) and Refundable Dividend Tax on Hand (RDTOH) account. In brief, the:

- CDA represents the non-taxable portion of net capital gains realized in a CCPC. The company can pay a tax-free dividend to its shareholders in the amount of the balance in the CDA. The CDA may contain amounts from other sources, such as the proceeds of corporate-owned life insurance; and
- RDTOH represents taxes paid by a CCPC on certain non-operating income, such as interest on investments. Essentially, a CCPC pays tax at a higher rate on investment income and receives a refund of the tax premium calculated at a rate of $1 for every $3 in taxable dividends paid to its shareholders. Therefore, while shareholders pay tax on dividends at the personal level, that tax essentially is offset by the RDTOH refund received by the company.

Importantly, the CDA and RDTOH are lost upon a change in control of a CCPC, so it is essential that any remaining balances in these accounts be cleared out prior to a sale so as not to lose the tax advantages associated therewith.

(iii) Transaction Advisors

Advisors that usually are involved in the private company sale process include lawyers, income tax experts, valuation experts and transaction intermediaries, among others. Each of these advisors is discussed below. The business owner might not require all of these advisors. Alternately, some advisors may be able to perform more than one of the functions.

The business owner should appoint one advisor, usually the intermediary, to coordinate efforts among the team of advisors and to champion the sale process. Appointing the right "coordinating advisor" is essential to ensuring that all of the important aspects of the sale process are duly addressed in an appropriate and objective manner and to increase the likelihood of value enhancement realization upon the sale.

Business owners often are reluctant to engage advisors when preparing for and selling their company for various reasons, including the costs involved, confidentiality and the desire to stay in control of the decisions affecting the sale of their company. While these things should be considered, the sale of a privately held company is a complex process, and for most business owners it is the largest single monetary event of their lifetime. Quality professional advice is fundamental to ensuring that value enhancement is being achieved and that the owner's needs are being met, including those they may not be aware of.

There is no shortage of advisors available to business owners who are seeking to sell their privately held company. Consequently, there is a wide variation in terms of their knowledge, expertise and cost. Engaging the right professionals is a matter of trust, so it is critical for the business owner to engage the advisors that are right for them in the context of the nature of their company, the industry in which it operates and the owner's personal situation.

It is important that the advisors retained to assist in the sale process have adequate knowledge and experience in the sale of privately held Canadian companies and who are known for offering their clients well-considered, objective advice. While there is a cost to engaging quality advisors, the business owner should weigh that cost against the expected value to be received in return. Good advisors should be able to "pay for themselves" through the enhanced value they bring to the business owner.

A clear engagement letter should be obtained with each advisor that is retained to assist in the sale process. The engagement letter should set out the deliverables, fees and costs, legal obligations and other important arrangements between the business owner and the advisor.

Fee arrangements should be established up front, in writing. Many advisors charge their fees on an hourly basis and therefore costs can escalate quickly with little or no apparent results. It is helpful to establish a budget for each advisor and have them agree to it in writing. This allows the business owner to manage costs and to review the advisor's performance on an ongoing basis throughout the sale process. Further, advisors normally charge for out-of-pocket disbursements, such as travel costs, photocopies and long distance calls. The business owner should ensure that there is an understanding, in writing, as to what the costs are expected to be. It usually is desirable for the business owner to pre-approve expenses that are beyond a certain monetary amount to ensure that these costs do not get out of control.

In some cases, business owners can recover some or all of their advisory fees (particularly the contingency fee paid to the intermediary) from the buyer. As part of the structure of the deal, a buyer may pay a slightly lower price for the company and pay the owner's transaction costs directly. This sometimes is advantageous to both the buyer and the seller from an income tax perspective, which can serve to enhance the overall value realized upon the sale.

Finally, confidentiality arrangements should be clearly established with advisors at the outset of their engagement. Each advisor should be aware of to whom they can or cannot speak regarding the sale of the company and the manner of communication (voice mail, e-mail and letters). Unclear confidentiality arrangements can result in employees, customers, competitors and others becoming aware of the pending sale prematurely, which might lead to significant problems for the business owner.

Exhibit III-2-4 summarizes the cornerstones for business owners to consider when engaging advisors to assist them in the sale of a privately held company.

Exhibit III-2-4

THE CORNERSTONES OF USING ADVISORS
IN THE PRIVATE COMPANY SALE PROCESS

Engage competent advisors that offer well-considered, objective advice	**Establish a written engagement letter that clearly sets out services, fees and costs**
Ensure that confidentiality arrangements are defined and understood	**Appoint one advisor (usually the intermediary) to act as the transaction coordinator**

Lawyers

Retaining appropriate legal counsel to assist in the sale of a private company is essential. Lawyers generally assist in many aspects of the sale process, from preparing for the sale through to closing. In particular, the business owner should engage a lawyer to review any legal documents, such as the purchase agreement, non-competition agreement and management contract, before the deal is finalized.

Business owners should ensure that the individual lawyer retained to assist in the sale process has sufficient experience in such matters. Therefore, the company's general counsel may or may not be the best choice, depending on the background of that individual and their legal firm. With the legal complexities and implications in the purchase agreement and other transaction-related documents, experience in handling such matters is essential.

Income Tax Experts

Obtaining sound advice on income tax structuring is essential, both in terms of preparing for the sale and when structuring the deal. Such advice may come from an accountant, lawyer or other professional who has in-depth tax knowledge. The degree of tax expertise required varies, depending on the size and nature of the company, the complexity of the transaction and the owner's personal affairs.

When preparing for the sale, income tax advisors can assist in ensuring that the owner's estate and the affairs of the company are organized in a way that will defer or reduce taxes and provide greater flexibility to the owner when negotiating with buyers. This may involve restructuring to ensure that the owner receives the benefits of the lifetime capital gains exemption and that excess cash or redundant assets are removed from the company in a tax-efficient way prior to the sale. These tax planning initiatives were discussed earlier in this stage.

Sound income tax advice also is essential in deal structuring. Common issues include whether the shares or the net assets of the company are sold, the tax implications of various forms and terms of payment and the taxation of amounts received under the management contract and other agreements. These tax issues are addressed in Stage 6.

Valuation Experts and Appraisers

Valuation experts normally are engaged where a business owner requires an independent valuation for purposes such as income tax and estate planning or shareholder buyouts. As discussed in Section II, there may be a substantial difference between the fair market value of a company as determined in an independent valuation and the price that the company will fetch when sold on the open market. However, an independent valuation sometimes is helpful to the business owner in assessing the reasonableness of offers submitted by prospective buyers. It may also be helpful before a company is exposed for sale because independent valuations, properly performed, should provide the business owner with an objective assessment of the key value drivers in their company and the risks and opportunities that a buyer likely will perceive. This information can be used to identify and undertake initiatives that increase the equity value of the company prior to the time buyers are solicited (see Stage 3).

In many cases, the intermediary may perform a valuation as part of their work in the sale process. A word of caution is warranted here — this would not be considered an "independent" valuation. Further, many intermediaries do not have formal business valuation training. In Canada, those having the requisite training usually hold the Chartered Business Valuator (CBV) designation. Some intermediaries (even those with professional qualifications) may be inclined to provide optimistic estimates of the value of a company to get the owner to "sign up" with them, so that the business owner is subsequently left to discover that their expectations were inflated.

If the company owns substantial real estate, it may be worthwhile to have it professionally appraised prior to exposing the company for sale. This is because there may be an opportunity to sell (or retain) the real estate separate from the company's principal operations (see Stage 3). A property appraisal may be necessary in order to evaluate the cost-benefit of such an alternative.

For capital-intensive businesses, it may be worthwhile to have an equipment appraisal completed to obtain an indication of its replacement cost. While underlying asset values generally are not the principal determinant of business value, higher underlying asset values may help to support a buyer's cash flow-based value determination. Furthermore, equipment appraisals can be used in support of obtaining bank financing by either the seller or the buyer. As discussed in Stage 3, the greater the perceived ability of a company to support debt financing, the lower the buyer's cost of capital, and the higher the resultant value.

Intermediaries

There are no stringent regulations in Canada that govern who can call themselves a business broker, investment banker or transaction intermediary (which are collectively referred to in this book as an "intermediary"). Many individuals and firms profess to offer intermediary services, yet they have little practical deal-making experience. Intermediaries who have a meaningful amount of deal-making experience usually have some formal certification, such as being registered as a Limited Market Dealer with a provincial securities commission.

The intermediary usually acts as the transaction coordinator when selling a privately held company. Buyers normally communicate with the intermediary in arranging meetings with the business owner, submitting letters of intent and conducting negotiations. Intermediaries generally are involved throughout the sale process, from pre-sale preparation through to closing. They work with the owner's other advisors (for example, lawyers and income tax experts) to facilitate the process and to ensure that value enhancement is realized. Therefore, it is of critical importance for the business owner to select the right intermediary to coordinate the sale process from planning through to execution and closing.

When selecting an intermediary, the business owner should consider their specific needs, and whether the intermediary is likely to be effective in achieving value enhancement realization as evidenced by their:

- experience in selling mid-sized privately held Canadian companies. The dynamics of selling a mid-sized Canadian company are different in many important respects than those of selling a small business, public company or a company based in the U.S. or elsewhere. This includes important differences in terms of tax and legal considerations, the types of buyers and negotiating strategies, all of which can have a significant impact on the terms of the deal;
- experience within the industry in which the company operates. Such experience, attained through transactions, valuation services, consulting or direct operating experience, makes it easier for the intermediary to understand the nature of the company's operations and to identify buyers that might have an interest in the company. It also helps the intermediary to coordinate the sale process by identifying lawyers and tax experts that possess relevant industry experience, as well as industry consultants and industry experts that can help in identifying and implementing initiatives to increase the intrinsic and strategic equity value of the company;
- professional qualifications, including whether they have earned the status of a Limited Market Dealer or similar formal recognition. These qualifications normally indicate that an intermediary is prepared to be bound by a professional code of conduct and that they perform a sufficient number of transactions in the Canadian marketplace to warrant the time and cost involved with maintaining that status;
- understanding of financial accounting and business valuation theory and practice, as evidenced by whether they hold a professional accounting designation (Chartered Accountant, Certified Management Accountant or Certified General Accountant) and professional valuation designation (Chartered Business Valuator). A strong technical finance and valuation background helps the intermediary to comprehend the financial drivers of a company's value, effectively convey those elements to prospective buyers and not become overwhelmed by a buyer's technical parlance involving financial matters;

- general understanding of Canadian income tax and legal matters. While the intermediary is not expected to be an expert in these areas, good working knowledge of these things will help the intermediary in identifying important issues and in coordinating efforts with legal and tax professionals. The intermediary should also have a good base of contacts (and referrals) among senior legal and income tax advisors in the event that they need to identify and recommend one or more such individuals that can assist in the sale process;
- research capabilities. The ability to effectively research the market and identify prospective buyers provides a knowledge base that is essential to effectively marketing the company for sale and negotiating with buyers in a manner that leads to value enhancement realization;
- experience in transactions involving the acquisition of privately held companies where the intermediary has acted on behalf of the buyer. First-hand knowledge of how buyers assess privately held companies is important to understanding what can be done to better position a company for sale, the financial models that buyers use when assessing value and price, determining how synergies are evaluated, and in negotiating and structuring the deal;
- ability to effectively communicate and negotiate, as evidenced by their mannerisms, reputation and referrals;
- approach to selling privately held companies, including who within their firm will be involved in the sale process, how they intend to identify and approach buyers, conduct negotiations, build deal momentum and create an effective auction; and
- ability to provide well-considered, objective advice that helps the business owner to realize their personal and financial goals. As a starting point, this requires that the intermediary take the time to understand the owner's particular needs, interest and circumstances. The intermediary should demonstrate to the business owner in a meaningful way that the sale of a privately held company is not a "cookie-cutter" process, but rather one that should be modified to meet the particular needs and interests of the business owner and their family. The intermediary selected should be one that the business owner believes will objectively advise them on the value of their company, the alternatives that are available, the attractiveness of proposals that buyers put forth and other things that influence both the economic and intangible elements of value in a deal.

These considerations are summarized in Exhibit III-2-5.

Exhibit III-2-5

INTERMEDIARY CHECKLIST

✓	Experience in selling mid-sized privately held Canadian companies
✓	Experience in the industry in which the company operates
✓	Professional intermediary qualifications
✓	Professional accounting and valuation qualifications
✓	Knowledge of Canadian income tax and legal matters
✓	Research capabilities
✓	Experience in the acquisition of privately held companies
✓	Ability to effectively communicate and negotiate
✓	Approach to the private company sale process
✓	Ability to provide well-considered, objective advice

Fees and costs

The fee charged by an intermediary usually is comprised of a work fee and a "success" or contingency fee. In most cases, the majority of the intermediary's fee is derived from the contingency component, which often is expressed as a percentage of the deal price. As such, understanding what the deal price represents is critical in assessing the reasonableness of the fee arrangement. Specifically, it is important to clearly establish:

- whether the contingency fee is calculated based on the enterprise value of the company or its equity value. As discussed in Section II, the enterprise value represents the total value of the company, including the debt and equity components, whereas the equity value refers only to the portion of the purchase price paid for the shares or net assets of the company;
- whether the price on which the contingency fee is calculated includes payments received by the owner under a post-transaction management contract, non-competition arrangements, rental income from the buyer on property that remains with the owner or similar arrangements; and

- when and how the fee is to be paid. As discussed in Stage 6, seldom is the price paid for a privately held company represented entirely in the form of cash at closing. Other forms of consideration often are used, which may include holdbacks, share exchanges, seller take-backs, earnouts and similar arrangements. This raises the issue of whether the intermediary receives their fee before the business owner collects the proceeds of sale.

While contingency fees help to align the interests of the business owner and the intermediary, a word of caution is necessary. The business owner should ensure that the intermediary's interests truly are aligned with their own. As noted throughout this book, the terms of a deal are just as important as the price that is paid (and perhaps even more so), as the highest price might not represent the best deal. Therefore, business owners should be comfortable that the intermediary whom they retain is objective and intent on serving their best interests, even if it means that the intermediary's fee may be somewhat reduced. A good intermediary will realize that, over the long term, the enhanced reputation they achieve from doing the right thing more than offsets the reduction in contingency fee earnings on a single assignment.

The intermediary engagement letter

Business owners should carefully consider the terms of the engagement letter that is signed with the intermediary. In addition to fees (discussed above), other important considerations include:

- whether the arrangements are on an exclusive or non-exclusive basis. Most intermediaries want to have exclusivity in order to protect themselves against a situation where the business owner (or other third party) identifies and consummates a transaction with another buyer, thereby bypassing the intermediary's contingency fee;
- the duration of the engagement and termination provisions. The agreement should set out the period in which the arrangements with a particular intermediary are in place, and the provisions for termination both during and after that time;
- the intermediary's right to receive the contingency fee on a transaction consummated after the end of the engagement. Most intermediary agreements specify that a fee will be payable for a specified time frame following termination if a transaction is completed with a buyer introduced by the intermediary; and

- the liability of the owner and the intermediary, including any release and indemnification granted by the business owner in favour of the intermediary.

Other Advisors

Other advisors that sometimes are helpful for a business owner to engage or consult when preparing for the sale include:

- **the company's accountants**, who might assist in preparing the company for sale and in preparing financial information for buyers to review as part of their due diligence investigation;
- **industry experts**, including those with technical or market expertise of the industry in which the company operates. Prior to the time the company is exposed for sale, industry experts can assist in objectively assessing the company's market position, competitive advantages and disadvantages, and so on. This will afford the owner more time to rectify or improve certain areas of their company in order to make it more attractive to prospective buyers;
- **business consultants**, who can assist in ensuring that the company is staffed and structured in a way that will be attractive to prospective buyers; and
- **financial planners**, who can assist the business owner in assessing their ongoing personal cash needs. The owner's need for cash on closing may affect the structure of the transaction that can reasonably be entered into with respect to the forms and terms of payment. Financial planners will also help in establishing an investment plan for the proceeds of sale.

The business owner must be satisfied that any advisors or consultants that are retained understand their personal and financial objectives and that they will act in the owner's best interests. In addition, the business owner and transaction coordinator must be satisfied that the advisors retained will be complementary to the sale process and that they will not take actions or make recommendations that will prove to be inconsistent or disruptive to the advancement of the owner's interests.

Summary

Adequate preparation for the sale of a privately held company is essential to realizing value enhancement. Preparing for the sale normally should begin at least one to three years prior to the time the company is exposed to the open market. The key to value enhancement is to structure the affairs of the company to increase its attractiveness to buyers. An attractive company is one that is perceived to have a sustainable competitive advantage that can be readily transitioned to a buyer.

Preparing the company for sale necessitates a comprehensive and objective review of the company's operations, including its customers, management structure and other operational and administrative aspects. The owner should determine which employees are critical to the company and enter into a formal employment contract where appropriate. Business owners should consider steps that can be taken to legitimately increase both the revenues and profits of their company in the years leading up to the sale. The balance sheet of the company should be reviewed in order to improve working capital management, manage capital expenditures and remove any redundant assets prior to the sale.

Preparing for the sale also should include a review of the owner's personal affairs to ensure that the ownership of the company is structured in a way that will provide flexibility when dealing with buyers and at the same time help to reduce the tax burden on the sale. This may include the use of holding companies, crystallizing the lifetime capital gains exemption and reviewing corporate income tax accounts.

Transaction advisors are an essential element to ensuring that the business owner realizes value enhancement. In particular, lawyers, income tax advisors and intermediaries are an integral part of the private company sale process. Other advisors, such as independent valuation experts, accountants and industry experts, may also play a role. One advisor, normally the intermediary, is appointed as the transaction coordinator and is responsible for working with the other advisors and facilitating the sale process from planning through to execution and closing. For each advisor, a clear understanding should be established with respect to work expectations, fees and confidentiality arrangements. Business owners should retain professionally accredited advisors that have experience in dealing with the sale of privately held Canadian companies and who are known for offering sound, objective advice to their clients.

SECTION III

Stage 3 | Estimating Value and Price

Introduction

Business owners often contemplate what their privately held company is worth. Unfortunately, there is no easy answer to that question. Estimating the value of a private company and the price that it might fetch in the open market is a complex task that necessarily involves an element of subjectivity. However, understanding how private company values are developed enables business owners to identify and undertake value enhancement initiatives that serve to increase the intrinsic and strategic equity value of their company prior to the time that it is exposed for sale in the open market.

Professional advice normally is required to deal with the many complex valuation issues that can arise during the course of the sale process. Furthermore, as discussed in Section II, there can be a substantial difference between the value of a company (normally defined as its "fair market value") and the price that might be paid for the company in the open market.

This Stage is intended to provide business owners with a basic understanding of how buyers generally value mid-size privately held Canadian companies. It is not intended to be comprehensive in scope. Readers can find a comprehensive guide to Canadian business valuations in *The Valuation of Business Interests*, Campbell and Johnson (Toronto: Canadian Institute of Chartered Accountants, 2001).

For a company that operates as a going concern, there are three underlying determinants to its equity value. Each of these elements is factored into the valuation methodologies explained in the following part of this Stage. While these factors were introduced in Section II, they are reiterated to highlight their importance. The three primary determinants of equity value are the:

- cash flow that the company is expected to generate in the future. "Discretionary cash flow", calculated as revenues less cash operating costs, capital expenditures, incremental working capital requirements and cash income taxes (but before debt servicing costs) ultimately is the primary determinant of economic value;
- rate of return (or its reciprocal, the valuation multiple) applied to the projected cash flow. The rate of return or valuation multiple is a function of the buyer's perception of the risk in achieving the projected cash flow, the company's growth opportunities beyond the projection period and the debt capacity of the company; and
- company's underlying financial position, including:
  - the extent to which the company's operations are financed by financial liabilities (i.e., interest-bearing debt and equivalents) as opposed to equity,
  - the adequacy (or inadequacy) of the company's net operating assets, given the nature of its operations, and
  - whether any redundant assets exist that will be extracted from or sold along with the company.

Recall from Section II that there is an important distinction between the enterprise value of a company and its equity value. The enterprise value of a company is a function of its prospective discretionary cash flow and the rate of return (or valuation multiple) applied thereto. The equity value of a company (i.e., the value of its overlying shares or underlying net assets) is equal to its enterprise value less its financial liabilities outstanding, plus or minus adjustments that are required to compensate for excesses or deficiencies in the company's net operating assets, plus redundant assets (if any). Each of the valuation methodologies discussed in this Stage distinguishes between the enterprise value and the equity value of a company.

Enhancing the intrinsic (or "stand-alone") equity value of a company requires that the business owner identify and undertake initiatives to increase its prospective discretionary cash flow and reduce the perception of business risk or better manage the net operating assets of the company, while at the same time recognizing that these things are all inter-related. Enhancing the intrinsic equity value of a company can be undertaken independently of the private company sale process. Increasing the equity value of a company prior to exposing it for sale sets the foundation for value enhancement. However, the realization of that value is dependent on conducting a well-managed sale process and appropriate deal structuring. Deal structuring is discussed in Stage 6. Estimating value and price within the context of the *Value Enhancement Framework*™ is depicted in Exhibit III-3-1.

Exhibit III-3-1

ESTIMATING VALUE AND PRICE WITHIN
THE *VALUE ENHANCEMENT FRAMEWORK*™

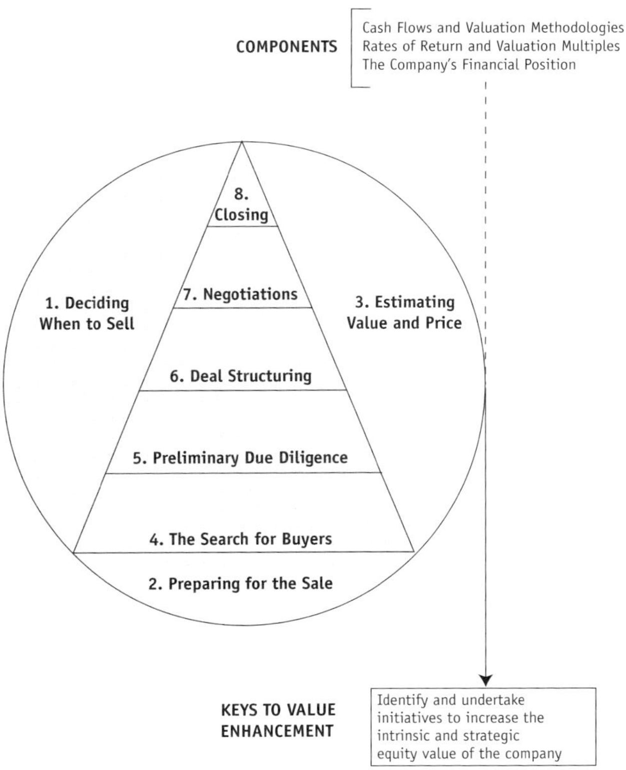

(i) Cash Flows and Valuation Methodologies

This section provides an overview of the methodologies that buyers commonly use to estimate the value of a mid-size privately held Canadian company. These include the multiple of earnings before interest, taxes, depreciation and amortization (EBITDA), multiple of earnings before interest and taxes (EBIT), capitalized cash flow and discounted cash flow methodologies. The calculations underlying these valuation methodologies can be complex, depending on the circumstances. For the purpose of this book, a basic version of these methodologies is presented to help business owners understand the principal determinants of equity value and how the equity value of their company might be increased.

The ordering of the valuation methodologies discussed below, beginning with the multiple of EBITDA, followed by the multiple of EBIT, capitalized cash flow and finally discounted cash flow, represents a build up from the simplest methodology to the most comprehensive. It is important to note that the discounted cash flow methodology is the preferred valuation methodology for most buyers of mid-size privately held companies. This is because, properly performed, the discounted cash flow methodology incorporates all of the elements that a buyer normally considers when assessing economic value.

Multiple of EBITDA Methodology

In its basic form, the multiple of EBITDA methodology involves applying an "EBITDA multiple" to normalized earnings before interest, income taxes, depreciation and amortization expense (EBITDA, sometimes referred to as the "operating cash flow" of the company). Normalized EBITDA multiplied by the EBITDA multiple generates the enterprise value of a company. Outstanding financial liabilities (i.e., interest-bearing debt and equivalents) are deducted in order to derive the equity value of the company. The basic form of the multiple of EBITDA methodology is illustrated in Exhibit III-3-2.

Exhibit III-3-2

MULTIPLE OF EBITDA METHODOLOGY

	Normalized EBITDA
x	EBITDA multiple
=	Enterprise value
–	financial liabilities outstanding
=	Equity value

A discussion of the normalized EBITDA calculation follows. Further details on the determination of the EBITDA multiple and the determination of financial liabilities are provided in subsequent parts of this Stage.

Calculating normalized EBITDA

An estimate of normalized EBITDA usually begins with a review of a company's operating results for its most recent fiscal years. Starting with income before taxes as reported on the income statement, adjustments are made to:

- add back depreciation and amortization expense, as these expenses do not represent current cash outflows of a company;
- add back interest expense. As explained in Section II, the enterprise value of a company is determined on a "debt-free" basis, and therefore interest and other financing charges are added back to the cash flow stream;
- normalize remuneration paid to owners and related parties. Owners of privately held Canadian companies often pay themselves amounts in excess of the market rate of remuneration that would be paid to an arm's length individual. Many business owners also employ their spouse or other family members and pay them salaries that are above market rates for income-splitting purposes. It is not uncommon for owners of privately held Canadian companies to declare year-end bonuses for themselves (or their families) to reduce pre-tax earnings to the "small business threshold" for income tax purposes. When a buyer assesses the cash flow generating capability of a company, it considers what that company can reasonably be expected to earn after paying market rate salaries and bonuses to arm's length managers and other employees who are required in its operations;
- normalize other related party payments. There may be other non-arm's length payments, such as building rentals from related parties or the purchase of goods or services from businesses owned by related parties. To

the extent that the prices paid to related parties are above or below market rates, the excess or deficiency is adjusted for when determining normalized EBITDA;

- add back other discretionary expenditures that were made, such as donations and discretionary travel, among others, which a buyer prospectively would not have to incur. In this regard, there sometimes is a debate between the business owner and prospective buyers as to the nature and amount of expenses that are considered to be discretionary. Likewise, where expenditures are considered to be inadequate to support the ongoing operations of a company, the EBITDA as reported is reduced by the amount of funds required to remedy the perceived deficiency;
- add or deduct unusual or non-recurring items. Companies sometimes experience anomalies in their operations, both in terms of revenues and operating expenses. Where such expenses (revenues) are not expected to recur in the future, they should be added back (deducted) when calculating normalized EBITDA. For example, if a company had a recall of its products (and it was an unusual event), the costs of the recall would be added back when calculating normalized EBITDA; and
- add back expenses and deduct the income relating to redundant assets. As subsequently discussed, where redundant assets exist they either are removed from the company prior to the sale, or they represent a separate source of value when sold along with the company. Since redundant assets are viewed in isolation, for the purpose of internal consistency, it is important that any related income or expense stream be removed from the calculation of normalized EBITDA.

Exhibit III-3-3 illustrates the calculation of normalized EBITDA.

Exhibit III-3-3

CALCULATION OF NORMALIZED EBITDA

	Pre-tax income as reported
+	depreciation and amortization expense
+	interest expense
=	Actual EBITDA
+ / −	excess (deficient) remuneration to the owner and related parties
+ / −	excess (deficient) payments to related parties
+ / −	discretionary (insufficient) expenditures
+ / −	unusual and non-recurring expenses (revenues)
+ / −	expenses (income) relating to redundant assets
=	Normalized EBITDA

It is important that normalized EBITDA reflect what a buyer reasonably would expect the company to generate each year in the future. Therefore, historical operating results are only relevant to the extent that they provide an indication as to future operating results. Where a company operates in a cyclical industry, prudent buyers normally take that fact into account by averaging the normalized EBITDA calculations for the past cycle period. However, where a company has experienced strong growth in recent years, its normalized EBITDA may best be represented by its most recent fiscal year, or its EBITDA for the past 12 months (which tends to provide a more current estimate). Normalized EBITDA calculations can also be prepared in respect of future periods where a meaningful budget or projection exists.

Example of the multiple of EBITDA methodology

Company X is a stable, mature business with reported pre-tax income of $2 million in its most recent fiscal year, which is believed to be reflective of its prospective operating results. Company X had no unusual or non-recurring items in its most recent fiscal year, but it paid above-market bonuses to its shareholders and related parties in the amount of $500,000. Further, Company X reported interest expense of $200,000 and depreciation and amortization expense of $300,000. Company X has $3 million of interest bearing debt on its balance sheet.

Assume that, following an analysis of the operations, risks and growth prospects of Company X, a buyer considers an EBITDA multiple of 5x to be appropriate. In this case, the buyer would determine the equity value of Company X as follows using the multiple of EBITDA methodology:

	Pre-tax income as reported	$ 2,000,000
	Adjustments:	
+	depreciation and amortization expense	$ 300,000
+	interest expense	$ 200,000
+	excess bonuses	$ 500,000
+/–	unusual or non-recurring items	nil
=	normalized EBITDA	$ 3,000,000
x	EBITDA multiple	5x
=	Enterprise value	$15,000,000
–	financial liabilities outstanding	$(3,000,000)
=	Equity value	$12,000,000

Other adjustments

The previous discussion and example provided an illustration of the multiple of EBITDA methodology in its basic form. In some cases, further adjustments are required in order to account for:

- prospective one-time items in terms of revenues, expenses or capital expenditures, where such items are not reflected either in normalized EBITDA or the EBITDA multiple. For example, a company that has to spend money on a one-time environmental clean-up would deduct that prospective expenditure from the enterprise value otherwise determined, rather than factor that cost into normalized EBITDA. Where revenues or expenses are non-recurring, they are not multiplied by an EBITDA multiple. From a technical standpoint, adjustments for one-time items should be made on an after-tax basis where the expenditure (revenue) is deductible (included) for income tax purposes;
- excess or deficient amounts in terms of the net operating assets of the company. For example, a buyer will reduce the amount it is willing to pay for the equity of a company where the company's working capital position is less than the buyer perceives is necessary to support its operations; and
- redundant assets, where such assets are sold with the company. The price for redundant assets as agreed to between the seller and the buyer is added to the equity value otherwise determined.

Shares vs. net assets

In theory, the equity value calculated pursuant to the multiple of EBITDA methodology illustrated above represents the value of all the issued and outstanding shares of the company. As discussed in Stage 6, there can be a significant difference in the price and terms of a deal depending on whether the buyer purchases the overlying shares of a company or its underlying net assets. Buyers normally are willing to pay a higher price for the net assets of a company because of the tax advantages that accrue to them pursuant to such a transaction. Specifically, where the shares of a company are purchased, the buyer assumes the existing tax base of the company's underlying assets. However, where the net assets of a company are purchased, the buyer and seller agree on the specific portion of the purchase price to allocate to each asset class being purchased. The buyer can increase the tax base of those assets to reflect the agreed purchase price. This provides a tax advantage to the buyer (to the detriment of the seller). Therefore, a buyer of net assets usually will make a separate adjustment to the equity value of the company otherwise determined to reflect the incremental tax benefits available from such a purchase.

Buyer synergies

An issue that arises in business valuation and pricing is the extent to which buyers are expected to realize synergies or other strategic advantages following a transaction. Buyers anticipate synergies in various forms, which might include headcount reductions of the combined entity, incremental revenue opportunities, a reduction in distribution costs and other benefits. Synergies are unique to every buyer, and the buyer is in a better position to determine what those synergies will be. Business owners should attempt to estimate what synergies a buyer believes it may realize following a transaction through research, negotiations and other tactics that are described in subsequent Stages.

When valuing a privately held company, buyers normally will attempt to quantify the synergies they expect to realize. They usually do this either by:

- increasing the normalized EBITDA of the company to reflect all, or a portion, of the anticipated synergies, and applying the EBITDA multiple to the higher level of normalized EBITDA; or
- applying a higher EBITDA multiple to the normalized EBITDA of the company, where normalized EBITDA is determined for the company on a standalone basis.

While buyers will estimate the value of synergies they expect to generate from an acquisition, they typically do not want to pay for those synergies. This is because most buyers perceive that the synergies are "theirs", and because most buyers perceive risks in realizing the synergy component. Ultimately, whether and to what extent synergies are paid for is a function of the relative negotiation strength of the buyer and the seller and the structure of the deal.

To increase the likelihood of getting paid for an element of synergies, the business owner should consider what synergies a particular buyer might realize and how they can create an operating structure so the buyer can more easily integrate the company with its existing operations. The greater the quantum of synergies and the lower the buyer's perceived risk of achieving same, the greater the likelihood that the buyer will offer a price for the company that incorporates at least a portion of its synergy value.

When estimating the equity value of their company, the business owner should consider separately both its intrinsic value and the price that a buyer would be willing to pay in light of the synergies that it expects to realize. The intrinsic equity value of a company can be assessed and enhanced independently of the sale process. The price that is paid for a privately held company, which incorporates the buyer's assessment of its intrinsic value and post-acquisition synergies, is a function of the effectiveness of the sale process and the structure of the deal. That said, the business owner normally can realize value enhancement by increasing the intrinsic equity value of their company prior to exposing it for sale and by undertaking initiatives that facilitate the buyer's realization of post-acquisition synergies.

Issues with the multiple of EBITDA methodology

The multiple of EBITDA methodology is attractive due to its simplicity. In addition, as a practical matter, buyers, sellers and their respective intermediaries often refer to the value of a given company and prices paid for similar companies in terms of EBITDA multiples in the course of negotiations. Therefore, it is important for business owners to understand the mechanics of this methodology and its shortcomings when talking "price" with buyers.

From a buyer's perspective, the multiple of EBITDA methodology has some significant shortcomings. Most notable among these shortcomings is that the multiple of EBITDA methodology does not explicitly address the capital expenditure requirements of a privately held company, any incremental working capital needs to finance growth, or the impact of income taxes. Rather, these things are implicitly incorporated in the EBITDA multiple. Furthermore, depending on the accounting standards adopted (which generally are more flexible in Canada than in some other jurisdictions) certain costs may be capitalized and amortized over a period of time, rather than being expensed in the period they are incurred (e.g., certain product development costs). Where such expenditures are not otherwise accounted for in the multiple of EBITDA methodology, the resultant value conclusion can be distorted.

As a result, sophisticated buyers usually adopt more comprehensive valuation models (such as the discounted cash flow methodology, discussed below) when estimating the value of a privately held company. However, buyers often will convert the valuation results derived pursuant to more sophisticated methodologies into a multiple of EBITDA equivalent when negotiating the purchase of the company with the business owner.

Multiple of EBIT Methodology

The multiple of EBIT (earnings before interest and taxes) methodology is similar to the multiple of EBITDA methodology except that the:

- earnings base adopted (normalized EBIT) is net of depreciation and amortization expense which, depending on the nature of the company, may provide the buyer with some indication of its ongoing capital expenditure requirements; and
- EBIT multiple adopted reflects the fact that capital spending has been considered (to some degree). Therefore, for a given company, the EBIT multiple should be higher than the corresponding EBITDA multiple.

The basic form of the multiple of EBIT methodology is illustrated in Exhibit III-3-4:

Exhibit III-3-4

MULTIPLE OF EBIT METHODOLOGY

	Normalized EBIT
x	EBIT multiple
=	Enterprise value
-	financial liabilities outstanding
=	Equity value

Again, the resultant value is adjusted to reflect prospective non-recurring revenues or expenses (net of tax), the impact of excess (deficient) net operating assets and the existence of any redundant assets.

Issues with the multiple of EBIT methodology

While the multiple of EBIT methodology does reflect historical capital expenditures and other capitalized costs through depreciation and amortization expense, there can be a significant difference between the ongoing capital expenditure requirements of a company and the depreciation and amortization expense that is recorded for financial accounting purposes. Furthermore, similar to the multiple of EBITDA methodology, the multiple of EBIT methodology does not explicitly consider such things as income taxes and working capital required to finance growth. Therefore, sophisticated buyers generally adopt the discounted cash flow methodology and convert those results to a multiple of EBIT (or multiple of EBITDA) when discussing value and price with the business owner.

Capitalized Cash Flow Methodology

The capitalized cash flow methodology normally is used by sophisticated buyers when valuing mature companies with flat or modest growth expectations. In addition, the capitalized cash flow methodology is used to derive the "terminal value" component of the discounted cash flow methodology (discussed below).

The mechanics of the capitalized cash flow methodology (sometimes referred to as the capitalization of discretionary cash flow methodology) can be complex. In order to avoid onerous detail in this book, a simplified version of the capitalized cash flow methodology is presented. In essence, the simplified version assumes that accounting income approximates taxable income. In most cases, the results obtained using the simplified version should approximate what would be obtained using the more comprehensive model.

The mechanics of the simplified capitalized cash flow methodology are illustrated in Exhibit III-3-5.

Exhibit III-3-5

CAPITALIZED CASH FLOW METHODOLOGY

	Normalized EBIT
−	income taxes
=	Adjusted income
+	depreciation and amortization
−	sustaining capital expenditures
=	Normalized discretionary cash flow
÷	capitalization rate
=	Enterprise value
−	financial liabilities outstanding
=	Equity value

As a starting point, an estimate is made of normalized EBIT, which as previously explained represents normalized EBITDA, net of depreciation and amortization expense. The corporate income tax rate is applied to this amount to determine the adjusted income of the company (before consideration of interest expense and similar financing charges).

However, buyers are primarily interested in the cash flow that a privately held company will generate as opposed to its accounting profits. Therefore, a further adjustment is made to add back the amount of depreciation and amortization expense embedded in the calculation of normalized EBIT and to deduct sustaining capital expenditures. Sustaining capital expenditures represent the estimated amount of cash that a company must spend on fixed asset additions, on average, each year in order to maintain its operations at current levels. In addition, where a company capitalizes certain expenditures (such as product development costs), the average annual cash outflow of such expenditures is deducted (given that the amortization of such costs was added back). The result of adding back depreciation and amortization and deducting sustaining capital expenditures (and capitalized expenses, where applicable) from adjusted income is the discretionary cash flow of the company. As explained in Section II, discretionary cash flow reflects the amount of cash that a buyer can withdraw from the company each year as a return on its investment, or reinvest into the company to generate incremental growth opportunities. Hence, discretionary cash flow is a true economic driver of business value.

Discretionary cash flow is divided by a "capitalization rate" which, as explained later in this Stage, reflects a buyer's after-tax cost of capital, net of the long-term expected growth rate of the company. The result is the enterprise value of the company. Where buyer synergies are believed to exist, these may be reflected in the buyer's quantification of the discretionary cash flow or by way of reducing its capitalization rate, which increases the enterprise value of the company.

Financial liabilities are deducted from enterprise value to determine the equity value of the company. Where necessary, further adjustments are made to reflect such things as prospective one-time revenues (net of tax), one-time expenses (net of tax), excess or deficient net operating assets and redundant assets.

Example of the (simplified) capitalized cash flow methodology

Company Z has normalized EBIT of $3 million, net of $250,000 in depreciation and amortization expense. The applicable income tax rate is 35%. Company Z's annual sustaining capital requirements are $300,000 and it has $5 million of financial liabilities outstanding.

Assume that a buyer uses a capitalization rate of 12.5% and that there are no redundant assets or prospective one-time revenues or expenses. However, an analysis of Company Z's balance sheet reveals that it has a working capital deficiency of $500,000. In this case, the buyer would determine the equity value of Company Z as follows pursuant to the capitalized cash flow methodology (before consideration of synergies):

	Normalized EBIT	$ 3,000,000
–	income taxes at 35%	$(1,050,000)
=	Adjusted income	$ 1,950,000
+	depreciation and amortization expense	$ 250,000
–	sustaining capital expenditures	$ (300,000)
=	Normalized discretionary cash flow	$ 1,900,000
÷	capitalization rate	12.5%
=	Enterprise value	$15,200,000
–	financial liabilities outstanding	$(3,000,000)
–	working capital deficiency	$ (500,000)
=	Equity value	$11,700,000

Discounted Cash Flow Methodology

The discounted cash flow (DCF) methodology generally is the preferred valuation methodology for buyers of privately held companies. This is because it captures all of the variables that ultimately influence the return that a buyer realizes on its investment. Sophisticated buyers normally adopt a DCF methodology as their primary valuation approach and then supplement their value conclusions with other methodologies, such as the multiple of EBITDA methodology. The mechanics of the DCF methodology can be quite complicated. Again, the approach illustrated in this book represents a simplified version and ignores some of the complicating technical factors, the impact of which will depend on the fact-specific circumstances of the company.

The DCF methodology begins with a forecast of the prospective discretionary cash flow that the company is expected to generate in each of the next few years, generally three to five years. As explained above, discretionary cash flow (in its simplified version) is calculated as EBIT less income taxes, plus depreciation and amortization expense, less capital expenditures. However, unlike the capitalized cash flow methodology, the determination of prospective discretionary cash flow pursuant to the DCF methodology not only considers the capital expenditures required to sustain the operations of the company, but also any incremental capital expenditures required to realize the growth set out in that cash flow forecast. Furthermore, pursuant to the DCF methodology, consideration also is given to any incremental working capital that is required to support the growth set out in the projections, which may include incremental accounts receivable, inventories and so on.

The prospective discretionary cash flow is discounted (i.e., converted to present value) using a discount rate that reflects the buyer's desired after-tax return on its capital (as discussed in the following section of this Stage).

A "terminal value" (or "residual value") is calculated by estimating the maintainable discretionary cash flow beyond the forecast period, which is capitalized at the buyer's capitalization rate, similar to the capitalization of cash flow methodology explained above. The resultant terminal value is discounted to a present value amount using the discount rate.

The sum of the present value of the forecast discretionary cash flow and the present value of the terminal value represents the enterprise value of the company. As before, financial liabilities are deducted from the enterprise value to derive the equity value of the company. The net realizable value of redundant assets is added to equity value, where applicable.

Note that, pursuant to the DCF methodology, no adjustments are required for prospective one-time items. This is because one-time revenues, expenses and capital expenditures should be captured in the forecast discretionary cash flow of the applicable year in which they are expected to occur. Furthermore, a separate adjustment for excess or deficient net operating assets (such as a net working capital deficiency) only would be made where such excess or deficiency had not been considered when determining the prospective discretionary cash flow of the company. The DCF methodology is illustrated in Exhibit III-3-6.

Exhibit III-3-6

DISCOUNTED CASH FLOW METHODOLOGY

<table>
<tr><th>Forecast Period</th><th>Terminal Value</th></tr>
<tr><td>Forecast discretionary cash flow for the next several years</td><td>Maintainable annual discretionary cash flow beyond the forecast period
÷ <u>capitalization rate</u>
= Capitalized cash flow beyond the forecast period</td></tr>
<tr><td colspan="2">Discounted by: Discount rate</td></tr>
<tr><td>= Present value of forecast cash flow</td><td>= Present value of terminal value</td></tr>
<tr><td colspan="2">present value of forecast cash flow + present value of terminal value</td></tr>
<tr><td colspan="2">= Enterprise value
– <u>financial liabilities outstanding</u>
= Equity value</td></tr>
</table>

Example of the DCF methodology

Company Q has forecast that its revenues will grow from $15 million this year to $20 million next year, $25 million in the following year and $30 million per year after that. Company Q expects that its EBIT margin will remain at 10% of revenues throughout the forecast period and that its depreciation and amortization expense represents 2% of its revenues. In order to achieve this rate of growth, Company Q has to invest $1 million in new equipment in each of the next two years. Thereafter, in order to sustain its operations, capital expenditure requirements will be $700,000 per year. Further, Company Q will have to support its growth with additional working capital, estimated at 10% of annual revenue growth, which translates into $500,000 per year. Company Q's income tax rate is 35% and it has $5 million of interest-bearing debt outstanding.

Assume that, given the risks involved in achieving these cash flows and the perceived strategic value of Company Q, a buyer believes that a discount rate of 15% is appropriate and that a capitalization rate of 12% is appropriate for the terminal value calculation. Under this scenario, the buyer would determine the equity value of Company Q as follows using the DCF methodology:

	Year 1	Year 2	Year 3	Beyond
Revenues	$20,000,000	$25,000,000	$30,000,000	$30,000,000
EBIT at 10%	$ 2,000,000	$ 2,500,000	$ 3,000,000	$ 3,000,000
Taxes at 35%	$ (700,000)	$ (875,000)	$ (1,050,000)	$ (1,050,000)
Adjusted income	$ 1,300,000	$ 1,625,000	$ 1,950,000	$ 1,950,000
Depreciation and amortization	$ 400,000	$ 500,000	$ 600,000	$ 600,000
Capital expenditures	$ (1,000,000)	$ (1,000,000)	$ (700,000)	$ (700,000)
Working capital	$ (500,000)	$ (500,000)	$ (500,000)	$ 0
Discretionary cash flow	$ 200,000	$ 625,000	$ 1,350,000	$ 1,850,000
Capitalization rate				12%
Terminal value				$15,416,667
Present value factor at 15%	0.8696	0.7561	0.6575	0.6575
Discounted cash flow	$ 173,913	$ 472,590	$ 887,647	$10,136,709
Enterprise value				$11,670,858
Less: financial liabilities				$ (5,000,000)
Equity value				$ 6,670,858

Note how the enterprise value of $11,670,858 is primarily driven by the terminal value component. This is not uncommon in the DCF methodology. Company Q's growth in the near term is eroded to a large extent by its capital expenditure and incremental working capital requirements. Also note that, in the terminal value period, no incremental working capital is deducted based on the assumption that annual cash flow, and hence working capital balances, remain relatively stable beyond that time.

In this example, a discount rate of 15% and a capitalization rate of 12% were adopted. The basis of these rates of return is discussed in the next section of this Stage. However, it was noted that the buyer considered the strategic importance of Company Q when determining these rates of return. Therefore, the resultant enterprise value and equity value include a component of buyer-perceived synergies. Alternatively, the buyer could have reflected some of or the entire synergy value component in the cash flow projections for Company Q.

For the purpose of this example, when applying the discount rate of 15%, year-end cash flows were assumed. However, it is not uncommon to assume that cash flows accrue evenly throughout the year (or mid-year), which typically has the impact of increasing the value conclusion. As a technical point, the present value factor beyond the final year of the projection period (year 3 in this case) is the same as that used in the final year. This is because the mechanics of the terminal value calculation already incorporate a one-year lapse beyond the end of the projection period.

As noted in the previous methodologies, while sophisticated buyers normally prefer the DCF methodology, they often convert the valuation result into a multiple of normalized EBITDA or some other measure when talking price with the business owner. In this case, Company Q's normalized EBITDA for its previous fiscal year would be calculated as:

	Last year's sales	$15,000,000
	Normalized EBIT at 10%	$ 1,500,000
+	depreciation and amortization at 2%	$ 300,000
=	Normalized EBITDA	$ 1,800,000

Therefore, the enterprise value calculation of $11,670,858 could be expressed as a multiple of approximately 6.5x Company Q's trailing EBITDA.

The DCF Methodology as a Tool for Value Enhancement

Developing a sound understanding of the underlying variables in the DCF methodology can help business owners in identifying and undertaking value enhancement initiatives prior to the time their company is exposed for sale. Even if their company is not being sold, the business owner can benefit from enhanced value through consideration of the DCF dynamics.

While growth in revenues may be of interest to business owners, such growth must be conducted in a manner that will create incremental value within the company. This requires consideration of all the costs associated with growth, including operating expenses, income taxes, incremental capital expenditure requirements and incremental working capital requirements. Value enhancement is more likely to be created where:

- economies of scale in terms of operating costs and other expenses are achieved through growth initiatives; and
- the underlying net operating assets of the company are closely managed so that incremental growth can be achieved without requiring a significant investment in capital expenditures and working capital, which in turn could serve to erode the benefits of that growth.

In addition, the business owner should consider what specific synergies buyers might anticipate if they acquire the company. To the extent that synergies and economies of scale can be meaningfully quantified, the business owner is in a stronger position to negotiate a price that incorporates some of that premium.

Business owners must be cognizant of the fact that cash flows and rates of return are inter-related (see Section II). Therefore, implementing growth strategies that increase the prospective cash flow of a company, but also serve to increase its perceived risk level, may result in an overall reduction in value.

By considering the variables of the DCF methodology and their interactions, business owners will be in a better position to identify and undertake initiatives that improve the perceived ability of their company to grow its prospective cash flow, regardless of the principal valuation methodology adopted by a buyer. Furthermore, by thoroughly understanding the DCF model, business owners will be able to realize on their value enhancement initiatives by better conveying to prospective buyers how such initiatives serve to increase the value of their company.

(ii) Rates of Return and Valuation Multiples

The valuation methodologies discussed in this Stage made reference to EBITDA multiples, EBIT multiples, capitalization rates and discount rates. These concepts are related, but they are not interchangeable. A common source of valuation errors made by business owners and their advisors, as well as buyers, stems from the commingling or inconsistent application of these concepts.

The derivation of rates of return and valuation multiples can be complex and a detailed discussion of the theory behind their development and application is beyond the scope of this book. However, the basic concepts are addressed here in order to provide business owners with a better understanding of what these terms mean and how they should be applied.

The starting point is an understanding of what is meant by discount rates and how such rates are developed. The discount rate is the primary indicator of the return that a buyer demands in order to place capital at risk in exchange for the prospective cash flows of the company being valued. Once an appropriate discount rate has been determined, the capitalization rate and valuation multiples (including multiples of EBIT and EBITDA) can be developed. This is the sequence in which these concepts are discussed below.

Discount Rates

A discount rate is the rate of return that a buyer requires to place its capital at risk in exchange for the prospective discretionary cash flow of a company. It is used in the DCF methodology. The discount rate normally represents a buyer's after-tax "weighted average cost of capital" (WACC). The WACC discount rate is applied to discretionary cash flow which, as previously discussed, is calculated after income taxes but before consideration of debt-servicing costs.

The WACC discount rate represents the mix of debt and equity that a buyer believes is appropriate with which to finance a company. In brief, the greater a buyer's ability to finance an acquisition with debt, the lower its cost of capital and hence the higher the value it places on a particular company. This is because the cost of debt financing is less expensive than equity financing and interest payments on debt financing are tax deductible. However, there is a limit to the extent that debt can be used to finance an acquisition. At some point, the risks associated with excessive debt financing offset the benefits. A buyer's ability to utilize debt to finance an acquisition depends on numerous factors, including the stability of the company's cash flows and the underlying tangible assets that can be used to secure debt financing. As discussed in the following section of this Stage, the company's existing financial position has an influence on the buyer's perceived ability to use debt to finance the acquisition.

The discount rate adopted by a buyer ultimately is subjective. It is influenced by the buyer's assessment of whether the company will achieve its discretionary cash flow forecast, which in turn is a function of the risks and opportunities affecting the company as well as current and prospective economic and industry conditions. The higher the perceived risk, the higher a buyer's discount rate, and vice versa. When developing discount rates, buyers normally give consideration to factors such as:

- the company's revenue stability, including whether it has established customer contracts or a recurring customer base. Greater predictability in future revenues reduces the perceived risk level of the company;
- whether the company has any proprietary products or services and whether its products are patented or protected. These things give rise to a company's sustainable competitive advantage, which reduces the risk that it will lose customers or have to drastically reduce prices to remain competitive;
- the company's technology and research and development capabilities, which also contribute to its sustainable competitive advantage;
- the operating cost structure of the company, including the degree to which operating costs are variable as opposed to fixed. A variable cost structure serves to reduce downside risk, since costs can more easily be reduced if revenue targets are not met. However, a variable cost structure also reduces the company's upside potential since there is less operating leverage as revenues grow;
- the level of competition faced by the company and any competitive advantages the company has in that regard;
- whether the company is economically dependent on certain customers, suppliers, the business owner or key employees. Such dependencies increase the company's risk level;
- the company's underlying financial position, as represented by the quantity and quality of its tangible assets and identifiable intangible assets (e.g., patents) less its liabilities. A stronger asset base increases the ability of a buyer to use debt to finance the acquisition, which in turn lowers the WACC discount rate and increases value and price. However, it is important that the company's financial strength or weakness not be double-counted pursuant to its inclusion in both the discount rate and by way of separate adjustment to the value calculation (e.g., a separate deduction to the equity value otherwise determined on account of a deficiency in working capital); and
- the strategic importance of the company to the buyer, which may cause the buyer to adopt a lower discount rate where such benefits have not been re-

flected in the cash flow projections. For example, where a buyer perceives that a company possesses innovative technology that can be leveraged in its existing operations, and the benefits of that technology cannot readily be quantified, the buyer might reflect the value of that technology pursuant to adopting a lower discount rate than might otherwise be the case.

While a buyer's discount rate can vary within a wide range, it is not unusual in the economic environment that has prevailed in recent years for buyers to adopt nominal (i.e., including inflation) after-tax WACC discount rates (sometimes referred to as "hurdle rates" or "threshold rates of return") in the range of 10% to 15% when valuing mid-sized privately held Canadian companies that have an established market presence. Higher discount rates may be used where the company is small or considered high-risk. Again, the discount rate adopted by a buyer is subjective and is based on its assessment of the fact-specific circumstances of the acquisition opportunity.

Capitalization Rates

A capitalization rate represents the buyer's after-tax required rate of return net of a growth allowance. It is used in the capitalized cash flow methodology and the terminal value component of the DCF methodology. A buyer derives its capitalization rate by subtracting long-term inflationary growth and real growth (i.e., growth in excess of inflation) from its WACC discount rate. In this regard, while buyers normally assume that a company will recover the cost of inflation over the long term (although this is not always the case), buyers also normally assume little or no long-term real growth (i.e., growth in excess of inflation) when valuing a privately held company. Over the past several years, it has been unusual for buyers to adopt a long-term real growth rate in excess of 2%, and many buyers assume no long-term real growth whatsoever. Therefore, for example, if a buyer determined that an appropriate discount rate to adopt when assessing a particular acquisition opportunity was 15% and that a long-term growth assumption of 3% was appropriate (including inflation and real growth), the buyer's after-tax capitalization rate would be 12% (calculated as 15% less 3%).

Valuation Multiples

A valuation multiple is the inverse of the capitalization rate (not the discount rate). As such, valuation multiples incorporate an element of long-term growth, where such growth is factored into the determination of the capitalization rate. For example, if a buyer determines its after-tax capitalization rate to be 12%, based on a WACC discount rate of 15% less 3% for long-term growth (as previously illustrated), the equivalent multiple of after-tax cash flow would be 8.3x (calculated as 1 divided by 12%).

Valuation multiples normally are expressed on a pre-tax basis and applied as a multiple of EBIT or EBITDA. Therefore, following from the current example, if a buyer has calculated its multiple of after-tax cash flow to be 8.3x and its income tax rate is 40%, the equivalent multiple of EBIT is 5x (calculated as 8.3 x (1 — 40%)). This calculation assumes that depreciation and amortization approximate sustaining capital reinvestment. A multiple of EBITDA would be derived on a similar basis, except that the multiple of EBITDA should implicitly consider a company's capital expenditure requirements. Therefore, for a given company, its EBITDA multiple should be lower than its corresponding EBIT multiple.

While valuation multiples can fall within a wide range, it is not unusual in recent years for mid-size privately held Canadian companies with an established market presence to transact in the range of 4x to 7x trailing EBITDA, depending on the industry. Lower valuation multiples sometimes are observed for smaller companies and those considered high risk, while higher valuation multiples sometimes are observed for companies that are believed to offer substantial near-term growth opportunities and those where buyer synergies are substantial and evident.

Comparable transactions

While buyers normally consider their own internal cost of capital and the risks and opportunities associated with a particular acquisition opportunity, most buyers also benchmark the valuation multiples implied by recent transactions involving companies operating in the same or similar industry as the acquisition target. In addition, intermediaries normally consider so-called "comparable transactions" when estimating the price that a company might fetch and when negotiating the sale.

Comparable transaction multiples normally are calculated based on information that is publicly disclosed following a transaction. For both the buyer and seller, valuation multiples derived from comparable transactions must be interpreted with caution, because the multiples derived can be distorted by a myriad of factors that may not be known to the general market, such as one party's compulsion to transact or certain aspects of the deal that affected the price paid and which were not publicly disclosed.

As discussed in Stage 6, the terms of the deal can have a significant impact on the stated purchase price and therefore the calculated valuation multiples. Furthermore, there are fundamental differences between any two companies in terms of their size, product offerings, geographic coverage and so on, which diminishes the usefulness of a direct comparison. Nonetheless, comparable transactions can sometimes provide valuable insight into the dynamics of a particular industry. In addition, comparable transactions can serve as a test against value conclusions derived pursuant to a DCF methodology or other valuation approach, and when negotiating the price and terms of a deal with prospective buyers. This latter point is further explored in Stage 7.

Public equity market multiples

A discussion of rates of return and valuation multiples would not be complete without addressing the implied valuation multiples of companies whose shares are publicly traded. As mentioned in Section II, there is a fundamental difference between public equity market multiples and the rates of return and valuation multiples applied when calculating the value of a privately held company. This is because public equity market multiples:

- reflect the trading of small lots of shares with varying degrees of liquidity. The same degree of liquidity may not be available for a privately held company when sold *en bloc*;
- are based on a limited amount of publicly available information. Buyers of privately held companies have access to non-public information on those companies, which impacts their view of risk and price;
- reflect a myriad of intended investment strategies and holding periods, from short term (a matter of days or even shorter time intervals) to long term (several years). Conversely, the purchase of a privately held company usually is associated with different investment strategies and a longer term intended holding period; and

- generally do not reflect buyer-perceived synergies that may be embedded in the multiples implied by transactions involving the purchase of privately held companies.

In any event, as in the case of comparable transactions, there are fundamental differences between any two companies in terms of size, products offered, geographic coverage and so on, that make any direct comparison potentially misleading.

While applying public equity market multiples and the implied rates of return and valuation multiples to a mid-size privately held company usually is not appropriate, public equity market multiples may provide some guidance for the reasonableness of valuation conclusions derived pursuant to a DCF methodology or other valuation methodology. Public equity market multiples may be somewhat meaningful for large private companies where an initial public offering is a viable option to a sale, assuming that reasonable public company comparables can be identified. Finally, buyers who are public companies themselves normally consider their own public equity market multiples and the impact thereon when determining the price they are willing to pay for an acquisition. As such, business owners should be aware of applicable multiples for public companies operating in their industry and the trends therein when negotiating the sale of their company.

Summary — Rates of Return and Valuation Multiples

Exhibit III-3-7 summarizes the relationship between rates of return and valuation multiples and the sequence in which they should be developed.

Exhibit III-3-7

RELATIONSHIP BETWEEN RATES OF RETURN AND VALUATION MULTIPLES

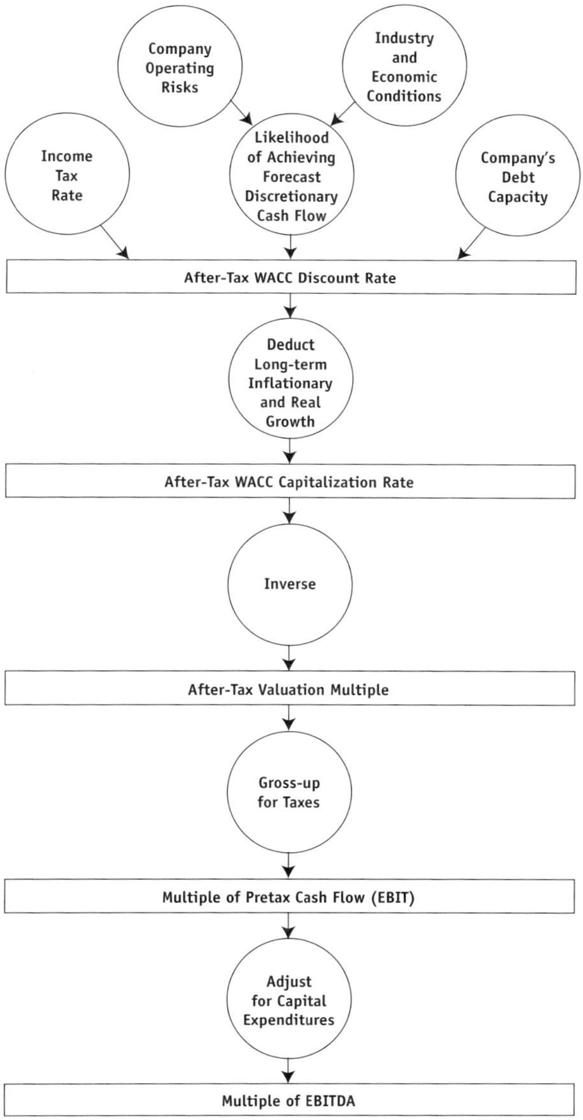

In the end, rates of return and valuation multiples are subjective. The important thing for business owners to remember is that rates of return and valuation multiples should be developed based on an informed and objective assessment of the risks and opportunities facing the company, and that they must be applied in a manner that is internally consistent.

With respect to internal consistency, a mistake that business owners (and their advisors) sometimes make is in commingling rates of return/valuation multiples and the cash flow against which they are applied. By way of example, assume that Company R had the following normalized operating results:

	Normalized EBITDA	$ 5,000,000
–	Depreciation (capital expenditures)	$ 1,000,000
=	Normalized EBIT	$ 4,000,000
–	income taxes	$(1,600,000)
=	Discretionary cash flow	$ 2,400,000

If the "correct" enterprise value of Company R is $20 million, that result could be derived as 4x EBITDA, 5x EBIT, or by dividing the normalized discretionary cash flow by a capitalization rate of 12%. The critical point to remember is that internal consistency is key. It would be incorrect, for example, to apply the EBITDA multiple of 4x to Company R's normalized EBIT of $4 million.

			Valuation Multiple	Rate of Return
	Normalized EBITDA	$ 5,000,000	4x	25%
–	Depreciation (capital expenditures)	$ 1,000,000		
=	Normalized EBIT	$ 4,000,000	5x	20%
–	income taxes	$ (1,600,000)		
=	Discretionary cash flow	$ 2,400,000	8.3x	12%

All results lead to a $20 million enterprise value

As previously discussed, rates of return and valuation multiples applied by buyers are a function of their perception of the risks facing the company, its growth prospects (to the extent that growth has not been incorporated in the projected cash flow of the company) and the ability of a buyer to finance the acquisition with debt. Therefore, the business owner can increase the equity value of their company by undertaking initiatives that:

- reduce the perceived inherent risk level of the company. This might be done by establishing and reinforcing the sustainable competitive advantages enjoyed by the company, which in turn will help to secure its customer base and reduce competition;
- increase the perceived future growth potential of the company. This might be done through tangible evidence relating to, for example, a growing order backlog or new product development; and
- increase the perceived ability for a buyer to use debt to finance the acquisition. This can be accomplished by strengthening the financial position of the company in the years leading up to the sale. Further, owners of capital-intensive businesses might consider requisitioning an independent asset valuation prior to exposing their company for sale in order to highlight the hidden value of the company's fixed assets.

(iii) The Company's Financial Position

Readers of financial statements usually are most interested in how much money a company is making, as reflected on its income statement. The balance sheet of a company often is not given the due consideration it deserves. However, the balance sheet sets out important information about the financial strength or weakness of the company. As a general rule, a stronger balance sheet (as evidenced through the quantity and quality of the company's net operating assets) lends to a higher value being ascribed to the company. Further, a strong balance sheet can lend support to greater debt capacity. As explained under the heading *Rates of Return and Valuation Multiples* above, increased debt capacity reduces a buyer's cost of capital, which in turn serves to increase its valuation of the company.

As explained under the heading *Valuation Methodologies* above, a company's financial liabilities, excesses or deficiencies in its net operating assets and the existence of any redundant assets account for the differences between the enterprise value of a company and its equity value. Each of these is discussed below.

Financial Liabilities

A company's balance sheet at the closing of the transaction will dictate the amount of financial liabilities assumed by the buyer (if any), which in turn reduces the amount paid for the shares of the company. Alternatively, where the net assets of the company are acquired, the financial liabilities assumed by the buyer will be as agreed with the seller. As discussed in Stage 6, financial liabilities that are not assumed by the buyer upon closing remain the obligation of the business owner and must be satisfied with the proceeds of sale. Therefore, whether or not the buyer assumes them, financial liabilities effectively reduce the equity value of the company.

Financial liabilities generally include both long-term and short-term interest-bearing debt obligations to banks and other lenders (e.g., operating lines of credit, term loans, mortgages and capital lease obligations). It also includes obligations of similar substance, such as loans and advances from shareholders and related parties, whether or not those things are interest bearing. When the company is sold, arrangements must be made to repay the outstanding financial liabilities or to assume those liabilities and to pay a commercial rate of interest thereon. In either case, the equity value of the company is reduced by the amount of financial liabilities outstanding.

Financial liabilities do not include accounts payable, accrued liabilities, or other similar liabilities. While such obligations do have to be paid, in most cases they will perpetuate as new obligations replace old. Where trade payables and similar liabilities provide the company with an ongoing interest-free source of financing, such obligations are considered operating liabilities and not financial liabilities. The existence of operating liabilities is considered in the calculation of net operating assets (see Section II), but they are not deducted from the company's enterprise value as are financial liabilities.

If the company has cash on its balance sheet, that amount normally is netted against any outstanding financial liabilities on the assumption that the cash could be applied to reduce those obligations. However, caution must be exercised in that buyers will not net cash against long-term financial liabilities where it would erode the company's net working capital position below an acceptable level.

Buyers and sellers sometimes disagree on whether a bank operating loan or similar form of debt should be considered a financial liability or an operating liability of the company. Since financial liabilities are deducted when determining the amount paid for the equity of the company while operating liabilities are not, this issue clearly is of concern to both buyers and sellers. However, the amount of operating liabilities owed by a company does affect its net operating assets, which may have an impact on the price that a buyer is willing to pay for the company. The situation can be particularly acute where the operations of the company are seasonal, and its bank operating line is at a seasonal high at the closing date of the transaction. The business owner may take the position that excessive operating debt is being used to finance higher assets (such as accounts receivable and inventories) at that point in time, which assets should serve to offset the excess debt. Alternatively, the business owner might be successful in convincing a buyer to deduct the cost of short-term debt (e.g., the interest paid on the bank operating line) when calculating cash flow, and not to deduct the principal amount of the loan from enterprise value.

As an example of the trade-off between deducting interest expense and deducting the outstanding principal amount of a bank operating loan, consider Company T, which has a normalized pre-tax cash flow from operations of $2 million (net of sustaining capital reinvestment, which approximates Company T's depreciation expense) and a bank operating loan of $3 million. The bank operating loan bears interest at a rate of 6% and Company T pays income taxes at a rate of 40%. If a buyer requires a 12% after-tax rate of return (i.e., a capitalization rate) it would determine the equity value of Company T as follows, based on the capitalized cash flow methodology:

Normalized pre-tax cash flow from operations	$ 2,000,000
– income taxes at 40%	$ (800,000)
= Discretionary cash flow	$ 1,200,000
÷ capitalization rate	12%
= Enterprise value	$10,000,000
– financial liabilities outstanding	$(3,000,000)
= Equity value	$ 7,000,000

Alternatively, if the business owner could convince the buyer to deduct the cost of financing from its cash flow base and not to deduct the principal amount of the bank operating loan, the business owner would argue that the equity value of Company T should be calculated as follows:

	Normalized pre-tax cash flow from operations	$ 2,000,000
-	cost of financing (6% x $3 million)	$ (180,000)
=	Adjusted pre-tax cash flow	$ 1,820,000
-	income taxes at 40%	$ (728,000)
=	Discretionary cash flow	$ 1,092,000
÷	capitalization rate	12%
=	Enterprise value	$ 9,100,000
-	financial liabilities remaining	$ (0)
=	Equity value	$ 9,100,000

While business owners will want to use this approach to increase the equity value of their company, sophisticated buyers will not accept such a proposition. Rather, a sophisticated buyer normally will argue that the applicable valuation multiple should decline (i.e., the required rate of return should increase) to reflect the higher level of risk being assumed due to the existence of the bank obligation (referred to as "financial risk"). In this example, if the capitalization rate increased to 15.6% to reflect the financial risk resulting from the bank operating line, the equity value of the company would remain unchanged at $7 million (calculated as $1,092,000 divided by 15.6%). That said, not all buyers have an adequately sophisticated technical valuation background to reflect an appropriate financial risk adjustment. Therefore, it sometimes is worthwhile for the business owner to put forth the argument that the cost of short-term debt should be deducted as opposed to the principal amount of short-term debt outstanding in the hopes of realizing an economic gain due to a buyer's naivety.

Net Operating Assets

As explained in Section II, the net operating assets of a company refer to its tangible operating assets (such as accounts receivable, inventories and fixed assets, but excluding intangible assets and redundant assets) less its operating liabilities (such as accounts payable and accrued liabilities, but excluding financial liabilities as discussed above).

A common misconception among business owners is that they will receive "extra" money for the net operating assets on the balance sheet, beyond the enterprise value of their company (i.e., they will be paid for the value of the shares in their company, plus the value of the accounts receivable, inventories and other operating assets of the company, net of its liabilities). However, the convention in transactions involving mid-size privately held companies in

Canada is that the buyer receives the company's balance sheet as part of the purchase price.

The balance sheet delivered to the buyer is subject to negotiation, but normally is comprised of net operating assets, including the net working capital that the buyer believes is necessary to support the company's ongoing operations. At the closing date of the transaction, the buyer will assume the balance sheet of the company, as agreed to with the business owner. This normally includes a minimum and/or maximum amount of net operating assets, net working capital, financial liabilities and other assets and liabilities to be delivered by the business owner at the closing date. The purchase price for the company is adjusted, upward or downward, for any excess or deficiency in the assets and liabilities delivered against the balance sheet targets, as agreed between the buyer and seller.

It is important that net operating assets, net working capital and other balance sheet target measures be appropriately defined so as to avoid any double-counting of adjustments to the purchase price. For example, where net working capital is defined to include a bank operating loan, the equity value of the company should not be reduced for both the amount of the bank operating loan and a working capital deficiency caused by the bank operating loan. Likewise, the business owner should be cautious that overlapping adjustments are not made on account of both the net assets and net working capital of the company.

Business owners can enhance the value they receive for the equity in their company by closely managing its financial position in the years prior to sale. In particular, efforts to legitimately reduce capital expenditure and working capital requirements of the company can cause buyers to perceive that prospective cash flows can be generated from a lower base of net operating assets. This can increase a buyer's expectations as to future cash flows of the company on the basis that growth in its operating profits will not be eroded by capital expenditure and incremental working capital requirements. A buyer's higher cash flow expectations may increase the price that it is willing to pay for the company.

Business owners can capitalize on better asset and liability management in the years prior to sale where they are able to negotiate the delivery of a "smaller" balance sheet at the closing date. This allows the business owner to extract net working capital and other net assets of their company in excess of the agreed levels, or to receive an upward adjustment to the purchase price to reflect the value of excess amounts delivered to the buyer. Balance sheet targets within the context of deal structuring are addressed in Stage 6.

Redundant Assets

Some privately held companies own assets that are not required in their ongoing operations (i.e., redundant assets). Examples of redundant assets might include marketable securities or vacant land that was purchased by the business owner through the company, as opposed to buying such assets outside of the company. In order to qualify as a redundant asset, the business owner must be capable of permanently withdrawing the asset from their company without impairing its longer-term viability. Excess assets that build up due to temporary surpluses (e.g., due to the seasonal nature of the company) are not considered redundant assets.

As a practical matter, redundant assets normally are removed from the company (on a tax-deferred basis) prior to its sale, as buyers seldom are interested in acquiring redundant assets. Removing redundant assets prior to the sale generally enhances the overall equity value realized by the business owner. This is because the buyer of an operating company usually seeks to pay a discounted price for any redundant assets that it agrees to acquire. However, where the redundant assets are withdrawn prior to sale, the business owner can sell those assets to another buyer that is willing to pay a higher price, or the business owner can continue to realize the income stream generated by those assets.

In circumstances where redundant assets are sold with the company, the equity value of the company is increased to reflect the price of those assets as agreed to between the buyer and the seller (which may be greater than or less than the book value of those assets for financial accounting purposes). Where redundant assets do exist, whether or not they are sold as part of the company or withdrawn prior to the sale, any revenues or expenses associated with those assets should be removed from the company's projected cash flow stream in order to avoid double-counting when estimating its value.

Real estate

In some cases, a company owns the real estate that is used to house its operations. In this regard, the real estate owned by the company may represent a "hidden" redundant asset.

Where the real estate is an attractive property that can be readily marketed for sale separate from the operating company, the owner should consider whether it is better to sell the real estate as part of their company or to remove the real estate beforehand and either rent the property to the buyer (or another tenant) or, alternatively, sell the real estate to a different buyer. This can result in a higher equity value being realized by the business owner.

As an example, assume that Company V owns the real estate that houses its operations. Company V generates normalized EBITDA of $5 million per year, net of all the costs of operating its facility. The market rent for the premises in which Company V operates is $1 million. The owner of Company V learns that companies similar to his are being acquired at a price of 5x EBITDA. However, real estate similar to Company V's premises is being valued in the order of 8x operating cash flow.

If the owner of Company V sold his company inclusive of the real estate, he could expect an enterprise value of $25 million, determined as follows:

Normalized EBITDA	$ 5 million
x EBITDA multiple	5
= Enterprise value	$25 million

However, if the owner of Company V sold the real estate separate from the operating company, the enterprise value that he realizes would increase to $28 million, as follows:

	Operations		**Real Estate**		**Total**
Normalized EBITDA	$ 5,000,000				
Rental income (expense)	$(1,000,000)		$ 1,000,000		
Adjusted EBITDA / operating cash flow	$ 4,000,000		$ 1,000,000		
x Multiple	5		8		
Enterprise value	$20,000,000	+	$ 8,000,000	=	$28,000,000

Therefore, depending on the nature of the real property owned by a company, it may be preferable to retain it or to sell it separately in order to realize value enhancement. In addition, the business owner's flexibility, in so far as offering buyers a choice of whether to:

- acquire the real estate along with the operating business (at a price that reflects the market value of that real estate);
- enter into a lease arrangement at market rates with the business owner who retains ownership of the property after selling the operating business; or
- allow the buyer to move the operations to another facility (and therefore to realize synergies),

can help in attracting a larger number of prospective buyers and in increasing the prices they may be willing to pay.

Summary

The enterprise value of a company is a function of its prospective cash flow (ultimately its discretionary cash flow) and the rate of return or valuation multiple applied thereto. The equity value of a company is a function of its enterprise value less its financial liabilities outstanding. Further adjustments are made where excess or deficient net operating assets exist (e.g., to reflect a working capital deficiency that has not been accounted for in the prospective cash flow calculation) or where redundant assets are sold with the company. Value enhancement is created where the business owner identifies and undertakes initiatives to increase the intrinsic and strategic equity value of their company prior to the time that it is exposed for sale in the open market.

Common valuation methodologies include the multiple of EBITDA, multiple of EBIT, capitalized cash flow and DCF methodology. Sophisticated buyers generally prefer the DCF methodology because it incorporates all of the elements that ultimately influence economic value. Business owners can gain important insights into how to enhance the equity value of their company by understanding the variables and dynamics of the DCF methodology.

Rates of return and valuation multiples are subjective. The discount rate is a function of the perceived likelihood that a company will achieve its prospective discretionary cash flow, given its operating risks and economic and industry conditions, and its debt capacity. The capitalization rate is determined as the discount rate less expected long-term inflationary and real growth. The valuation multiple is the inverse of the capitalization rate. It normally is converted to a pre-tax basis and expressed as a multiple of EBIT or EBITDA. In order to reduce the discount rate (or increase the multiple) applied to the prospective cash flows of a company, the business owner should focus on initiatives that will cause buyers to perceive a lower risk level and strong growth prospects for the company, and by improving its effective debt capacity.

The financial position of a company influences the rates of return and valuation multiples adopted by a buyer, and defines the debt, net operating assets and working capital assumed by the buyer upon closing. Business owners should recognize that their company's net operating assets influence its equity value. Therefore, it is important to effectively manage both the income statement/cash flows of the company as well as its underlying assets and liabilities in the years prior to sale in order to create and realize value enhancement.

SECTION III

Stage 4 | The Search for Buyers

Introduction

The search for buyers is the first stage in the execution phase of the private company sale process. At this point, the business owner begins transitioning from being an operator of their company (either passively or actively) to being a "seller". The key to value enhancement in the search for buyers is for the seller to attract a sufficient number of qualified buyers so as to establish the platform for an effective auction. Therefore, the seller and their intermediary should consider in broad terms which types of buyers might be interested in purchasing the company.

Sellers should consider what their company has to offer in terms of its customer base, technology, businesses processes and other intangible attributes that may be of interest to buyers, both within and outside of their company's industry segment. In many cases, a buyer from outside of the industry is the one that perceives the greatest value in the company because it offers that buyer the opportunity to expand into new markets or to access new customers.

It is not sufficient to simply identify which buyers might be interested in the company. Preliminary research also must be done to assess whether they are qualified prospects. A qualified buyer is one that is believed to have well-founded reasons for its interest in the company (such as the opportunity to realize synergies) and the ability to consummate a transaction on terms that would be acceptable to the seller. Preliminary research allows the seller to rank prospective buyers in relative terms, and to tailor the way each buyer is approached.

Initial contact with qualified buyers should be conducted to engage their interest such that they agree to execute a non-disclosure agreement in order to receive further information. The seller and their intermediary must ensure that sensitive information about the company is not disclosed until after a non-disclosure agreement has been signed.

The search for buyers stage, including identifying prospective buyers, qualifying prospective buyers and initial buyer contact, normally takes about one to two months to complete. The search for buyers stage of the private company sale process within the *Value Enhancement Framework™* is depicted in Exhibit III-4-1.

Exhibit III-4-1

THE SEARCH FOR BUYERS STAGE WITHIN THE *VALUE ENHANCEMENT FRAMEWORK™*

(i) Identifying Prospective Buyers

Types of Buyers

The first step toward building deal momentum and creating an effective auction process is for the seller and their intermediary to identify potential buyers. This includes obvious prospects (such as competitors) as well as other potential buyers that may foresee a strategic fit with the company.

Owners of privately held Canadian companies often believe they know with certainty which prospective buyers will be interested in their company. As such, they sometimes choose to restrict their search in that regard for reasons such as expediency or to preserve confidentiality. In many cases, however, the ultimate buyer is one which the seller never expected. This is because the buyer willing to offer the best value to the seller may be from outside of the company's industry segment, thereby bringing a much different perspective compared to a competitor as to the benefits to be realized from the acquisition. Therefore, a broadly based search for buyers usually works best, including the identification of some prospective buyers through "out-of-the-box" type thinking.

The market for mid-size privately held companies is made up of a variety of different types of buyers. This includes strategic buyers, non-strategic buyers, small corporate buyers and individuals, financial buyers and the management and employees of the company. While each prospective buyer is unique, generalities can be made regarding the types of buyers in the marketplace and their expectations.

Strategic buyers

"Strategic buyers" refers to competitors, customers, suppliers, organizations with complementary products and other prospective buyers that are believed to have the opportunity to realize synergies by combining the company with their existing operations. Sellers often are hesitant to approach these prospects because they are wary about word of a sale spreading in the marketplace, resulting in a loss of revenues, employees, trade secrets and other negative effects. While the method in which these parties are approached can help reduce the risks of the market becoming aware that the company is for sale (as discussed later in this Stage), such risks can never be eliminated altogether.

The identification of strategic buyers requires creative thinking by the seller and their intermediary. While suppliers, customers and competitors are obvious choices, other prospects should be considered as well. In this regard, it is helpful to consider the strengths and intangible assets that the company has to offer. For example, owners of companies that have a broadly diversified customer base should think about what other types of businesses would benefit from access to that customer base by considering other products or services that are (or could be) sold to those customers. Alternatively, owners of companies with proprietary technology should consider horizontal applications of that technology into other industries.

The key point is that strategic buyers come from a variety of sources. The identification of strategic buyers from different types of industries or sectors may help the seller to more fully understand the reasons for buyer interest in their company, which in turn can be emphasized in discussions with all prospective buyers. In addition, strategic buyers from outside of the company's industry might be willing to pay a premium for both prospective cost reduction opportunities as well as the strategic value to them of gaining access to a new market segment.

A sub-set of strategic buyers is those buyers actively pursuing a roll-up or consolidation strategy. As discussed in Stage 1, industries sometimes go through a period of consolidation that results in additional liquidity for sellers and higher prices being paid for companies than ordinarily may be the case. The key to value enhancement realization during a consolidation phase is timing, that is, not selling the company too early or too late in the process. It also is important to ensure that more than just the roll-up buyers are solicited to create an effective auction and to maintain viable alternatives throughout the sale process.

Non-strategic buyers

A non-strategic buyer refers to a corporation that is unlikely to realize any material synergies or strategic advantages in buying the company. Non-strategic buyers undertake acquisitions primarily to earn an acceptable return on their investment, viewed on a stand-alone basis. Consequently, they tend to look for acquisition opportunities that can be consummated at low prices and on terms that are favourable to them, so as to shorten the payback period for their investment.

While non-strategic buyers generally comprise those from outside of the company's immediate industry segment, depending on the industry, they can include a company's competitors, suppliers, customers and other participants. The economics of certain industries make synergies difficult to realize. This is not to suggest that non-strategic buyers should be avoided, but rather that the seller should understand the premise of the valuation model used by these buyers, being one based on the intrinsic value (i.e., "stand-alone" value) of the company. Value enhancement opportunities may still be available to the seller where they are able to demonstrate strong intrinsic growth potential for their company and reduced risk. When dealing with a non-strategic buyer outside of the seller's industry, it may be possible to negotiate a premium for the diversification opportunity that their company presents to that buyer. Finally, for those buyers that might have an opportunity to realize synergies but that are unwilling to pay for those synergies due to the high level of uncertainty that they will materialize, it may be possible to structure the transaction so that the seller receives a cash payment (or equivalent) for the intrinsic equity value of their company on closing and the value of any synergies is shared between the buyer and the seller only if and when they are realized.

Small corporate buyers and individuals

Small corporate buyers and individuals who want to own a mid-size private company (apart from management and employees of the company, discussed below) essentially are a sub-set of the non-strategic buyer group. Small corporate buyers and individuals seldom can generate significant post-acquisition synergies due to the relatively small size of their existing operating base (if one exists at all). Therefore, such buyers normally are prepared to only pay for the intrinsic value of a company, if that. Small corporate buyers and individuals normally are risk-averse and are hesitant to invest a substantial portion of their wealth in an acquisition opportunity. Typically, deals are done only where small corporate buyers and individuals are able to negotiate what they believe to be a very attractive price and deal terms.

Small corporate buyers and individuals frequently have limited financial resources. Therefore, the terms of a transaction with these buyers normally involves a significant portion of the purchase price being paid over time or being contingent upon the future operating results of the company. As discussed in Stage 6, the value received by the seller in such deal structures often is much lower than the stated price paid for the company.

For these reasons, small corporate buyers and individuals usually are not the best means for enabling the seller of a mid-sized privately held company to realize value enhancement in a transaction. That said, there can be instances where a well-financed small corporate buyer or individual is interested in the company and has the ability and interest to transact at a meaningful price and deal terms. While these types of buyers should not be dismissed altogether, it is important to be selective when dealing with them and to ensure adequate pre-qualification of their ability to consummate a transaction on reasonable terms.

Public vs. private company buyers

Strategic and non-strategic buyers may be publicly or privately held companies. While for the most part public and private company buyers assess acquisition opportunities in a similar way, there are some differences between the two that are important to recognize. The principal differences revolve around their decision-making process, the impact of accounting earnings and access to capital.

Buyers that are private companies normally have a single owner or are closely held by a family or group of individuals. Therefore, decisions can be made relatively quickly. Conversely, depending on the size of the acquisition, the decision-making process for publicly held companies can be quite lengthy, particularly where board approval is necessary. In today's environment, public companies generally are more concerned with proper due diligence and fiscal prudence than was the case in the 1990s, which may further lengthen the approval process. Therefore, it is important for the seller to recognize and plan for possible delays when dealing with buyers that are public companies in so far as their negotiations and due diligence are concerned.

Owners and managers of private companies tend to emphasize cash flow when assessing acquisition targets and also tend to be driven, at least to some extent, by tax minimization opportunities. While managers of public companies also tend to emphasize cash flow, they are cognizant about the impact that an acquisition will have on post-acquisition profits. Profit maximization generally is the primary goal of public company managers, as opposed to income tax minimization. Public companies generally are reluctant to do a deal that will result in an erosion of their earnings per share on a near-term basis. Accounting rules often influence the price that a public company is willing to pay for an acquisition and sometimes even whether it will enter into a transaction at all. This can present a value enhancement opportunity for skilful negotiators who are able to employ deal structuring alternatives that will allow a public company to report favourably to its stakeholders from a financial accounting perspective, while providing enhanced value to the seller from a cash flow perspective. In addition, public companies usually consider the valuation multiples implied by the market price of their own outstanding share capital and they normally seek to consummate a transaction at lower multiples in the hope of gaining a "lift" on the earnings of the acquired company (immediately "accretive" earnings) when consolidated with their existing business.

While private companies usually will rely on their own sources of capital to finance a transaction (or alternatively borrow from banks or other sources), public companies have access to the public equity markets for capital. Depending on the status of the financial markets at a given point in time, this can facilitate a major acquisition. In addition, some public companies finance some or all of their acquisitions through share exchanges, particularly when their shares are trading at high multiples. Share exchanges are further discussed in Stage 6.

There are several other advantages to dealing with public company buyers. Because such companies must publicly disclose their financial statements, sellers generally have a better opportunity to assess their likely interest in acquiring and their ability to finance a transaction. Further, managers of public companies sometimes feel compelled to transact, particularly during periods of high profitability. This is because shareholders of public companies generally expect that profits will be reinvested in new opportunities, used to repay debt or distributed back to shareholders. Managers of public companies sometimes prefer the reinvestment option in order to grow the business so that they can manage a larger organization. Some public companies announce that they are actively pursuing acquisition opportunities. This sometimes causes public company managers and directors to be pressured into paying a premium in order to consummate a transaction and meet shareholder expectations.

Financial buyers

Financial buyers include private equity funds, investment companies, pension funds and other groups whose mandate includes investments in privately held companies. Financial buyers have become much more prominent in recent years and now represent a viable alternative for many mid-size privately held Canadian companies.

Financial buyers may seek a minority interest, controlling interest or the outright ownership of a privately held company. While this book focuses on the last of these three avenues, these other alternatives may be worth exploring. Financial buyers often require that the seller or the management team maintain an equity interest in their company to ensure loyalty and proper alignment of objectives between management and the financial buyer.

Financial buyers have the advantage of ready access to capital. Further, many of these organizations are compelled to invest in order to satisfy their stakeholders. Consequently, in recent years, financial buyers have become more aggressive both with respect to their pricing and in the types of investments they are prepared to make.

While financial buyers may not have the same degree of industry knowledge that a competitor of the company has, they often specialize in certain industry sectors in order to better understand the operating dynamics and risks involved. For those that do specialize in an industry sector, there may be an ability to realize operating synergies where two or more of the financial buyers' investee companies can be combined.

When dealing with financial buyers it is important to understand their investment criteria and objectives. In most cases, financial buyers seek companies with an established management team in place. While financial buyers normally will insist on having board level representation in the investee company, they generally do not want to be involved in its day-to-day management. Therefore, financial buyers may not be interested in a company where the seller is not willing to remain following the transaction or where a capable successor cannot be identified. Financial buyers also tend to have a different expectation as to investment time horizon. Most financial buyers expect to resell the acquired company (or possibly take it public) within about three to seven years of making an investment. Therefore, they tend to prefer growing companies that will enjoy a higher "exit multiple" (in terms of a multiple of EBITDA, for example) than they originally paid. Simply put, financial buyers seek to invest in private companies that can be resold within the next few years at a higher valuation multiple and with higher cash flows, thereby generating a substantial return on their investment. In addition, financial buyers are more inclined to finance a larger portion of the acquisition price with third party debt so as to leverage the return that they generate on the equity portion of their investment.

When dealing with financial buyers, the seller should emphasize the organic growth potential of their company, the various exit strategy alternatives that are available and synergies with other investments in the financial buyer's portfolio, where applicable. The seller might also consider selling a controlling interest in their company to a financial buyer and retaining a minority interest position that could be crystallized upon the subsequent sale of their company to a strategic buyer or an initial public offering. Such a structure usually is more attractive to a financial buyer and it allows the seller to realize upside potential on a subsequent transaction, as long as the seller is satisfied that the potential rewards outweigh the risks that are involved.

Domestic vs. foreign buyers

Owners of privately held Canadian companies should not only consider domestic buyers, but those based in other countries as well. Foreign-based buyers may be attracted to a Canadian company where they do not have an existing platform in the country. This is true not only for U.S. buyers, but also for those in Europe and other parts of the world. Many foreign companies have Canadian subsidiaries that they are looking to grow.

With recent trends in globalization and freer trade, many mid-size Canadian companies have become more attractive to foreign buyers than previously had been the case. Further, in recent years, mid-size Canadian privately held companies with an established market presence are attracting a growing number of foreign-based financial buyers, some of which perceive that Canadian companies are undervalued relative to companies in other jurisdictions.

Foreign-based buyers tend to be more interested in Canadian private companies where they are larger businesses with an established market presence. This is due to the relatively high costs of pursuing smaller-sized foreign acquisitions versus the benefit that they receive. That said, a smaller privately held Canadian company might be of interest to a foreign buyer where the company offers proprietary technology or some other intangible benefit that the buyer can leverage in its existing business.

Management and employees

A natural buyer for many companies is the management team or employee group that runs the company on a day-to-day basis. Business owners consider selling to management and employees for various reasons, including their belief that these individuals are owed the chance to buy the company, or because they believe the sale process will be facilitated given that management and employees are already familiar with the company. While this may be true, it also results in the loss of the ability for the seller to enhance value through creating an effective auction among external buyers.

Management and employees suffer from many of the same drawbacks as small corporate buyers and individuals, including the lack of financial resources and limited opportunity for synergies. However, depending on the size and nature of the company, management and employee buy-outs may be aided by financial buyers who can provide the needed resources.

A difficulty that sellers sometimes face is where they are actively soliciting third party buyers, but management (or the employees) also is bidding for the company. In some cases, third party buyers will not bid against the management team, particularly where some or all of those management individuals will be required to operate the company after the sale. This can hamper the seller's ability to build deal momentum and create an effective auction. Furthermore, management is placed in a position of conflict given that it is in their interest to reduce the operating results or outlook for the company where possible, in order to negotiate a better deal for themselves.

Sellers faced with having to deal with management or employees as a prospective buyer should identify this group's interest at an early stage in the sale process and carefully consider how they should deal with the situation. This is one reason why it generally makes sense for the seller to inform key employees about the possible sale of their company prior to negotiations with third party buyers. In order to diminish the natural conflict of interest that managers may have where they are prospective buyers for the company, the seller might consider sharing a portion of the sale proceeds received from a third party buyer with some of the company's managers and employees. In particular, the seller may allow management to participate in the portion of the purchase price that is in excess of the price that management had bid for the company. Once again, every situation is fact-specific. The important point is that when management or employees present themselves as potential buyers, the situation must be carefully handled so that it does not impede the open market sale process. If managed properly, the existence of a possible management or employee buy-out provides another party to the auction process that can serve to generate greater value enhancement opportunities for the seller.

Summary – types of buyers

Exhibit III-4-2 summarizes the types of buyers that normally exist for mid-size privately held companies and the factors that the seller should focus on when dealing with these various groups in order to create the platform for value enhancement realization:

Exhibit III-4-2

TYPES OF BUYERS AND FACTORS TO FOCUS ON

Type of Buyer	Key Factors
Strategic	Synergies and the strategic importance of the company's intangible assets (e.g., customer base, technology and other advantages) to the buyer.
Non-Strategic	Organic growth potential and risk reduction factors
Small Corporate or Individual	Pre-qualification regarding their level of interest and ability to transact
Financial	Organic growth potential, synergies with other investments, exit strategies
Management and Employees	Ability to transact or to obtain a financial backer. Not allowing the management and employee group to become an impediment to the open market sale process.

Sources of Prospective Buyers

The identification of prospective buyers should commence in the planning phase of the private company sale process, specifically during the sale preparation stage (Stage 2). Early identification of possible buyers can help the business owner better understand the particular valuation dynamics in the company's marketplace and to identify and undertake initiatives that make their company more attractive to a particular group of buyers.

Prospective buyers can be identified from many sources. As a starting point, the business owner may have received previous offers for their company prior to the time that a sale had been contemplated. Ideally, the names and contact information of those interested parties were retained.

Customers, suppliers and competitors are also obvious possibilities. As noted above, sellers sometimes are reluctant to contact these parties because of the possible repercussions if the marketplace learns that their company is for sale. The issue of contacting prospective buyers is addressed later in this Stage.

As discussed above, strategic buyers are well positioned to optimize value for the seller. Identifying the best strategic buyers often requires some creative thinking. In this regard, it is helpful to consider the entire supply chain of an industry and buyers that offer complementary products and services that may benefit from the company's intangible assets, such as its customer base, technology, work force and so on. Other potential buyers may be identified through industry journals and by contacting industry associations.

Where there are publicly traded companies within an industry, their annual reports and regulatory filings should be reviewed to determine whether they are potential buyers. Many public companies disclose their intent to make acquisitions as part of their growth strategy.

There are a large number of financial buyers that exist. Many of them are listed on websites and databases that are dedicated to the financial buyer segment. Most financial buyers disclose their general investment criteria, which should be reviewed to establish whether or not there is a reasonable likelihood of a fit with their objectives.

A good source of prospective buyers often can be found by examining merger and acquisition transactions that have taken place within a particular industry over the past several years. Acquirers of privately held companies within a given industry often have an active acquisition mandate and the available capital to consummate transactions on reasonable terms. Many intermediary firms subscribe to databases and information services that provide regular updates of merger and acquisition transactions that have occurred throughout a wide array of industries.

Finally, as noted earlier in this Stage, when identifying potential buyers it is important not to limit the scope of the search based on geography. Buyers located in the U.S., Europe and other regions often seek to acquire mid-size Canadian privately held companies. As a general rule, the larger the company, the greater the likelihood that it will attract the interest of one or more foreign buyers.

(ii) Qualifying Prospective Buyers

While it is important to identify a sufficient number of prospective buyers in creating the platform for the effective auction, it is also important to determine which of those buyers are qualified prospects. A qualified prospect is one that is believed to have well-founded reasons for its interest in the company (such as the ability to generate post-acquisition synergies) and the ability to consummate a transaction on terms that are acceptable to the seller. Preliminary research should be conducted on prospective buyers to establish the reasons why they may be interested in acquiring and also their ability to transact.

An important element of realizing value enhancement is the research and analysis conducted on prospective buyers early in the sale process. Research can assist in identifying those buyers best positioned to benefit from an acquisition of the company and aid in quantifying the synergies they will expect to generate. This information can be used to rank prospective buyers as high, medium and low prospects. Further, such research is valuable so that specific features of the company can be highlighted to each buyer when it is first contacted, which may increase the likelihood of capturing their initial interest.

Websites are a useful place for gathering information. While the quantity and quality of the information set out on a prospective buyer's website can vary substantially, it usually provides some indication as to the principal markets it serves and its perceived strengths. Other sources of information on prospective corporate buyers includes trade associations, industry publications, articles written by or about that company and direct knowledge of the buyer where the seller has had dealings with that company in the past.

Where the prospective buyer is a privately held company, there usually is no publicly available financial information. In some cases it is possible to obtain public information about such things as the number of employees, number and size of facilities and breadth and depth of product and service offerings. These things can provide some indication as to the size of the buyer and its areas of interest. Credit reports may also be available for some private companies, however, caution must be exercised not to place too much reliance on a credit report, as it can be outdated or inaccurate. At this point in the sale process, the objective is only to establish whether there is a reasonable expectation that a prospective buyer will be interested in the company, the synergies that it might expect to realize, and to obtain a general sense of the buyer's ability to consummate a transaction on reasonable terms. In addition, while it is helpful to consider the types of synergies that could be available to a specific buyer, the seller should not view these things as a foregone conclusion, since buyers may change their strategy or outlook.

For publicly held companies, information-gathering is facilitated due to regulatory filings. This includes annual reports, management circulars, press releases and other communications. Some public companies openly announce that they are actively pursuing acquisition opportunities and disclose their investment criteria.

Details on recent merger and acquisition transactions consummated by a particular buyer can provide some insight into its motives, expectations and pricing strategies. In general, more details regarding a transaction are available where one or both parties were public companies. However, even transactions among two privately held companies can offer an indication as to the reasons for the buyer's interest and the types of synergies that it expects.

With respect to financial buyers, their websites usually are designed with the intention of openly communicating their industries of interest and general investment criteria. Many financial buyers disclose their portfolio of investments, which may provide some insight into synergy or roll-up opportunities. However, details of transactions involving the purchase of privately held companies by financial buyers usually are limited.

Finally, where small corporate buyers and individuals are identified, it usually is difficult to obtain any meaningful public information on their objectives or ability to transact. Accordingly, when first contacting small corporate buyers and individuals, it is not uncommon for the intermediary to request further information on their background and financial resources so as to gain some comfort that they may be a qualified prospect.

(iii) Initial Buyer Contact

Initial contact with qualified buyers must be done in a way that will capture their initial interest and set the groundwork for future discussions. In this regard, it is important that the acquisition profile (discussed below) convey the nature and attractiveness of the opportunity to the buyer, while not revealing details about the company until a non-disclosure agreement (discussed below) has been signed.

Who to Approach and How

When first contacting prospective strategic or non-strategic buyers, it usually is best to do so via a direct telephone call to a senior management individual, such as the president, chief financial officer or a division executive of that organization. The seller's intermediary normally initiates the call. There are several reasons for the direct contact approach. First, sending out "blind" company profiles via e-mails and faxes to a large number of possible buyers undermines credibility and often results in those solicitations being missed, deleted or ignored. Second, while a follow-up fax or e-mail may be appropriate, it is best to first establish direct contact. Most senior executives will accept calls dealing with an acquisition opportunity.

Importantly, direct contact allows the seller and their intermediary to gather information regarding the prospective buyer and the market for companies within the industry. Questions can be asked about the buyer's interest in acquisitions as a general strategy, the acquisitions it has made in the past and its strategic direction. This serves to confirm or dispel initial belief as to whether a particular buyer represents a qualified prospect. Senior executives sometimes disclose more than they should during an initial phone call, which information can be useful in subsequent discussions with that buyer. Furthermore, senior executives often will provide their view on the prevailing merger and acquisition activity within their industry and the multiples that are being paid to acquire privately held companies. This information can be useful in future discussions and in negotiations with that buyer and other prospective buyers. Finally, those buyers that are not interested in the company may offer some suggestions as to other organizations that would be interested.

Large corporate buyers sometimes employ individuals within their organizations who are dedicated to looking at acquisition opportunities. While these individuals may take an active role at some point, as a first step it generally is best to present the opportunity to senior operating management, such as a divisional executive, because senior operating management usually has a better understanding of the strategic fit between their organization and the company. Further, senior operating management are more likely to champion the acquisition opportunity within their organization, which is important to moving the process forward and building deal momentum. Corporate acquisition departments may service a range of business segments within a particular organization and therefore its staff may not understand the strategic fit to the same degree as operating management, or they may get side-tracked with other projects.

Sellers sometimes contemplate advertising the sale of their private company in newspapers or websites that list companies for sale. While such an approach may be appropriate for small businesses, it seldom proves worthwhile for mid-size private companies. This is because buyers of mid-size private companies seldom look at those sources for acquisition opportunities. Furthermore, this medium does not allow the seller to determine who has accessed those information sources, which hinders the seller's ability to control the sale process. An approach that consists of researching the market, identifying qualified prospective buyers and soliciting those buyers directly usually works best.

During the initial contact with the prospective buyer, it is customary to convey the information set out in the acquisition profile, but not to disclose the identity of the company until the buyer has verbally agreed to execute a satisfactory non-disclosure agreement. Each of these things is discussed in the parts that follow.

An issue that often arises is if, and when, to contact direct competitors of the company, as well as customers and suppliers to the company which could be considered as potential buyers. Sellers usually are wary about approaching these parties for fear of having word of a sale spread within the industry and the risk that key employees of the company may learn of the pending sale, worry unnecessarily about it, or leave.

The right time to approach competitors, customers and suppliers depends on the number and quality of other potential buyers that have been identified. Where a large number of qualified prospects have been identified, it usually is preferable to begin with those that are not competitors, customers or suppliers. In circumstances where other possible buyers represent strong prospects, it allows the seller to gather some indication as to the general level of interest that exists for their company and then to approach direct competitors, customers and suppliers, knowing that sensitive information regarding their company will only be provided if such buyers exhibit a genuine interest in the opportunity. This allows the seller to shorten the timeline afforded to direct competitors, customers and suppliers so as to reduce the risk that word of the sale spreading through the marketplace, which usually escalates with the passage of time.

When first contacting direct competitors, customers and suppliers, it is best to make the acquisition profile vague so as to better protect the identity of the company until the buyer has proclaimed an interest and has verbally agreed to sign a non-disclosure agreement. Caution must be exercised however to ensure that the description of the acquisition opportunity remains attractive to those prospective buyers who genuinely would be interested. As a practical matter, greater synergies may be available to direct competitors, customers and suppliers, which in many cases represent strategic buyers, and hence these parties may be willing to offer the best value to the seller.

When approaching direct competitors, customers and suppliers, the intermediary must endeavour to establish that the party is a qualified buyer and is not simply looking to receive information about the company for its own internal use (even though such use of the information would be contrary to the non-disclosure agreement). This is done through preliminary research (such as researching prior transactions undertaken by the prospective buyer) and in the initial telephone discussions with the prospective buyer, with inquiries directed to the buyer's strategic direction and the size and type of business that it would be interested in acquiring (to the extent that the buyer is willing to disclose such information). There is nothing wrong with conveying to a prospective buyer that such pre-qualification is necessary due to the sensitivity of the information involved. It also provides the seller with information that can be used in subsequent discussions and negotiations with that buyer.

In circumstances where small corporate buyers and individuals are contacted, it is usual to engage in a fairly comprehensive pre-qualification process to try to establish their level of interest in the opportunity and the financial resources they have with which to consummate a transaction. It is also important to determine the acquisition criteria of the small corporate buyer or individual. As a general rule, where a small corporate buyer or individual has stated acquisition criteria that are fairly broad, they are unlikely to transact unless they perceive that they are getting a bargain price. Conversely, small corporate buyers and individuals with specific interests in terms of the industry segment, transaction size, and other defined investment parameters, may prove to be worthwhile prospects. The other caveat in this regard is to establish whether those buyers have adequate capital readily available or whether any offer will be contingent upon their ability to secure financing.

When approaching financial buyers, the seller must be cognizant of the fact that such buyers normally see a large number of opportunities. Therefore, attracting a financial buyer's interest may require tailoring the acquisition profile and initial telephone discussion to meet that firm's specific investment criteria, where such information has been disclosed. As mentioned previously in this Stage, financial buyers typically have time horizon objectives between three to seven years and therefore the initial contact should address the company's organic growth potential, exit strategy opportunities and possible synergies with other companies in the financial buyer's portfolio.

The Acquisition Profile

The realization of value enhancement depends on the ability of the seller and their intermediary to attract a sufficient number of qualified buyers to establish the platform for the effective auction. In order to do so, it is necessary to capture the initial interest of buyers that are believed to be qualified prospects so that they will agree to execute a non-disclosure agreement. Capturing the initial interest of prospective buyers depends to a large degree on the content of the acquisition profile (sometimes referred to as the "teaser").

The purpose of the acquisition profile is to provide prospective buyers with an indication of the type of company that is for sale, without revealing its identity until the buyer has agreed to execute a non-disclosure agreement. Therefore, the acquisition profile must be worded to balance the risk of premature identification against the risk of not attracting a qualified prospect by being too vague. Furthermore, the acquisition profile should be tailored as necessary, depending on the prospective buyer. For example, direct competitors may not require as much information about the company as a prospective buyer that is within a different industry segment or a financial buyer.

In its written form, the acquisition profile usually is no more than one to two pages in length. It normally sets out the company's industry segment, its geographic location in general terms (e.g., the city or region in which it operates), an overview of the company's operations, summary financial data and other information to gain the interest of prospective buyers, while maintaining anonymity. It should be succinct. With respect to financial data, it is common to provide limited information, such as the range of revenues in the past year (or past few years) and some indication as to the company's level of profitability. This usually is done through mentioning the normalized operating profit margin (such as the percentage of earnings before interest, taxes, depreciation and amortization, i.e., EBITDA) achieved in the past few years, or just mentioning whether the company is cash flow positive. Selected balance sheet information, such as total assets, may also be conveyed.

While the acquisition profile is a written document, it may be conveyed verbally to prospective buyers. Recall that it normally is best to approach buyers directly to gauge their level of interest and to obtain additional information about their operations and the marketplace. While the written acquisition profile may be sent to a prospective buyer following the initial telephone call, in some cases a prospective buyer's interest is satisfied from the conversation with the intermediary that the acquisition opportunity is of interest and the buyer is prepared to execute a non-disclosure agreement. A direct approach also allows the intermediary to modify the discussion points so as to highlight those areas of greatest interest to a particular buyer. In this regard, the seller should provide direction to their intermediary in so far as the nature and extent of information that can be conveyed to prospective buyers prior to the execution of a non-disclosure agreement.

The Non-disclosure Agreement

The non-disclosure agreement (sometimes referred to as the NDA or the confidentiality agreement) is a legal document intended to prevent the disclosure of sensitive information about the company to unauthorized parties, or the use of that sensitive information in a way that would be harmful to the seller, including the very fact that the company is for sale. It is important for the seller to recognize that a non-disclosure agreement cannot afford absolute protection on these things. Furthermore, even if there is a breach of the agreement, it may be difficult to prove or to recover damages from the other party. The seller and their intermediary must actively manage the flow of information to the buyer to limit the likelihood of a breach occurring and the extent of damage to the seller in the event that a breach does occur.

Since the non-disclosure agreement is a legal document, the seller and their lawyer should be satisfied with its contents. In general, the non-disclosure agreement states what does, and does not, constitute confidential information, and that the recipient will not:

- use the confidential information for any purpose other than assessing the acquisition opportunity;
- disclose the confidential information to any party other than its employees and representatives who have a need to know the confidential information for the purpose intended, and who agree to be bound by the provisions of the non-disclosure agreement; or
- communicate directly with the seller or the company's employees, suppliers, customers or other specified parties, except where authorized to do so by the seller and the intermediary.

The non-disclosure agreement also specifies that the prospective buyer will return or destroy any confidential information upon request, the period of time that the agreement is in force and other pertinent terms and conditions attached to the receipt of non-public information regarding the company.

In some cases, buyers are hesitant to execute a non-disclosure agreement put forth by the seller. Some corporate buyers have internal legal departments whose mandate includes the review of non-disclosure agreements prior to their execution. Not only does such a review sometimes cause delays, but the buyer's legal advisors may object to certain provisions in the seller's non-disclosure agreement. It is not unusual for buyers that are in the same industry as the seller to express concern that there may be an unfounded perception that confidentiality has been breached simply because the buyer may be in the process of developing similar technology or services many of the same customers. Therefore, the buyer and its legal advisors sometimes will demand changes to the non-disclosure agreement. The seller and their lawyer and intermediary must be satisfied that the proposed changes to the non-disclosure agreement do not compromise their company's proprietary information.

In some cases, a buyer supplies its own non-disclosure agreement and requests that the seller execute same. This is common where the buyer has made an unsolicited offer to the business owner. In addition, some buyers will demand that the seller also execute a non-disclosure agreement in respect of confidential information that the seller may receive from the buyer during the sale process. Again, the seller and their lawyer and intermediary should be satisfied in so far as the protection of confidential information and liability are concerned.

Finally, some financial buyers have a policy of not signing non-disclosure agreements. Therefore, the seller and their team of advisors must satisfy themselves as to the integrity of these organizations and their commitment to maintaining confidentiality in the absence of a formal written agreement.

Following the execution of the non-disclosure agreement or other arrangements that are satisfactory to both the seller and the buyer, the buyer is given the opportunity to conduct preliminary due diligence on the company, which is the subject of the next Stage.

Summary

Several types of prospective buyers normally exist for privately held companies. These include strategic buyers, non-strategic buyers, small corporate buyers and individuals, financial buyers and management and employees of the company. Strategic buyers tend to be preferred, although financial buyers are gaining more of a presence among mid-size privately held companies. Owners of Canadian private companies should not only consider prospective buyers based in Canada, but in the U.S. and other countries as well.

Prospective buyers can be identified through many sources, including prior solicitations to the business owner, competitive analysis, supply chain analysis and industry associations. When identifying prospective buyers, it is important for the seller to consider what their company has to offer in terms of its customer base, technology, workforce and other attributes, and to think creatively about the types of organizations that would be attracted by those intangible assets.

It is not sufficient to merely identify a large number of possible buyers. It also is important to undertake preliminary research on each buyer that is identified in order to assess whether or not they likely are a qualified prospect. A qualified buyer is one that is believed to have well-founded reasons for its interest in the company and the ability to consummate a transaction on terms that are acceptable to the seller. This allows the seller and their intermediary to rank prospective buyers and to tailor the solicitation approach to each.

The manner in which qualified buyers initially are contacted is important in order to capture their interest. Attracting a sufficient number of qualified prospective buyers establishes the platform for creating the effective auction and ultimately value enhancement realization. Direct telephone contact normally is the preferred form of communication, preferably to senior operating management within the buyer's organization. When soliciting financial buyers, emphasis should be placed on the company's organic growth potential, exit strategy alternatives and possible synergies with other companies in that financial buyer's portfolio.

The acquisition profile must be carefully worded so as to convey the attractiveness of the acquisition opportunity while maintaining the company's anonymity until the buyer has agreed to execute a non-disclosure agreement. The acquisition profile is a succinct document that provides a general description of the company and limited financial information. The written acquisition profile and the verbal conveyance of same should be tailored as necessary, depending on the prospective buyer.

Finally, the non-disclosure agreement is a legal document intended to protect (at least to some degree) the confidential information provided by the seller to the buyer during the sale process. Where the buyer modifies the terms of the non-disclosure agreement or provides its own such agreement, the seller and their lawyer and intermediary must be satisfied that the confidential information of their company will be adequately protected.

SECTION III

Stage 5 | Preliminary Due Diligence

Introduction

Preliminary due diligence refers to the information provided to the buyer from the time that the non-disclosure agreement is signed to the time that a letter of intent is agreed to. This includes information set out in the confidential information memorandum, information conveyed during initial meetings between the seller and the buyer and other information provided both prior to and during negotiations with the buyer. The key to value enhancement in preliminary due diligence is for the seller to control the flow of information to increase the perceived value of the company among buyers.

Typically, the first tranche of non-public information about the company that is provided to the buyer is contained in the confidential information memorandum. As such, this document plays a key role in positively influencing the buyer's perception of the company and it must be well prepared to ensure this is achieved.

Buyers that continue to be interested in the company will request one or more meetings with the seller. The seller's conduct during those initial meetings can also have a substantial bearing on a buyer's perception of the company. The ability to realize value enhancement will depend on how the seller addresses the company's strengths and weaknesses and the opportunities and threats that it faces, as well as how the seller uses those initial meetings to learn of the buyer's interests, motivations and negotiating position.

Following the initial meetings (and sometimes prior to), buyers that continue to be interested in the company will request additional information. The issue to be addressed from the seller's perspective is how much information to provide and what to expect from the buyer in return. The general rule is that the seller should provide sufficient information about their company to enable the buyer to prepare a letter of intent that reflects all material considerations in the proposed deal. However, the seller should convey information to a buyer gradually, with more sensitive information being provided as the probability of a transaction with that buyer increases. This reduces the risk that highly sensitive information will be disclosed to a buyer that does not consummate a transaction.

The preliminary due diligence stage normally runs for about two to four months, depending on the size of the company, the complexity of its operations, the number of qualified buyers and scheduling logistics. The preliminary due diligence stage of the private company sale process within the context of the *Value Enhancement Framework™* is depicted in Exhibit III-5-1.

Exhibit III-5-1

PRELIMINARY DUE DILIGENCE STAGE WITHIN THE *VALUE ENHANCEMENT FRAMEWORK™*

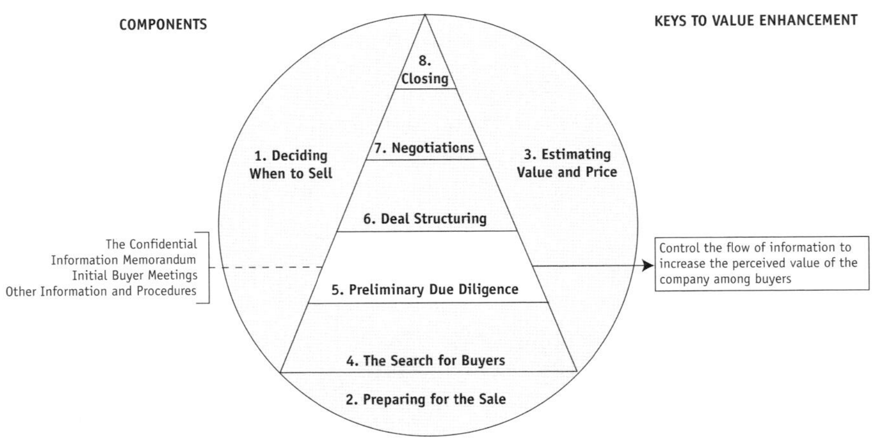

(i) The Confidential Information Memorandum

Purpose of the Confidential Information Memorandum

The confidential information memorandum (sometimes referred to as the "CIM") is first and foremost a selling document. As such, it is intended to cause the recipient to take action. However, the desired action at this point is not the acquisition of the company, but rather the creation of sufficient interest among prospective buyers to entice them to obtain additional information about the company and arrange an initial meeting with the seller.

Since the confidential information memorandum is the first document that prospective buyers receive containing meaningful non-public information about the company, the seller and their intermediary should carefully consider its content and presentation. The opportunity for value enhancement is created where the confidential information memorandum positions the company in a way that creates a positive perception to buyers. This serves to fuel the buyer's interest in the company and encourages them to react quickly to ensure they do not miss out on the acquisition opportunity. Generating strong interest among buyers helps in creating an effective auction. Creating a positive initial perception is important because, at a relatively early stage, buyers will begin contemplating the price range for the company and the resources they will need to consummate a transaction. These things will influence a buyer's starting point in the negotiations.

Another important function of the confidential information memorandum is to help the seller set the agenda for the sale process. Control of the sale process is key to building deal momentum. As such, the confidential information memorandum should clearly convey the rules, guidelines and principles that will govern the sale process. Recall from Section II that there is a difference between a formal auction and an informal auction. The rules and deadlines set out in a formal auction are rigid. The seller should be careful not to establish parameters that are too rigid, as these could restrict flexibility or result in a loss of credibility in the event that stated deadlines have to be amended. For these reasons, an informal auction generally is preferred when selling a privately held company.

In an informal auction, the seller and their intermediary endeavour to set the agenda in more subtle ways, such as the process in which the confidential information memorandum is issued, controlled and followed up. Specifically, the intermediary should follow up with the buyer within a few days of sending the confidential information memorandum to get a sense of whether or not the buyer is interested in pursuing the opportunity further. If the buyer remains interested, it creates an opportunity for the intermediary to obtain some initial views from the buyer as to the reasons for their interest and motivation. If the buyer is not interested in pursuing further discussions, the confidential information memorandum should be returned to the intermediary.

Content of the Confidential Information Memorandum

The confidential information memorandum sets the stage for future discussions with buyers. It contains both public and non-public information about the company and deals with matters such as the motivation for selling. Buyers use the confidential information memorandum to establish whether there is a fit between their own operations and those of the company, and as a basis for beginning to develop an offer for the company.

The confidential information memorandum normally is between 10 to 25 pages in length, plus appendices where appropriate. Graphs, charts and diagrams are used to convey the essence of the company in a straightforward manner. While the confidential information memorandum may contain publicly available information about the company, it should not simply reproduce the contents of the company's website or marketing materials. While it should reference some of these items, the confidential information memorandum should convey a deeper level of disclosure about the company's operations and competitive advantages. It should disclose the material attributes about the company that will allow the buyer to make an informed decision whether or not to proceed further with its preliminary due diligence investigation.

While the confidential information memorandum should portray a positive image of the company overall, it should avoid overstatement or hyperbole as this harms credibility. The seller also will lose credibility where, upon receiving subsequent information, the buyer perceives that it was mislead in its initial views of the company. Further, the confidential information memorandum should in no way mislead or contain inaccuracies as this will likely lead to a loss of qualified buyers. While the intermediary normally drafts the confidential information memorandum, the seller should review its content to ensure that the final product portrays an accurate, objective and positive image of the company.

The confidential information memorandum should not include highly sensitive information that, once disclosed, could harm the company. For example, details about the company's proprietary technology, customer-specific pricing strategies and labour costs should be excluded. This is because, during the course of the sale process, it is likely that several buyers who receive the confidential information memorandum will not pursue the opportunity further. While such parties should return the confidential information memorandum and are bound by the provisions of the non-disclosure agreement, non-interested buyers inevitably will retain some of what they have read. This is of particular concern where the non-interested buyer is a competitor, customer or supplier of the company. Therefore, the information set out in the confidential information memorandum should avoid disclosing any information that a non-interested buyer could use in such a way that could prove harmful to the seller.

The exclusion of detail in the confidential information memorandum also serves another important purpose. It will lead interested buyers to specifically request additional information about the company. This provides an opportunity to obtain initial feedback from the buyer regarding the reasons for its interest and to gather intelligence about the buyer's motivation and negotiating position. Such information can be valuable to the seller in developing a negotiating strategy for that buyer.

While the specific content of the confidential information memorandum will vary depending on the specifics of the situation, it generally includes the following:

- **restrictions on the use of the document.** For legal reasons, recipients are reminded of their obligations under the non-disclosure agreement to use the information only for the purpose of determining whether they wish to engage in further discussions regarding a possible transaction;
- **a disclaimer regarding the information contained in the document.** Much of the information contained in the confidential information memorandum will not have been independently verified. The disclaimer places the onus on the buyer to perform its own due diligence prior to finalizing a transaction;

- **contact protocol.** The confidential information memorandum normally states that the buyer should only contact the intermediary regarding any further information requests or to follow up, and that the buyer should not directly contact the seller or the company's employees, customers or suppliers;
- **an executive summary**, which usually is one to two pages in length and highlights the principal attractive features of the company. The executive summary normally includes high level financial information, such as the company's most recent revenue and normalized earnings before interest, taxes, depreciation and amortization (EBITDA) figures, a brief description of its products, services, markets, customers, facilities and operations, as well as its key strengths and competitive advantages. The wording of this part must be particularly well crafted, as it establishes the basis for a buyer's level of interest in the company, or even whether it is interested at all;
- **products or services offered**, including the company's brand names, trademarks, and other proprietary assets. This description should address how the company's product and service offerings are different from those of its major competitors, be it in their design, functionality, technology or even the way they are sold and serviced. It is important to remember that buyers are more attracted to companies that are perceived to have a sustainable competitive advantage as opposed to those that only offer pure commodity-type products and services. Where the company sells a variety of different products or services, it generally is helpful to provide a general indication of the overall revenues derived from each major product or service category;
- **customer and market analysis**, which normally sets out the company's target market and major customers, although the dollar amount sold to specific customers usually is not specified at this stage. Where the company enjoys a diversified base of repeat customers, that fact should be highlighted as it contributes to revenue stability and hence value perception. Other noteworthy items also should be mentioned as appropriate, such as any awards the company received from its customers or a growing order backlog;
- **sales and marketing information**. The company's major sales and marketing initiatives should be discussed, including means of distribution (e.g., whether resellers, manufacturers' representatives, commissioned sales agents or similar third parties are used), advertising and promotional strategies and customer value proposition. The seller must be careful not to divulge marketing and pricing plans that it does not want to become generally known in the marketplace;

- **operational information**, including a general description of the company's facilities (e.g., size, location and production capacity), principal physical assets, research and development efforts and major suppliers, again being sensitive as to the amount and type of information provided;
- **information pertaining to management and employees**. A brief summary of each key management individual within the company should be provided including, where appropriate, their age, number of years with the company, areas of responsibility and relevant business and educational background. Ideally, the seller will be able to portray a company with strong management depth which is not dependent on one or more individuals. It is customary to provide an organizational chart that indicates the number of employees in the company, with a breakdown between those in operations, administration, sales and marketing, and other areas. This part should state whether or not the employees are unionized and, if so, provide a brief overview of the prevailing collective bargaining agreement;
- **ownership information**. Buyers want to know who the owners of the company are and, if there is more than one owner, whether all owners are willing to sell. The reasons for selling also should be explained. Owners that are actively involved in the company should state whether they have an interest in remaining involved with the company after it is sold and any significant restrictions in that regard. While the nature and level of a seller's post-acquisition involvement is subject to negotiation, buyers want some indication as to the seller's level of flexibility near the outset of their due diligence investigation;
- **selected financial information**. The nature and extent of financial information provided in the confidential information memorandum must be carefully considered. It usually is preferable to provide limited financial information, such as revenues, gross profit, normalized EBITDA and summarized balance sheet information, for the past three to five years. This allows the seller to obtain some initial feedback from the buyer before providing additional details (e.g., whether the business appears too large or too small to be of interest to the buyer). When determining the nature and extent of financial information to provide in the confidential information memorandum, the following factors should be considered:
  - where the company has a limited product or service offering, it may be prudent to exclude gross margin information so that recipients cannot decipher the company's pricing strategy,

- when calculating normalized EBITDA, it usually is helpful to demonstrate the reconciliation between pre-tax income as reported on the company's income statements, and adding back interest expense, depreciation and amortization and adjusting for discretionary, unusual or non-recurring items, with an explanation as to their nature (see Stage 3). Further, it is common to calculate normalized EBITDA before remuneration to shareholders, as the terms of any post-acquisition involvement of the seller is subject to negotiation,
- with respect to balance sheet information, it is customary to show major asset and liability categories, such as current assets, fixed assets, other assets, current liabilities, long-term debt and shareholders equity for the past several years, consistent with the years of income statement data provided,
- as a supplement to the balance sheet information, it is helpful to set out sources of available financing for the company and capital expenditures for the past several years,
- where there are reasonably evident sources of cost savings or synergies available to buyers, such opportunities should be noted and, where appropriate, the financial impact of these things should be estimated, and
- it is helpful to provide a brief discussion of certain financial highlights, such as the reasons for sales growth (or decline) and explanations of major changes in profitability.

In some cases, budgeted or projected results are provided in addition to historical operating results. While such information may help to convey the growth prospects of the company, caution must be exercised. Several months may pass between the time that budgets or forecasts are prepared and when a buyer undertakes its detailed due diligence of the company (as part of the closing stage). At that time, buyers may be in a position to compare actual results against what was budgeted or forecast. Where actual results have fallen short of expectations, it can impair the seller's credibility and negotiating position. Therefore, the seller should have a reasonably high level of confidence that any near-term budgets or projections set out in the confidential information memorandum will be met or surpassed;

- **SWOT analysis**. Recall from Stage 2 that, when preparing for the sale, the owner and their team of advisors should prepare an analysis of the company's strengths, weaknesses, opportunities and threats. The confidential information memorandum normally should set out a summary description of these things (possibly in chart form to communicate the key points).

  While the benefits of highlighting the company's strengths and opportunities in the confidential information memorandum are evident, it may seem counter-intuitive to mention its weaknesses and threats. However, mentioning the company's weaknesses and threats can bolster the seller's negotiating position if presented properly. Weaknesses can be portrayed as attractive opportunities for buyers. For example, an admission that the company has limited financial resources to finance growth could be presented as "incremental growth opportunities are possible given the availability of additional financing".

  In addition, it is advisable to disclose significant weaknesses and risks near the outset of the sale process in order to quickly eliminate those buyers that cannot see past those issues. Further, discussing weaknesses and threats in a constructive way at the outset allows the seller to build value momentum as they proceed through the sale process by dealing with the negative aspects near the beginning. It also prevents a prospective buyer from retracting previous indications of value in light of new (negative) information regarding the company or the industry.

  While weaknesses and threats generally should be addressed near the outset of the sale process, the seller should consider when that information should be conveyed. That is, whether such information is better included in the confidential information memorandum or at a later stage, such as during initial buyer meetings or when providing a buyer with supplementary information in the preliminary due diligence stage. As a general rule, major weaknesses and threats that are self-evident should be set out in the confidential information memorandum and discussed with interested buyers shortly thereafter. However, weaknesses and threats that are sensitive and that generally are not known within the industry usually are best addressed during initial buyer meetings or later in the sale process. This allows the seller to limit the number of parties that become aware of this negative information; and

- **industry information**. The amount of industry information contained in the confidential information memorandum, and whether it is even included at all, varies depending on the anticipated scope of distribution. Where the document is being sent to industry participants, it is usual to have little, if any, industry information. However, where the intended recipients of the confidential information memorandum include organizations from other industry segments, the inclusion of some industry information is more common. Furthermore, financial buyers often like to receive an overview of the industry in order to determine whether they are interested in further pursuing an investment opportunity.

  Where industry information is provided, it generally includes such things as market size, growth rates and principal competitors. Reference can also be made to industry websites or trade associations. When providing industry statistics, it is helpful to draw that information from credible sources that a buyer can verify independently if it so chooses. Where the information is derived from sources such as the seller's knowledge of the industry, care must be taken to ensure that a credible information source does not contradict the information provided, which could cause the buyer to question the seller's credibility; and
- **appendices.** Supplemental information contained in the confidential information memorandum commonly includes company brochures, articles written about the company, additional industry statistics and similar types of information. For the most part, appendices normally contain information that is available in the public domain and that further serves to convey the attractiveness of the company.

A summary of the usual content of a confidential information memorandum is provided in Exhibit III-5-2.

Exhibit III-5-2

USUAL CONTENT OF A CONFIDENTIAL INFORMATION MEMORANDUM

Restrictions on the use of the document
Disclaimer
Contact protocol
Executive summary
Product and service offerings
Customer and market analysis
Sales and marketing information
Operational information
Management and employees
Ownership information
Selected financial information
SWOT analysis
Industry information
Appendices

(ii) Initial Buyer Meetings

Meeting Protocol

Following their review of the confidential information memorandum (and possibly other information provided to the buyer thereafter), buyers that remain interested will want to arrange a meeting (or more than one meeting) with the seller. The considerations to be addressed by the seller include: who should attend those initial meetings, where they should be held and what information regarding the company should and should not be provided. The key to value enhancement in initial buyer meetings is the manner in which the strengths, opportunities and threats facing the company are addressed and the seller's ability to gather information regarding the buyer's interests, motivation and negotiating position. This information can later be used by the seller to better convey the attractiveness of the acquisition opportunity to the buyer and when negotiating the deal with the buyer.

In most cases, initial buyer meetings should be held away from the seller's place of business, such as at the intermediary's office or a third party location where a discussion can be held in confidence. This helps to prevent speculation among the company's employees as to the reasons for the meeting. If the meetings are held at the buyer's place of business, the seller must be comfortable that confidentiality will be maintained. The meeting facilities must be conducive to allowing an open conversation about the company and, if appropriate, a slide presentation (or other form of presentation) by the seller.

In many cases, the buyer and seller have more than one meeting prior to the time that formal negotiations commence. Follow-up meetings tend to focus on more specific issues that the buyer has identified during the course of its preliminary due diligence investigation.

The attendees on the seller's side normally are restricted to the seller and their intermediary but, in some cases, key management personnel who are aware of the pending sale also attend. However, as a general rule, it is preferable to have only a few people involved to prevent any inconsistency in the information that is conveyed to the buyer.

On the buyer's side, the attendees normally include senior management representing the buyer's organization and may also include lower-ranking individuals (such as analysts) and the buyer's intermediary or advisors, if they are used. The seller should request a list of those planning to attend the meeting beforehand, including their position within the buyer's organization, so as to better prepare for the meeting.

During the initial meetings, most of the discussion should take place between the seller and senior management acting for the buyer. The discussion should focus on the operations of the company itself and not on valuation, pricing or deal structuring. The intermediary generally has limited input during the initial meetings, except for asking specific questions of the buyer regarding its interest, acquisition process and related matters, and to deflect questions that the buyer asks of the seller that are not appropriate at the time.

It should be made clear at the outset of the initial meetings that any discussions as to price and terms of sale are premature. Rather, the main purpose of the initial meetings is for both the buyer and the seller to establish whether or not there is a fit between their respective organizations, and the basis for further discussions. However, it is important for the seller to remember that anything said during the initial meetings will influence subsequent negotiations with that buyer.

Preparing for Initial Buyer Meetings

Preparation for initial meetings is critical to ensure that the seller is successful in portraying their company in its best light and in gathering intelligence regarding the buyer's interest, motivation and negotiating position that can be used in future discussions. Prior to the initial meeting, there needs to be agreement among the seller and their team of advisors as to the amount and type of information that will be conveyed during the course of the initial meetings. It is important that the seller and their intermediary control the agenda for the meeting. Therefore, the seller should present a written agenda at the outset of the meeting to ensure that information is both conveyed to, and received from, the buyer. In this regard, it usually is better to have the buyer begin with an overview of its business and an explanation of why it is interested in the acquisition opportunity, and then for the seller to discuss their company. This allows the seller to highlight those areas that the buyer has indicated to be of particular interest.

It often is helpful for the seller to prepare a formal presentation for the buyer as this ensures that the meeting agenda does not go too far off track. However, flexibility in the presentation is important, in order to allow the seller to expand on those areas that are of interest to the buyer. The usual content of the seller's presentation is addressed in the following part. As a general comment, the presentation should not be overly detailed so that the discussion remains at a fairly high level. The initial meetings are not the time to become lost in details that are unlikely to be material to the buyer's value perception of the company.

The seller should prepare supplementary charts, schedules and other documents that, depending on how the discussions are proceeding, may be provided to the buyer during the meeting. Again, this additional documentation should not be so detailed that it requires a long time for the buyer to digest during the meeting. Rather, each document should be prepared in a simple, straightforward manner for the purpose of effectively communicating an important point that ultimately will influence the buyer's perception of the company's value.

Initial meeting preparation also involves the seller and their intermediary conducting research on the buyer beforehand. This includes publicly available information regarding the buyer's business (its website, annual reports if the buyer is a public company, articles written about the buyer and so on as well as an analysis of any transactions that the buyer has been involved in over the past several years). Such information (much of which may already have been gathered when conducting preliminary research in order to qualify prospective buyers – see Stage 4) is helpful in formulating specific questions to ask the buyer about the reasons for its interest in the company, how it foresees the operations of the company following the transaction and possible synergies it might be anticipating.

Conveying Information to the Buyer

As mentioned above, during the initial meetings the seller normally conveys information to the buyer in a formal presentation format with supplementary documents that may or may not be provided, depending on how the discussions are proceeding. The seller's presentation normally covers much of the same information that was provided in the confidential information memorandum in terms of the company's operations, sales and marketing, management, employees and financial results. However, these things typically are expanded upon during the presentation and the seller should highlight those areas that will serve to raise the buyer's perception of the company's value. This includes the company's key drivers, such as revenue stability, growth opportunities, the competitive advantages enjoyed by the company and factors that help to mitigate perceived business risk.

The seller should discuss the operations of their company candidly with the buyer. While it is important to highlight the company's competitive advantages and opportunities, it also is important that weaknesses and threats to the company be tabled at a relatively early stage of the initial meetings. If a buyer takes the position that one or more weaknesses or threats to the company overshadows the positive points, it is better for the seller to know this early in the discussion, before too much sensitive information is conveyed to the buyer or time is expended unnecessarily.

The timing and extent to which weaknesses and threats facing the company are discussed is a function of their nature and sensitivity. For example, if initial buyer meetings are held with a direct competitor, it is prudent to ensure that the prospective buyer has a genuine interest in a transaction before disclosing issues that could prove harmful to the seller. However, it is important that negative points affecting the company be addressed with the buyer prior to the time that a letter of intent is agreed. Where a buyer submits an offer and subsequently discovers a material weakness or threat facing the company that previously was undisclosed, the buyer will use that information to reduce the value it previously was willing to offer. This issue is further discussed in Stage 7.

Prior to closing a deal, buyers likely will identify the major risks and issues facing the company, whether the seller discloses them or not. The important point from the seller's perspective is to demonstrate to the buyer that such risks are recognized and that they are being managed proactively and effectively. Further, when discussing these issues with prospective buyers, the seller should consider how weaknesses and threats faced by their company can be positioned as opportunities for the buyer. For example, if the company has a lease contract with above-market rents for the next three years, that issue can be presented as an opportunity for the buyer to reduce rental expense in three years time.

Finally, when discussing weaknesses and threats facing the company, it is helpful to provide the buyer with an indication as to the potential financial impact of these things or how they can be resolved (or turned into opportunities). Candidly discussing the issues faced by the company and presenting possible solutions can help ease a buyer's concerns regarding the severity of those matters, rather than allowing the buyer to speculate as to the level of uncertainty that exists.

Obtaining Information from the Buyer

The seller and their intermediary should use initial buyer meetings and the preliminary due diligence process in general to better understand each buyer's interests and motivations. This will assist the seller in presenting their company in a positive manner and provide a better indication as to the buyer's key parameters for establishing value and price, which can subsequently be used in negotiations with that buyer.

Throughout the seller's presentation, it is desirable to obtain specific feedback from the buyer on the positive and negative factors affecting the company. The seller should strive to understand the specific reasons underlying each buyer's interest in the company and the buyer's expectations as to how the company will be operated following a transaction. It is particularly helpful for the seller to get an indication of how the buyer intends to integrate the company with its existing operations following an acquisition, in order to get a better idea of the types and quantum of synergies that the buyer might be anticipating.

It also is important for the seller to understand the buyer's investment decision process, including who will ultimately decide to proceed with an offer and what internal approval processes the buyer must go through prior to finalizing a transaction. This helps the seller to convey information in a way that will better promote their company to specific individuals within the buyer's organization and helps orchestrate the timing among buyers, all in aid of building momentum as the auction progresses.

While buyers typically will provide some information on their intentions and expectations, they usually are reluctant to provide too much information in fear of compromising their negotiating position. Where a buyer is not being receptive to direct questions, some information may be obtained through indirect questioning. For example, where a buyer has consummated other transactions in recent years, questions can be asked about the underlying reasons for those transactions, whether the buyer's expectations were met, and what the buyer would have done differently in hindsight. Questions can also be constructed in the form of a general discussion with a buyer as to how it perceives the state of the industry and recent developments involving mutual customers, competitors and suppliers.

The seller and their intermediary should pay close attention to non-verbal signals given by the buyer's representatives during initial meetings, such as body language, notes passing among the buyer's management team and so on. These things provide clues into the buyer's specific interests and concerns.

As the discussions progress, at some point the parties should address the seller's prospective role within the buyer's organization in greater detail and the resources that the buyer has with which to finance a transaction. This discussion often serves as a segue to the negotiation stage, which is discussed in Stage 7.

(iii) Other Information and Procedures

The seller may provide each prospective buyer with additional information both before and after the initial meetings and through the negotiation stage. Further, at some point, the buyer may be invited for a tour of the company's facilities or to conduct other procedures (such as a review of the company's technology) in order to better understand the company's operations. It is important that the seller and their intermediary orchestrate this process and control the flow of information (and the timing of other procedures undertaken by the buyer) so as to create an effective auction for the company. This is done by obtaining feedback from each prospective buyer on an ongoing basis, so that the nature and extent of information provided can meet each buyer's unique interests and needs. This serves to increase the perceived value of the company among buyers and builds the deal momentum through the course of ongoing discussions and negotiations. The timing of information dissemination to each buyer also is important in order to try to coordinate negotiations with multiple buyers around the same time frame, thereby creating a competitive bidding environment.

The information provided by the seller at the preliminary due diligence stage should be sufficient to allow the buyer to assess the prospective cash flows and risks inherent in the company and to enable the buyer to reasonably estimate the synergies that it might expect. Sensitive details regarding the company's operations (such as detailed payroll information) usually are not disclosed at this stage. Rather, such information can be provided during the buyer's detailed due diligence efforts following an agreed letter of intent. As a general rule, information that a buyer can obtain during its detailed due diligence investigation that simply serves to confirm the seller's representations is not disclosed during the preliminary due diligence stage. However, recall that weaknesses or threats facing the company should be discussed during the initial buyer meetings or otherwise conveyed during the preliminary due diligence stage (or prior to the time that a letter of intent is agreed to), in order to prevent the buyer from using these issues as a basis for renegotiating the deal when the buyer subsequently discovers their existence in its detailed due diligence.

In exchange for information that is provided, the seller should expect to receive feedback from the buyer in terms of its observations, concerns, plans and ongoing interest in the company. This information will assist the seller in determining what further information should be provided as part of the preliminary due diligence and in the seller's negotiations with the buyer. The seller normally should provide information to the buyer in tranches, beginning with general information regarding the company and moving to greater disclosure as the level of comfort with a particular buyer increases. This way, the seller is less likely to disclose highly sensitive information about their company to a buyer that ultimately does not proceed with a transaction.

During the planning phase of the private company sale process and, in particular, when preparing for the sale and estimating value and price, the seller and their intermediary should begin gathering the information that they anticipate buyers will want to review during the preliminary due diligence stage. The following part of this stage sets out a list of the information that normally is provided as part of the preliminary due diligence information package.

Preparing the preliminary due diligence information package before soliciting prospective buyers is important for several reasons. First of all, it allows the seller to take more time in preparing the information, so that it can be presented in a way that best highlights the attractive features of the company. Second, it prevents the seller from having to scramble to get a lot of information ready in a short period of time, which can cause concerns among the company's employees. Third, it allows the seller greater flexibility in controlling how quickly or how slowly the information is disseminated to buyers, which helps in creating an effective auction. Finally, where usual due diligence information is not readily available, it might cause a buyer to suspect that no other parties are interested in the company, which may negatively impact the seller's negotiating position.

In some cases, preliminary due diligence information is made available in a "data room", which normally is located away from the seller's premises, such as at the intermediary's office. Data rooms help in controlling access to the company's information and are particularly useful when a large amount of information must be conveyed to the buyer in a relatively short time frame. The existence of a data room often helps in creating the appearance of an effective auction, which in turn may cause buyers to put forth better proposals than they might otherwise have done. However, data rooms are more common during the closing stage of the private company sale process, in order to expedite the buyer's detailed due diligence investigation.

When used in the preliminary due diligence stage, the materials provided in a data room setting must be carefully considered and prepared, in order to portray an attractive image of the company, while not disclosing highly sensitive information too early in the process. The "rules" of the data room must be established with each prospective buyer, which normally include the provision that information cannot be copied or removed without the consent of the seller or their intermediary.

Much of the information provided during the preliminary due diligence stage is prepared in summary form, such as an outline of key provisions governing significant contracts, rather than providing details or copies of the contracts themselves. There are two main reasons for providing summary information as opposed to details. First, it helps to expedite the buyer's preliminary due diligence process so that the seller can obtain feedback more quickly. Second, it allows the seller to retain more sensitive information until a later stage in the sale process, such as when the buyer is conducting its detailed due diligence. In this regard, it is important that the summary information provided to prospective buyers accurately conveys the company's prospective cash flows and business risks, and that there are no material discrepancies between the summary and detailed information that would later provide a buyer with the justification for reconsidering its proposal. It also is important to ensure that the information provided to buyers is internally consistent, as inconsistencies lead to confusion and can compromise the seller's credibility and their negotiating position.

Prospective buyers may request information that had not been previously contemplated by the seller. Prior to providing such information, the seller should seek to understand the reasons for the buyer's request and how it will affect the buyer's level of interest and value perception of the company. The nature and extent of information requested during the preliminary due diligence stage can vary considerably, depending on the interests and motivations of the buyer. Every situation is unique and the seller must strike a balance between providing the buyer with sufficient information for its analysis, while not disclosing highly sensitive information prematurely. It is important to maintain well-documented records of the information provided to each prospective buyer in order to facilitate continuing discussions and to ensure that all information is returned in the event the buyer and/or the seller elect to discontinue the discussions.

The seller should recognize that buyers will actively gather publicly available information about their company during the preliminary due diligence stage. This includes information contained on the company's website, in industry or trade association publications and any public news items involving the company or its owner. The seller and their intermediary should be cognizant of the information that buyers likely will find in their public information search and should ensure that issues arising from that information are dealt with accordingly.

The Preliminary Due Diligence Information Package

This part summarizes some of the financial, operational, sales and marketing and other information that normally is provided to buyers during their preliminary due diligence of the company. This list is not intended to be exhaustive, but rather to provide the seller with an indication of the type of information that normally is contained in a preliminary due diligence information package or data room. The intermediary normally will have a list that will be customized based on the nature of the company and prospective buyers. While this information normally is provided in written form, there may be circumstances where some of it is better provided verbally. This can be the case where a fairly complicated explanation accompanies the information. In such cases, it may preferable to meet with the buyer, explain the information and then provide a summary of the information and explanation in written form.

Some of the information set out in this part may already have been included in the confidential information memorandum. The purpose of a preliminary due diligence information package is not to simply repeat what had previously been provided, although there may be some overlap for clarity reasons. Once again, internal consistency is important.

Financial information

This should include:

- historical annual financial statements for the past several years (normally three to five). Details of unusual, non-recurring and discretionary items should be provided, with support, to allow the buyer to calculate the normalized cash flow for the company (i.e., normalized EBITDA, EBIT or discretionary cash flow – see Stage 3);

- management's internal financial statements, to the extent that they provide additional meaningful information. Such internal financial statements should not be so detailed that they disclose highly sensitive information, such as pricing strategies for particular customers or the details of production costs for specific products;
- information regarding the company's income tax situation, including tax rates and income tax pools;
- budgets and forecasts, including capital spending projections, along with supporting assumptions and a brief narrative setting out why the projections are believed to be achievable. As previously noted, caution must be exercised when providing budget and forecast information, as buyers will compare near-term forecasts against actual results at a later stage in the sale process. To the extent that near-term forecasts are not met, the seller's credibility and negotiating position may be compromised;
- additional details of major asset categories, such as accounts receivable, inventories and fixed assets;
- a summary of major banking terms and conditions, including borrowing capacity, security and covenants;
- a description of important financial policies, such as customer credit terms; and
- a description of the basis for determining the amount of contingent liabilities, warranty reserves or like items.

Operational information

This should include:

- a summary of the company's operating facilities, such as the size and square footage of each facility, production capacity, number of shifts and age and condition of equipment;
- information on the company's key management personnel, including their age, the number of years they have been with the company, their responsibilities, and relevant business and educational background. Detailed payroll information normally is not provided at this stage;
- a summary of employee pension and benefit plans;
- a list of principal suppliers (normally the top five or ten), including the amount purchased from those organizations in each of the past few years;
- a summary of major lease terms (e.g., lease rate, expiry date and extension provisions) or, alternatively, copies of the actual leases themselves;

- a summary of ongoing research and development projects – again being cautious about sensitive plans and trade secrets; and
- a summary of key performance indicators that the company's management team use to manage its operations. This may include indicators such as capacity utilization, sales per employee and other non-financial measures.

Sales and marketing information

This should include:

- a breakdown of historical revenues by product or service category, geographic region, distribution channel or other meaningful classification for each of the past several years;
- a list of key customers (normally the top ten or so), including dollar sales to each of them over each of the past few years. Caution should be exercised not to disclose sensitive information to direct competitors or customers, such as detailed pricing information;
- a description of the company's sales team, distribution channels, sales agents, and so on, including a summary of the basis for remuneration (i.e., salary, commissions and incentives);
- a description of the primary and secondary target markets, the principal competitors within those markets, and how the products and services offered by the company are differentiated in those markets; and
- a summary of the major terms of existing contracts with customers, including order size, duration and other important terms. Copies of the actual contracts themselves normally are not provided until the buyer's detailed due diligence investigation.

Other information

This should include:

- general corporate information, such as incorporation documents and minute books;
- a summary explanation of outstanding legal claims and contingent liabilities;
- a summary of the terms of major contracts and commitments;
- general industry information, which may include industry research studies, an overview of the product and service offerings of competitors and a description of important industry regulations. This information generally

is provided where the buyer does not actively operate within the company's industry segment, such as a financial buyer; and

- business plans, board presentations and other documents that summarize the company's current situation and its plans. Once again, caution must be exercised in providing sensitive information to direct competitors too early in the sale process.

Other Preliminary Due Diligence Procedures

In addition to the documentation set out above, buyers may want to conduct other preliminary due diligence procedures such as:

- touring the company's facilities and operations. Depending on whom the prospective buyer is, this can lead to rumours being spread among the company's employees. Sometimes such tours are conducted after-hours or on weekends in order to reduce such risks;
- discussions with key employees, customers and suppliers. Such discussions normally are held as part of the buyer's detailed due diligence investigation, following an agreed letter of intent with the seller. However, in some cases, such procedures may be conducted prior to the letter of intent. If so, in the case of employees, the seller should ensure that the employee is coached beforehand as to the nature and depth of company information that can be disclosed. In the case of customers and suppliers to be interviewed by the buyer, it is important to ensure that they are contacted by the seller beforehand in order to state the nature and reasons for the buyer's pending call; and
- product demonstrations to illustrate the technical capabilities of the company's products, such as software and hardware capabilities. Smaller demonstrations can be done at the initial meetings with buyers, while more comprehensive demonstrations may require special arrangements. Product demonstrations should be geared towards conveying the functionality, benefits and competitive advantages of the company's products as opposed to the details of how they are designed.

The Seller's Due Diligence of the Buyer

As previously discussed, throughout the buyer's preliminary due diligence on the company, the seller and the intermediary should be conducting their own due diligence on each prospective buyer. This type of information helps the seller to better understanding the fit between their company and the buyer's organization, and in assessing the price that the buyer might be willing to pay. In addition to the information gathered when initially researching and contacting buyers (see Stage 4) and the feedback obtained from buyers during initial meetings and in the discussions and correspondence thereafter, the seller should consider the following:

- touring the buyer's facilities to understand how the buyer operates and the synergies available to the buyer by combining the company's products and services with its own;
- meeting with senior management of the buyer who were not part of the due diligence team but who are aware of the possible acquisition to discuss the buyer's longer-term vision, strategy and other aspects about the buyer's organization. This can ensure consistency with what the buyer's due diligence team has represented to the seller. In some cases, the buyer may permit the seller to have an open discussion with the owner of another private company that it acquired in recent years; and
- requesting financial information regarding the buyer's organization. This is more common where the buyer is a privately held company and its financial statements are not publicly disclosed.

Not surprisingly, buyers are reluctant to provide the seller with non-public information regarding their operations, particularly non-public financial information. However, buyers will sometimes accommodate a seller's request (at least to some extent) to demonstrate their openness, particularly where it is expected that the seller will become an important part of the buyer's organization following the sale and the buyer wants to relieve some of the concerns that the seller might have in making that transition.

Summary

Preliminary due diligence consists of the information provided to the buyer from the time the non-disclosure agreement is signed to the time that a letter of intent between the parties is agreed to. It includes the confidential information memorandum, initial meetings between the buyer and seller and other information and procedures. Opportunities to realize value enhancement are created where the seller controls the flow of information so as to increase the perceived value of the company among buyers.

The confidential information memorandum is, for the most part, a sales document used to convey a positive perception to prospective buyers about the company. It also serves to establish the guidelines to ensure that the seller controls the sale process. The contents of the confidential information memorandum must strike a balance between providing adequate information to allow a buyer to assess its level of interest in the company, while not disclosing sensitive information that may prove harmful to the seller should the buyer choose not to proceed further.

Initial buyer meetings require considerable preparation to ensure that the company is presented in a positive manner and to obtain a better understanding of what each buyer is seeking. The discussions at the initial meetings should be restricted to operational matters about the company and the industry. Specific discussions on valuation, pricing and deal structuring should be deferred to the deal structuring and negotiation stages that follow. Weaknesses and threats faced by the company should be addressed relatively early in the discussion and presented as opportunities where possible. It is important that the seller control the meeting agenda and that the initial meetings be used to gather information about the reasons for the buyer's interest in the company, its motivations and how it would expect the company to operate if a transaction does proceed.

During the preliminary due diligence stage, the seller should convey sufficient information about their company to allow the buyer to prepare a meaningful letter of intent. Information normally is provided in tranches, with more general information conveyed up front and greater details disclosed as the discussions progress. A preliminary due diligence information package, which sometimes is provided in a data room setting, should be prepared beforehand so that its content and presentation style help to convey the attractiveness of the acquisition opportunity and therefore raise the buyer's perception as to the value of the company. However, it is important that weaknesses and threats to the company be addressed prior to the letter of intent to prevent a buyer from using new information to subsequently renegotiate the deal.

During the preliminary due diligence stage, the seller should create an atmosphere of give-and-take in order to obtain feedback from the buyer regarding its areas of interest and concern. This allows the seller to customize the information content, presentation and flow in order to increase the perceived value of the company among buyers. Creating an atmosphere of give-and-take also allows the seller to better assess the strategic fit between their company and the buyer's organization and the price and terms that a buyer might be willing to offer.

SECTION III

Stage 6 Deal Structuring

Introduction

The highest price offered for a privately held company may not represent the best deal for the seller, because the value received by the seller is highly dependent on when, how and under what conditions the purchase price will be paid. Therefore, price and deal structure must be considered in tandem when negotiating the sale and evaluating offers from buyers.

While the structure of the deal is formally negotiated between the buyer and the seller at a later stage in the private company sale process, it is important that the seller define the general parameters of an acceptable deal structure prior to the time that the company is exposed for sale. An acceptable deal structure depends on the personal situation of the business owner, including the amount of cash required to support their lifestyle or financial commitments, and whether or not the owner is prepared to remain involved with the company following the sale. It is harmful to the seller's negotiating position where they change the acceptable terms of a deal after negotiations are underway. Furthermore, by considering deal structuring from the outset of the sale process, the seller can undertake income tax and estate planning initiatives that may ultimately result in greater negotiating flexibility. This in turn will improve the seller's negotiating position and may reduce the taxes payable on the sale.

The three major parameters of deal structuring are: (1) whether the overlying shares or the underlying net assets of the company are sold; (2) the forms and terms of payment; and (3) the provisions of the post-transaction management contract. The key to value enhancement in deal structuring lies in evaluating each proposal based on its risk-reward parameters and income tax efficiency to the seller.

Any portion of the purchase price not received in the form of cash on closing is subject to risk. The seller must consider the quantum, timing and conditions under which any deferred portion of the purchase price may ultimately be received and be satisfied that the potential rewards are sufficient, given the time value of money and the risk of non-realization. The assessment of risk and reward should take into account all aspects of value to the business owner, including the stated purchase price, the economic terms of the deal and the intangible aspects of the deal.

In terms of tax efficiency, when analyzing a buyer's proposal, the seller and their team of advisors must consider how and when the various components of the purchase price will be taxed and what opportunities are available to reduce the overall tax burden. Deal structuring often involves significant legal and income tax considerations. While this stage briefly addresses some of the more common tax and legal aspects, a detailed discussion of these subjects is beyond the scope of this book. Where a transaction involves a complex payment structure, expert legal and income tax advice should be obtained. It is also important to note that the rules and regulations in respect of income taxes and legal matters are ever-evolving, and therefore the discussions and calculations set out in this stage may be significantly affected by changes in this regard.

The deal structuring stage is done in tandem with negotiations, and normally lasts for about one to two months. The deal structuring stage of the private company sale process within the context of the *Value Enhancement Framework™* is depicted in Exhibit III-6-1.

Exhibit III-6-1

THE DEAL STRUCTURING STAGE WITHIN
THE *VALUE ENHANCEMENT FRAMEWORK™*

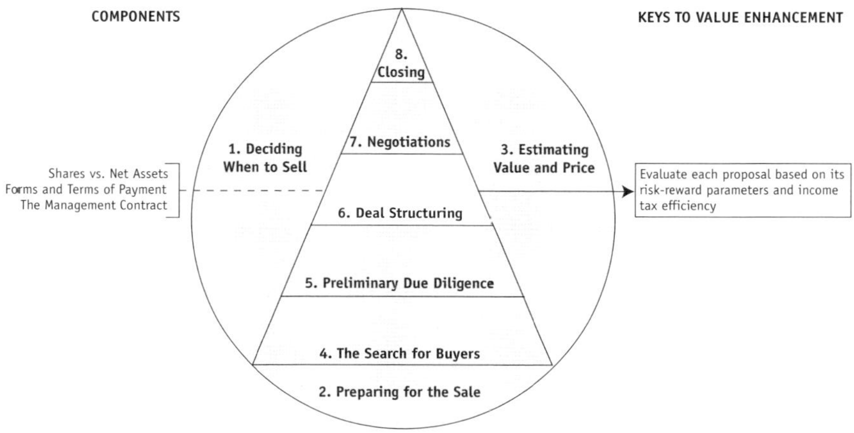

(i) Shares vs. Net Assets

One of the first issues to be addressed in deal structuring is whether the shares or the net assets of the company will be sold. As a general rule, sellers of privately held Canadian companies prefer to sell shares, whereas buyers prefer to buy assets. This is because:

- from the seller's perspective, a sale of shares is taxed as a capital gain, which generally results in lower income taxes on disposition. In addition, a sale of shares is necessary for a seller who wants to take advantage of the lifetime capital gains exemption (see Stage 2); and
- from the buyer's perspective, a purchase of assets provides the buyer with a tax advantage pursuant to its ability to "bump up" the cost base of the assets acquired for income tax purposes and generally allows it to avoid hidden liabilities. However, the ability of the buyer to bump up the cost base of the purchased assets gives rise to adverse tax consequences to the seller. In addition, a sale of assets in Canada may be subject to a provincial *Bulk Sales Act*, which can result in the buyer assuming certain liabilities, whether or not it had been specifically agreed to do so.

Consequently, a buyer normally is prepared to pay a higher price for the net assets of a company, as opposed to its shares. Where the net assets of the company are sold, the seller has the option of retaining the proceeds of sale within the remaining "shell" company (which can be used for post-transaction investment purposes) or winding up the remaining shell company and distributing the proceeds of sale to the shareholders. Either alternative has income tax consequences, which are discussed in the following part.

Where the net assets of the company are sold, the buyer and seller must mutually agree on the specific portion of the purchase price to be allocated to each asset class being acquired. Buyers normally seek to allocate a higher portion of the purchase price to assets such as machinery and equipment, where the capital cost allowance (CCA) rate (i.e., the depreciation rate allowed for Canadian income tax purposes) is higher. Depending on the nature of the assets and the tax base of the assets involved, this can result in recaptured CCA and, over and above recaptured CCA, possibly a capital gain to the seller. Sellers generally prefer to allocate a higher portion of the purchase price to assets such as land and "goodwill", which receive more favourable tax treatment from their standpoint, but which are not as favourable to the buyer.

When purchasing the net assets of a company, the buyer and seller must specifically agree on which liabilities the buyer will assume. The liabilities assumed by the buyer reduce the net purchase price paid to the seller. Any liabilities not assumed by the buyer remain the obligation of the seller, who must satisfy them from the proceeds that are received. Likewise, any assets not acquired by the buyer remain the property of the seller, who can realize on their value.

In many cases, buyers are selective in the specific assets they are prepared to acquire and the liabilities they are willing to assume. It is not uncommon for a buyer to offer to purchase only the principal operating assets of a company, such as its accounts receivable, inventories and certain fixed assets. A buyer usually does not want to acquire a company's redundant assets or to acquire certain operating assets, such as prepaid expenses and tax recovery amounts receivable. While the seller is free to realize on the non-acquired assets, they must consider the risk in their realization. For example, while assets such as prepaid insurance premiums may have an inherent value at a point in time, that value will erode once the insurance coverage period has elapsed unless the seller is able to obtain a refund for the unused portion. Similarly, leasehold improvements may be of little value (and may in fact become a liability to the seller) where the buyer does not take over the company's building lease.

With respect to intangible assets, it is common for buyers to allocate a portion of the purchase price to "goodwill" and to specify that such amount is in exchange for the company's contracts, customer base, technology, intellectual property and other specifically designated intangible property. However, intangible assets that have no underlying substance, such as "deferred costs" (being expenses that are incurred by the company but that are capitalized as opposed to being expensed for accounting purposes), rarely are acquired. Such "non-identifiable intangible assets" have no value in and of themselves, and the seller should recognize that no incremental amount would be realized from such assets. However, the inherent value of non-identifiable intangible assets may lie in the resultant cash flow that the company prospectively is able to generate as a result of their incurrence. For example, where start-up costs associated with a new product line are capitalized for financial accounting purposes, such deferred cost has no value in and of itself, but may lead to incremental cash flow for the company in the future as revenues from the new product line are generated. Therefore, the seller should be satisfied that any value inherent in non-identifiable intangible assets is adequately reflected in the amount paid for "goodwill".

On the liability side, it is not uncommon for buyers to assume only certain operating liabilities, such as accounts payable and specific accrual amounts. Financial liabilities, such as bank operating loans, mortgages and term debt, often remain with the seller. Therefore, when evaluating an offer received for the purchase of the net assets of their company, the seller must understand which assets are being acquired and which liabilities are being assumed in order to assess the equity value implied by the offer.

Example of equity value comparison

The balance sheet of Company I is as follows:

COMPANY I
BALANCE SHEET ($000)

Current Assets		
Cash	$	800
Accounts receivable	$	4,700
Inventories	$	3,300
Deferred marketing costs	$	900
Prepaid expenses	$	300
Advance to shareholder	$	1,000
Total current assets	$	11,000
Fixed assets (net)	$	4,000
Total assets	$	15,000
Liabilities		
Accounts payable	$	4,000
Accrued liabilities	$	2,000
Total current liabilities	$	6,000
Bank term loan	$	3,000
Total liabilities	$	9,000
Shareholders Equity		
Share capital	$	100
Retained earnings	$	5,900
Total equity	$	6,000
Total liabilities & equity	$	15,000

Mr. Eye, the sole owner of Company I has received two cash offers. Buyer A is prepared to buy the shares of Company I for a cash price of $10 million, payable on closing. Buyer B is prepared to pay $15 million for certain assets of Company I, as follows:

Purchase price offered		
Accounts receivable	$	4,700
Inventories	$	3,300
Fixed assets	$	5,000
Goodwill	$	2,000
	$	15,000
Payment of purchase price		
Assumption of accounts payable	$	4,000
Cash paid on closing	$	11,000
	$	15,000

In order to make a meaningful comparison of the two offers, Mr. Eye should assess the equity value implied by each. In the case of Buyer A, the equity value is represented by the $10 million offer price for the shares. In the case of Buyer B, the equivalent equity value offered is calculated as follows:

Equity value calculation of Buyer B's offer:

Cash paid on closing			$	11,000
Add: estimated realizable value of assets not acquired:				
Cash	$	800		
Deferred marketing costs		nil		
Prepaid expenses (assume)	$	200		
Advance to shareholder	$	1,000		
			$	2,000
Deduct: value of liabilities not assumed:				
Accrued liabilities	$	2,000		
Bank term loan	$	3,000		
			$	5,000
Implied equity value			$	8,000

The starting point for determining the implied equity value of Buyer B's offer is the cash price payable on closing of $11 million, which is net of the accounts payable that Buyer B will assume. The estimated realizable value of the assets not acquired by Buyer B is added to this amount. The cash balance and the advance to shareholder are stated at their book value on the basis that they can readily be realized. However, no value is afforded to the deferred marketing costs because there is nothing that can be realized independent of Company I. The value of the prepaid expenses has been discounted by $100,000 to reflect the seller's assumption in this case that a portion of such prepaid amounts is not recoverable.

The liabilities that Buyer B does not assume, being the accrued liabilities and the bank term loan, remain with the seller who must satisfy those obligations from the proceeds received. Therefore, the equity value that Mr. Eye would realize on a sale to Buyer B is only $8 million, which is significantly less than the amount offered by Buyer A. Further, the two offers have different income tax consequences to Mr. Eye, given that Buyer A has offered to purchase the shares of Company I while Buyer B has offered to purchase its net assets. This issue is addressed in the following part.

Income Tax Comparison – Shares vs. Net Assets

When evaluating offers received from buyers, the seller should consider the net after-tax proceeds that they will retain from a sale of shares of their company as compared to a sale of its underlying net assets. Value enhancement opportunities may be available through pre-sale preparation, which may lessen the tax burden to the seller regardless of whether the shares or the net assets of the company are sold. As discussed in Stage 2, pre-sale planning normally includes initiatives such as crystallizing the lifetime capital gains exemption, which may reduce the differential tax consequences between a sale of shares and a sale of net assets. In some cases, it may be possible for the seller to negotiate the buyer into paying a higher purchase price, based on the purchase of the company's net assets, while paying little more tax than would otherwise have been the case had the shares of the company been acquired.

There are two levels of taxation when the net assets of a company are sold – at the company level and at the shareholder level. Assets that are sold for an amount higher than their tax base give rise to income or a capital gain (depending on the nature of the asset) within the company itself. Once the assets of the company are sold, the seller is left with a shell company, consisting of cash from the sale and any assets and liabilities that were not acquired. The seller then has the option of retaining those assets within the shell company (for investment purposes) or withdrawing them. Where investments are made through an investment company based in Canada, there may be further tax considerations at the corporate level in the form of "additional refundable tax". Therefore, sellers should consult their tax advisor to determine whether it is better to make post-transaction investments through the remaining shell company or, alternatively, to make such investments personally, following the withdrawal of the net proceeds from the shell company.

A seller can withdraw the proceeds received from a sale of net assets either by way of a dividend or bonus. While the tax rate paid by Canadian residents on dividends from Canadian companies is lower than the tax rate on ordinary income, dividends are paid from the after-tax profits of a corporation, which means that the seller effectively is subject to double taxation. Where the seller declares themselves a salary, that amount is deductible to the corporation, but taxed in the hands of the owner at a higher rate. Deal structuring involving asset sales can be complex from a tax perspective and therefore professional tax advice usually is required.

Example of the tax implications of shares vs. net assets

Mr. Tee is the sole shareholder of Company T. He has received one offer of $10 million for the shares of Company T and another offer for $12 million for the net assets of Company T. The net asset offer would be allocated as follows:

- $3 million for the net working capital of Company T, which is the same as the value of those net assets for income tax purposes;
- $7 million for the fixed assets of Company T, which approximates their original cost. Those assets have a cost base for tax purposes (i.e., their undepreciated capital cost) of $2 million; and
- $2 million for goodwill.

Company T pays corporate income tax at a rate of 40%. Mr. Tee pays personal income tax at a rate of 50% on income and 33% on dividends. The cost base of Mr. Tee's shares for tax purposes is $10,000 and no other assets or liabilities would remain in Company T following the sale.

Assuming that Mr. Tee could take advantage of the lifetime capital gains exemption (as discussed in Stage 2), his net proceeds on the sale of shares would be as follows:

Price offered for the shares of Company T		$10,000,000
Income Taxes Paid by Mr. Tee:		
Cost base of shares	$ 10,000	
Gain on sale	$ 9,990,000	
Less: capital gains exemption	$ 500,000	
Capital gain	$ 9,490,000	
Taxable portion (50%)	$ 4,745,000	
Personal income taxes at 50%		$ 2,372,500
Net proceeds to Mr. Tee under a share sale		$ 7,627,500

Alternatively, if Mr. Tee sold the net assets, it would give rise to income in Company T of $6 million, consisting of a gain on:

- fixed assets of $5 million, being the difference between the allocated purchase price of $7 million and their cost base for tax purposes of $2 million; and
- goodwill of $1 million. While $2 million was allocated to goodwill as part of the purchase price, at present in Canada, only 50% of the proceeds received by a company on account of goodwill are subject to corporate income tax. The other 50% accrues to the company's capital dividend account (see Stage 2) and can be paid out to shareholders on a tax-free basis.

To avoid double taxation, Mr. Tee declares himself a bonus of $6 million (to offset the income in Company T arising from the asset sale, as explained above) and withdraws the other $6 million by way of dividend. The net proceeds retained by Mr. Tee are calculated as follows:

Offer price for net assets		$12,000,000
Taxes paid by Mr. Tee on bonus:		
Bonus paid to Mr. Tee	$ 6,000,000	
Taxes thereon at 50%		$ 3,000,000
Taxes paid by Mr. Tee on dividend:		
Dividend to Mr. Tee	$ 6,000,000	
Less: non-taxable dividend (50% of goodwill)	$ 1,000,000	
Taxable dividend	$ 5,000,000	
Tax on dividend at 33%		$ 1,650,000
Net proceeds to Mr. Tee under a net asset sale		$ 7,350,000

Given Mr. Tee's situation, the offer of $10 million for the shares of Company T is more favourable, on an after-tax basis, compared to selling the net assets of Company T for $12 million and distributing the proceeds to Mr. Tee.

(ii) Forms and Terms of Payment

Few private company sales are completed where the stated purchase price is entirely paid in the form of cash on closing. At the very least, the buyer usually retains some portion of the purchase price for a period of time in the form of a hold-back. In addition, other forms of consideration may be used, including a seller take-back, share exchange and earnout. These alternative forms of consideration and the issues that normally should be considered when they are being negotiated are discussed below.

When evaluating an offer received from a buyer, the seller should consider the following:

- the aggregate payment to be received and in what form (e.g., cash, shares of the buyer's organization, etc.);
- when the payments(s) will be received, and whether the portion not received on the closing of the transaction bears interest (or some other form of return) to account for the time value of money;
- the nature and amount of security offered by the buyer for that portion of the purchase price not received on the closing of the transaction;
- the conditions (if any) that must be satisfied in respect of the amounts to be received and, if they do exist, the likelihood that they will be achieved; and
- the income tax implications of the proceeds to be received, and how much will be retained after income taxes have been paid.

The seller and their team of advisors should carefully weigh the risks and rewards associated with the various forms and terms of payment of a given offer. Such consideration should take into account the nature of the company (e.g., highly cyclical or relatively stable), the type of buyer and the payment terms of other merger and acquisition transactions known to have occurred in the industry. It also is important for the seller to consider the impact of various forms and terms of payment on the intangible aspects of value, given their personal situation, tolerance for risk and so on. In essence, the potential reward for accepting non-cash consideration should compensate the seller for the risk of not realizing on those amounts.

When comparing offers received for the company, the seller and their advisors should estimate the cash equivalent value of each offer. This is done by estimating the risk-adjusted present value of any component of the purchase price not received in the form of cash on closing.

Example of a cash-equivalent value calculation

Mr. Jay, the owner of Company J has been presented with three different offers for the shares of his company:

- Offer A is for $10 million, comprised of $9 million in cash on closing and a $1 million hold-back, payable 12 months after the closing date. The hold-back will be placed in escrow and used to purchase a risk-free government bond bearing interest at a rate of 5%, which interest will accrue in favour of Mr. Jay;
- Offer B is for $12 million, comprised of $6 million on closing and $2 million in each of the following 3 years. No interest is payable on the deferred amounts. While Offer B comes from a large credit-worthy corporation, there is no specific security offered on the payment of the deferred purchase price amounts. Mr. Jay and his team of advisors believe that a commercial rate of interest of 8% is appropriate; and
- Offer C is comprised of $4 million on closing and an earnout arrangement whereby Mr. Jay is entitled to 10% of the revenues generated by Company J in each of the next 3 years, subject to certain minimum revenue levels. Company J normally generates around $40 million in revenue each year. Mr. Jay and his team of advisors believe there is a 75% likelihood that this trend will continue. However, Offer C comes from a smaller, less credit-worthy corporation. Therefore, Mr. Jay believes that a commercial rate of interest of 15% is appropriate, given the credit risk involved.

A comparison of the three offers (before consideration of income tax consequences to Mr. Jay) on a cash-equivalent basis is as follows:

CASH-EQUIVALENT VALUE OF OFFERS RECEIVED FOR THE SHARES OF COMPANY J

		Timing of Payment			Total Cash
	Closing	**Year 1**	**Year 2**	**Year 3**	**Equivalent**
Offer A					
Nominal Amount	9,000,000	1,050,000	0	0	
Present Value at 5%	9,000,000	1,000,000			10,000,000
Offer B					
Nominal Amount	6,000,000	2,000,000	2,000,000	2,000,000	
Present Value at 8%	6,000,000	1,851,852	1,714,678	1,587,664	11,154,194
Offer C					
Nominal Amount	4,000,000	4,000,000	4,000,000	4,000,000	
Probabilized Amount	4,000,000	3,000,000	3,000,000	3,000,000	
Present Value at 15%	4,000,000	2,608,696	2,268,431	1,972,549	10,849,675

The assessment of Offer A is relatively straightforward. The $9 million cash received on closing is worth that amount. While the hold-back payable in one year bears interest at a risk-free rate, that interest essentially serves to compensate for the time value of money to Mr. Jay. Therefore, the present value of the hold-back in Offer A is worth $1 million, for a total cash-equivalent offer price of $10 million.

The assessment of Offer B depends on the assumption of the appropriate commercial interest rate used. At a rate of 8%, the present value of the cash flows to be received pursuant to Offer B amount to approximately $11.15 million, which is better than Offer A. In fact, the interest rate used when evaluating Offer B would have to be approximately 24% per annum to cause the present value of Offer B to be less than the $10 million under Offer A. Therefore, so long as Mr. Jay is comfortable that the appropriate interest rate on Offer B is less than 24% and, subject to his personal cash needs and other personal factors that may be appropriate for Mr. Jay to consider, Offer B is preferable to Offer A.

The assessment of Offer C is more subjective. The cash-equivalent value of that offer is influenced by the probability factor assigned to the earnout amounts and the interest rate adopted to account for collection risk. These assumptions do not apply to the $4 million received at the closing date, but do apply to each of the contingency payments in the following three years. Based on the assumptions made by Mr. Jay and his team of advisors (being a 75%

probability factor for the earnout and a 15% interest rate to compensate for the credit risk of the buyer), the cash-equivalent value of Offer C is approximately $10.85 million, which is higher than Offer A, but less than Offer B. However, Mr. Jay should recognize that the cash-equivalent value of Offer C is highly sensitive to the assumptions that were used. Therefore Mr. Jay and his team of advisors should perform sensitivity analysis on those assumptions. Again, it is important for Mr. Jay to consider his personal situation and other pertinent factors when assessing the risk-reward parameters of Offer C.

Hold-backs

A hold-back refers to the portion of the purchase price that is not paid until a point in time after closing, and which is dependent upon the outcome of certain issues. Most buyers use hold-backs to insure against the risk of assuming hidden liabilities of the acquired company, and/or to insure that the accounts receivable, inventories and other assets that they acquire can be realized within a reasonable period of time.

Hold-backs are particularly common where the shares of a company are acquired because the buyer is at greater risk of assuming hidden liabilities. The provisions of a hold-back normally provide that its payment is conditional on the findings of an audit of the company's accounts as of the closing date of the transaction, which audit normally begins shortly after the closing date. The hold-back may extend beyond the finalization of the audit, on account of the existence or valuation of other assets or liabilities that cannot be determined at the audit completion date. In addition, hold-backs often are used where the company is a defendant to an outstanding legal claim. The buyer might set aside a portion of the purchase price pending the outcome of the claim or the settlement thereof.

Where no adjustment to the purchase price is required (i.e., the buyer realizes on the acquired assets and no hidden liabilities are uncovered within the time frame specified), the seller receives the entire hold-back amount. Alternatively, the buyer will draw against the hold-back to compensate for hidden liabilities that are uncovered and other adjustments arising subsequent to the closing date, in accordance with the terms of the purchase agreement.

The key issues for the seller to consider when negotiating a hold-back include:

- the portion of the purchase price that is subject to a hold-back. Hold-backs in the range of 5% to 15% of the stated purchase price are not uncommon, although hold-backs can be greater or less than this proportionate amount;
- the period of time that the hold-back will be in place. This normally depends on the nature of the company and the purpose of the hold-back. A period of 6 to 12 months is not uncommon for hold-backs relating to undisclosed liabilities and unrealizable assets. However, a longer period may be required in respect of hold-backs on account of outstanding legal claims;
- whether the hold-back amount bears interest in favour of the seller and, if so, at what rate;
- the conditions under which the buyer can make a claim against the hold-back amount (e.g., undisclosed liabilities or unrealized assets). These conditions must be clearly established in the purchase agreement in order to prevent disagreement as to what constitutes a legitimate draw against the hold-back;
- whether there are minimum and/or maximum amounts that can be claimed against the hold-back amount. For example, the buyer and seller sometimes will agree that an adjustment must exceed a specified amount in order for the buyer to make a claim against a hold-back. If this is the case, there must be agreement as to whether the specified amount is calculated on a cumulative basis or in respect of each individual adjustment; and
- the nature and amount of security afforded by the buyer to the seller to ensure that the hold-back amount will be paid, assuming that payment conditions are met. In this regard, hold-back amounts often are placed in escrow in order to satisfy the seller that the buyer has the funds available.

When negotiating the terms of a hold-back, the seller should consider the real cost of adjustments that may give rise to a buyer's entitlement to a claim against the hold-back. Specifically, while the buyer may look to the hold-back to offset the gross amount of an undisclosed liability or unrealized asset, the after-tax cost to the buyer may be less than that amount. For example, if a buyer is exposed to a "hidden liability" of $1 million, the settlement of that liability may be a tax-deductible expense to the buyer. If the buyer's tax rate is 35%, then the after-tax cost to the buyer is only $650,000. Accordingly, the seller should attempt to negotiate that the after-tax cost to the buyer represents the amount deducted from the hold-back, and not the gross amount of $1 million.

It is important that tax implications such as these be clearly stated in the purchase agreement.

Seller Take-backs

A seller take-back (or "vendor take-back") refers to an arrangement whereby the seller agrees to accept payment for some (or perhaps all) of the purchase price over a period of time. This arrangement usually is structured as a promissory note from the buyer that is payable to the seller at a specified point in time or made on an instalment basis over time. The seller take-back may also be structured as redeemable preferred shares in the seller's company or in the buyer's company.

When negotiating a seller take-back, the seller should consider the following:

- the time period over which payment will be made to repay the principal amount of the note or to redeem the preference shares;
- the rate of interest that will be paid on the note (or alternatively the dividend yield on the redeemable preferred shares) issued to the seller. The interest rate (or dividend yield) must be sufficient to compensate the seller for both the time value of money and the credit risk associated with collection of the principal amount under the note (or redemption price of the preferred shares);
- the circumstances or conditions under which the buyer could reduce the amount paid on account of the seller take-back, similar to a hold-back; and
- the nature and amount of security provided by the buyer against the outstanding value of the seller take-back. This issue is particularly important where the seller take-back represents a significant portion of the purchase price.

When agreeing to a seller take-back, the seller should be satisfied that they are being fairly compensated for accepting the risk involved. This can be accomplished either by way of the interest rate on the note, the face value of the note, or both.

The seller should consider the tax implications arising on payments received pursuant to a seller take-back. Interest paid on a seller take-back note normally is taxable to the seller at their top marginal personal income tax rate, while such interest normally is tax deductible to the buyer. However, an increase in the face value of the note (reflecting a higher purchase price for the company) normally is treated as a capital gain to the seller, and therefore subject to a lower effective tax rate. The buyer, however, cannot deduct the face value of the note for income tax purposes. Therefore, when considering the trade-off between accepting a higher face value for the note (which relates to the stated purchase price for the shares or net assets of the company) and a higher rate of interest on the note, the seller must take into account the differing tax consequences between the two.

Also in respect of taxation, the seller should consider when they will have to pay tax on the principal amount of the note. The proceeds of sale generally are taxed in the year that the deal is closed, regardless of when such proceeds are received. Consequently, the seller may have a personal tax liability to pay, without the necessary funds to pay it. Some relief may be available pursuant to provisions of the Canadian *Income Tax Act* that allow the seller to defer income taxes on a portion of the proceeds not yet received over a maximum five-year period. Specifically, the seller may claim a reserve for income tax purposes in the year of the transaction for up to 80% of the purchase price. This reserve declines to 60%, 40% and 20% of the purchase price in each successive year, subject to the provision that the amount of the reserve cannot exceed the amount of deferred proceeds.

Finally, the seller also should consider their interest and ability to accept payment over time. While more flexible payment terms may help to attract a greater number of potential buyers, the seller must be comfortable with the fact that any portion of the purchase price not received on closing is at risk of never being received. In addition, the seller must consider their own personal situation in terms of the amount of cash required to support a desired lifestyle, financial commitments and personal goals.

Share Exchanges

Share exchanges involve the buyer exchanging shares of its company for the shares of the seller's company. Share exchanges tend to be popular when public equity markets are buoyant, as a public company buyer can capitalize on the "inflated" value of its own shares as currency to acquire another company.

Share exchanges between Canadian corporations normally can be structured as a tax-deferred transaction, provided the seller does not receive any consideration other than shares (i.e., the seller cannot receive a portion of the purchase price in cash, a seller take-back or other form of payment other than shares of the buyer's company). In a tax-deferred share exchange, the seller must pay income taxes when the shares received as consideration ultimately are disposed of, which tax would be calculated at the capital gains rate. In most cases, a tax-deferred share exchange can also be orchestrated with a foreign buyer, although the costs of doing so (including legal and other expenses) sometimes are prohibitive. Where shares that are received represent one component of the purchase price (and hence do not qualify as a tax-deferred share exchange), they are taxable to the seller based on their market price at the closing date of the transaction. However, that market price sets the seller's cost base for those shares, which is used when calculating the capital gain or loss to the seller when those shares subsequently are disposed of (taking into account the lifetime capital gains exemption, where applicable).

Sellers sometimes become enamoured about the prospect of a share exchange because of its tax-deferral feature and the hope of participating in the buyer's rising stock price. However, share exchanges also involve risks that a seller must consider. These risks include:

- restriction periods. In some cases, the seller is restricted from divesting of the buyer's shares, often for a period of between three to twelve months. This is often the case where the buyer is a relatively small public company and the seller's interest represents a considerable portion of the buyer's outstanding share float. It is possible that the buyer's share price may decline significantly by the time the seller is cleared to liquidate the shares that were received upon the sale; and
- market liquidity. Even if the seller is not precluded from disposing of the shares received, it may not be practical to do so where the buyer's shares are thinly traded and a significant trading volume would place downward pressure on the market price.

Therefore, the seller must be satisfied that the premium received for accepting shares of the buyer in lieu of cash adequately compensates them for the risks involved.

While share exchanges are usually the domain of public company buyers, in some cases share exchanges take place among privately held companies. This usually results in the seller going from a control position in a relatively mid-size private company, to being a minority shareholder in a large private company. The risks entailed in such an arrangement can be significant to the seller, since it is unlikely that a ready market for the disposition of a minority position in a privately held company exists. Therefore, the seller cannot be assured of either the price or timing of proceeds derived from the shares received as consideration. In addition, when consummating a share exchange between privately held companies, there is the challenge of valuing the shares received from a privately held buyer. Such value determination is subjective compared to the readily discernible value of shares that trade on the public equity markets.

Private company share exchanges are uncommon due to the risks and complexities involved. However, they sometimes are used by privately held companies pursuing a "roll-up" or "consolidation" strategy, who manage to convince the seller that the value of shares given in exchange will be realized when an initial public offering or sale to a strategic buyer is completed in the coming months or years. The seller must bear in mind that there is considerable risk attaching to the timing and price that ultimately will be received under these scenarios. Therefore, the seller must be satisfied that the prospective return adequately compensates for these risks.

In circumstances where the seller agrees to a share exchange with another privately held company, the importance of the shareholders' agreement becomes paramount. The shareholders' agreement must provide the seller with ample protection as a minority shareholder in the buyer's company. In particular, the shareholders' agreement should include provisions that allow the seller to influence the decision-making process of the buyer's company. Further it should ensure the seller's right to liquidate the shares of the buyer's company on reasonable terms at some point in time.

Earnouts and Similar Arrangements

An earnout refers to an arrangement whereby payment of some (or all) of the purchase price is conditional upon the future operating results of the company (or some other performance measure). Earnouts are often used to bridge the expectation gap on price between the buyer and seller, particularly where there is a fairly high level of uncertainty attaching to the future operating results of the company.

Buyers tend to favour earnout arrangements because they serve to shift the risk of the company's post-transaction performance from the buyer back to the seller. Not surprisingly, sellers tend to frown on earnout arrangements due to the uncertainty that they create. Where an earnout is agreed to, the seller must carefully reflect on whether the potential upside of an earnout adequately compensates for the risks and uncertainties involved.

The tax consequences of an earnout arrangement must be carefully considered. When structured properly, payments received under an earnout are taxed as a capital gain to the seller when received (assuming that the shares of the company are sold). If not structured properly, the seller might risk having to pay taxes on contingent earnout payments prior to the time that the related proceeds are received. Again, professional income tax advice normally is required. Further, it is important that the purchase agreement be carefully reviewed to ensure that the provisions governing the earnout are clearly established and that they will not cause the Canada Revenue Agency to adopt a differing, and less favourable, view of how proceeds pursuant to the earnout should be treated for income tax purposes.

When negotiating an earnout, the seller should consider the following:

- the portion of the purchase price represented by the earnout. From the seller's perspective, the earnout should ideally be used to bridge the operating performance expectation gap between the buyer and seller. Therefore, the seller should strive to receive cash (or equivalent) for at least the intrinsic value of their company. The earnout should represent the "price premium" that is realized where performance targets beyond those incorporated in the company's intrinsic value are met or surpassed;
- the time period of the earnout. Earnouts commonly range from one to five years. As a general rule, the longer the earnout period, the greater the risk that the earnout will not be realized due to the higher uncertainty associated with longer time frames;
- the basis for measuring the earnout payment. Generally, sellers prefer the earnout to be calculated based on revenues or other top-line performance measure. Buyers prefer measures such as EBIT (earnings before interest and taxes) or EBITDA (earnings before interest, taxes, depreciation and amortization). In some cases, a compromise may be reached by using gross profit as the performance measure. From the buyer's perspective, a gross profit measure reduces the risk that a seller who remains active in the company following the sale will lower the selling price of the company's products or services in order to meet earnout revenue targets, with no regard to profitability. From the seller's perspective, the gross profit measure reduces the risks associated with operating expenses (such as general and administrative costs) that are beyond their control;

- the level of control the seller will have over the earnout performance measures. In this regard, earnout arrangements are more common where the seller will continue to be actively involved with the company following the transaction; and
- whether there is a minimum and/or maximum earnout level, and whether the seller is given the opportunity to recoup shortfalls in the performance measure experienced in one particular year by over-performing in the following year.

Royalty arrangements

There are numerous other structures that that the buyer and seller can use, which in substance are similar to an earnout. For example, the parties might agree to an arrangement whereby the seller receives a royalty calculated at a fixed dollar rate per unit sold or as a stated percentage of revenues (or some other performance measure).

Royalty agreements have many of the same characteristics as earnouts and must be carefully structured to ensure that the seller is protected, particularly if they intend to retain the rights to the property. Furthermore, the tax consequences of royalty payments must be considered. Royalty payments usually are taxed as ordinary income to the recipient, while being tax-deductible to the payer.

Partial sales and put-call arrangements

Another type of arrangement that, in substance, has similar risk-reward parameters to an earnout is where the seller initially agrees to sell a controlling interest in their company at the closing date, and enters into a "put option" whereby the seller has the right to sell the remaining shares of their company to the buyer at a later date. Alternatively (or in conjunction with the seller's put option), the buyer may have a "call option" to acquire the remaining shares at a later date. The price for the seller's remaining interest at the subsequent sale date may be based on a pre-set formula, established by way of agreement, or based on an independent valuation or arbitration.

This form of arrangement allows the seller to participate in the upside potential of the company, while retaining the tax advantages of a capital gain. Where such an arrangement is struck, the seller must be satisfied that the terms of the shareholders' agreement protect their interest as a minority shareholder in the company, and that the provisions governing the circumstances under which the seller is entitled (or obligated) to divest of their remaining interest are acceptable.

It is important to note that pre-set "put-call" valuation formulas can prove dangerous to the seller (and to the buyer). Pre-set formulas can create an unrealistic (and often unforeseen) valuation result due to unexpected changes in business and industry conditions. Therefore, where the put-call agreement is established by way of a pre-set formula, the seller should insist on protection via an arbitration clause in case the valuation result proves to be unreasonable.

Summary — Forms of Consideration

The key considerations when assessing the various non-cash forms of consideration are summarized in Exhibit III-6-2.

Exhibit III-6-2

KEY CONSIDERATIONS IN NON-CASH FORMS OF CONSIDERATION

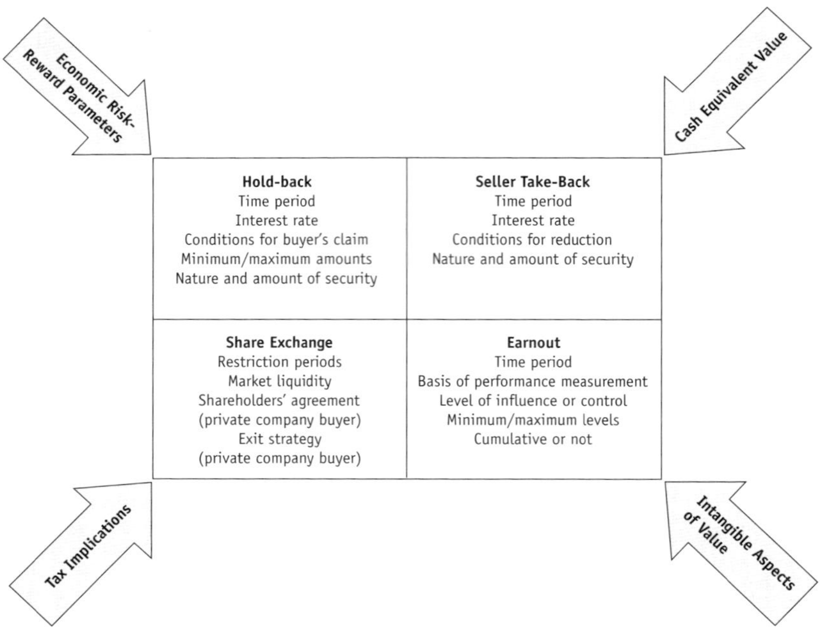

(iii) The Management Contract

Where the seller has been actively involved in their company, it is common for a buyer to request that the seller enter into a management contract following the closing of the transaction. From the buyer's perspective, the seller's ongoing involvement facilitates the transition of the company's customers and employees to the buyer, and helps to preserve the goodwill of the company. In some cases, a buyer may not be willing to consummate a transaction unless the seller is prepared to enter into a satisfactory management contract.

The terms and conditions of a management contract can vary widely with respect to the seller's responsibilities following the sale, the duration of the contract and compensation levels. The seller's role can range from occasional consulting to a full-time management position. The duration of the management contract may range from a few months to several years. As mentioned in Stage 1, when deciding when to sell, the business owner should decide on acceptable parameters in terms of the role, responsibilities and the duration of involvement that would be acceptable, given their personal goals, interests, health and other important factors.

The seller typically is paid for the services provided under a management contract, however, the amount and basis of payment can vary widely. In many cases, the seller is remunerated at a higher rate than would be paid to an arm's length individual for the same service provided. If so, a portion of the purchase price for the company may effectively be embedded in the management contract remuneration. In addition, the basis for compensation under a management contract often includes significant incentives for meeting performance targets. This causes the management contract to be similar in many respects to an earnout arrangement.

The terms of the management contract should be considered in conjunction with the overall deal. There often is a trade-off between the purchase price for the company and the payments made under the management contract. From a buyer's perspective, it is preferable to compensate the seller through a management contract as opposed to a higher purchase price or earnout arrangement. This is because payments made under a management contract are tax-deductible to the buyer. Conversely, the income received under a management contract is taxable to the seller as ordinary income. Therefore, the seller should consider the tax implications of payments received under a management contract and determine the amount that will be received on an after-tax basis.

Example of the management contract remuneration trade-off

A buyer is prepared to pay Mrs. Kay, the sole shareholder of Company K, a cash purchase price calculated as 5x EBIT (earnings before interest and taxes), based on the normalized operating results of Company K for the past 12 months. Company K's normalized trailing 12-month EBIT is $5 million before management salaries. The buyer has offered Mrs. Kay latitude in terms of the amount paid to her pursuant to a 5-year management contract that will be agreed to. The minimum that Mrs. Kay must take in terms of her annual salary is $100,000 and the maximum is $500,000. Under this scenario, Mrs. Kay should consider the following:

PROCEEDS TO MRS. KAY UNDER DIFFERENT MANAGEMENT CONTRACT STRUCTURES

	Low Salary	High Salary
Normalized EBIT before salary	$ 5,000,000	$ 5,000,000
Less: annual management salary	($100,000)	($500,000)
Normalized EBIT	$ 4,900,000	$ 4,500,000
EBIT multiple	5x	5x
Purchase price	$ 24,500,000	$ 22,500,000
Add: Salary received (over 5 years)	$ 500,000	$ 2,500,000
Total proceeds	$ 25,000,000	$ 25,000,000

On the surface, Mrs. Kay may be indifferent as to the choice between a higher annual salary or higher purchase price for Company K, since the total proceeds under either scenario are $25 million. The only difference is a trade-off between the purchase price and aggregate salaries of $2 million. However, the low salary scenario likely would be preferable to Mrs. Kay because:

- an additional $2 million is received in the form of the purchase price on closing, which Mrs. Kay can invest in her personal account. On the contrary, payments to Mrs. Kay under the management contract are made over a five-year period;
- further to the point above, Mrs. Kay may not receive all of the payments under the management contract should she depart prior to its five-year duration for reasons such as performance or health. Often sellers do not remain for the entire duration of the management contract because of the difficulty in making the transition from owner to employee, or as a result of differences that arise between the buyer and the seller over time; and

- the tax consequences to Mrs. Kay are more favourable. Assuming that ordinary income is taxed at a rate of 50% and capital gains at an effective rate of 25% (recognizing that only 50% of capital gains are taxable), Mrs. Kay would save $500,000 in taxes under the low-salary scenario (calculated as $2 million of income x [50% tax rate on salary income less 25% effective tax rate on capital gains]).

One final point with respect to management contracts pertains to contingencies. There may be circumstances where, for reasons beyond the seller's control, they are unable to fulfill the terms of the management contract (e.g., due to serious health issues). Where payment under the management contract effectively includes an element of the purchase price, the seller should be satisfied that ample protection is afforded so that the purchase price is not unduly eroded in unforeseen circumstances. Where the buyer is unwilling to guarantee payment under the management contract, the seller should consider life and disability insurance coverage to protect them against a loss in value arising from death or disability.

Summary

Deal structuring is a fundamental determinant of the value received by the seller of a privately held company. The highest stated offer price may not represent the best value to the seller. From the seller's perspective, it is important to be satisfied that the rewards associated with any portion of the purchase price that are not received in the form of cash on closing compensate for the time value of money and the risk that such amounts may not be received. It also is important to consider the tax consequences attaching to various forms of consideration and tax planning opportunities that may be available. In the context of deal structuring, value enhancement is realized where proposals are evaluated based on their risk-reward parameters and income tax-efficiency to the seller. Professional advice is required due to the income tax and legal complexities involved and because the rules and regulations governing such things are always evolving.

As part of deal structuring, the seller should first consider whether the shares or the net assets of the company will be sold. The seller should compare the after-tax equity value under both scenarios. Since most transactions involve terms of payment in a variety of forms other than cash on closing, the seller and their team of advisors should carefully consider the terms and conditions attaching to non-cash forms of payment, including hold-backs, seller take-backs, share exchanges, earnouts and similar arrangements. Any portion of the purchase price not received in the form of cash on closing is subject to risk. Therefore, competing offers should be compared on a cash-equivalent basis, with sensitivity analysis performed on key assumptions that influence the calculation of the risk-adjusted present value of a non-cash offer. Finally, the seller should consider the provisions of a post-transaction management contract that they are willing to enter into, and be satisfied with the terms of the management contract in the context of the entire deal.

Preparations for effective deal structuring and tax planning should commence in the planning phase of the private company sale process. In addition to pre-sale tax structuring for the company and organizing the personal affairs of the business owner, the owner should consider the forms and terms of payment that would be acceptable and the parameters of a management contract they would be willing to accommodate prior to the time that prospective buyers are actively sought out. The foundation for value enhancement creation that is set in the planning phase of the private company sale process is fundamental to realizing value enhancement in deal structuring.

SECTION III

Stage 7 | Negotiations

Introduction

Following the initial buyer meetings and after providing other preliminary due diligence information to the buyer, the formal negotiations of the purchase price and the terms of the deal begin. The issues to be addressed from the seller's standpoint include: what should be done to prepare for the negotiations; what negotiating strategies and tactics should be deployed; and what should be included in the letter of intent that is agreed to with a particular buyer.

Effective negotiations begin with adequate preparation. The seller must clearly define their own needs, interests and negotiating position, and understand those of each prospective buyer. The negotiating strategies and tactics that are deployed by the seller and their negotiating team are a function of the perceived relative negotiating position of the buyer and seller, which stems from the alternatives available to each party and their desire to transact. Ideally, the negotiations should culminate in the execution of satisfactory letter of intent (LOI). The execution of the LOI represents the apex of deal momentum in the private company sale process.

The key to value enhancement realization in the negotiation stage is to secure a comprehensive LOI that offers the best value to the business owner. That is, an LOI that addresses all significant aspects of the deal and provides the best overall value to the business owner, having regard to the stated purchase price, economic terms of the deal (i.e., when, how and under what conditions the purchase price will be paid) and intangible aspects of the deal.

Securing a comprehensive LOI that offers the best value is achieved where the seller and their intermediary build deal momentum through creating a competitive bidding environment, where buyers submit proposals with relative concurrency. This allows the seller to negotiate effectively among several potential buyers. Creating a competitive bidding environment is best facilitated where the seller is prepared to offer buyers flexibility with respect to the purchase price and the terms of the deal.

The negotiations stage (done concurrently with the deal structuring stage) normally lasts between one to two months from the time that negotiations with buyers effectively begin to the time that an agreed letter of intent is executed. The negotiations stage of the private company sale process within the context of the *Value Enhancement Framework™* is depicted in Exhibit III-7-1.

Exhibit III-7-1

THE NEGOTIATIONS STAGE WITHIN
THE *VALUE ENHANCEMENT FRAMEWORK™*

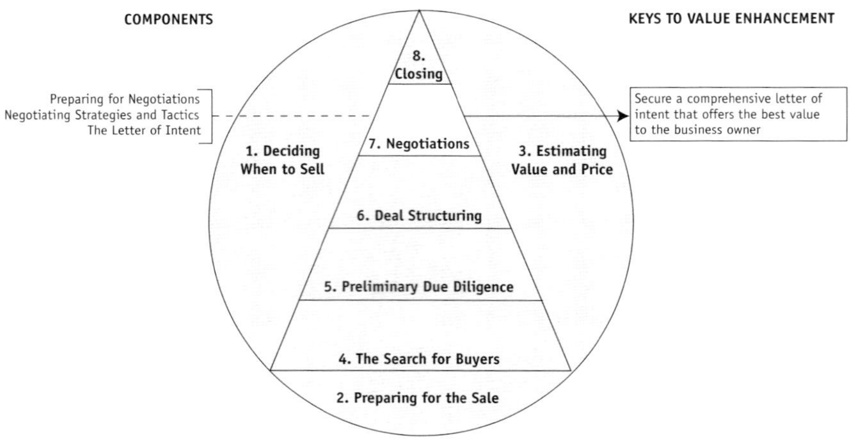

(i) Preparing for Negotiations

Prior to entering into negotiations with a buyer, the seller and their team of advisors must decide on who should be directly involved in the negotiations, what should and should not be said, and the style and posture that will be adopted. To meaningfully prepare for these things, the seller must establish their own interests, needs, alternatives and negotiating position, and those of each buyer with whom negotiations take place.

The seller's advisory team normally consists of an intermediary, lawyer, tax expert and other professionals as required. However, only one or a select few of these individuals should directly engage in negotiations with the buyer. In most cases, it is best that direct negotiating be conducted between the intermediary and the buyer's representatives. The seller normally is not directly engaged in the negotiations. However, the seller does maintain control of whether or not to transact at the price and terms that are offered.

The reasons for limiting the number of persons directly involved in the negotiations include:

- the fewer individuals directly involved, the less likely it is that someone will say or do something that negatively affects the momentum of the negotiations;
- it provides the intermediary with the opportunity to discuss issues and proposals with the seller and to renegotiate certain issues separately. However, the intermediary must be selective in renegotiating the deal after conferring with the seller. Excessive use of such a tactic can lead to a loss in the intermediary's credibility;
- business owners sometimes find it difficult to separate their emotional ties with their company from the practical aspects of negotiating the economic parameters of a deal. This may impair the seller's ability to negotiate objectively, particularly if the buyer's representatives are seasoned negotiating experts who are tuned to the seller's body language and other non-verbal indicators; and
- where the seller and other advisors are not directly involved in the negotiations from the outset, it leaves open the opportunity for those individuals to deal directly with the buyer at a later date if an impasse arises in the negotiations between the intermediary and the buyer.

The intermediary should clearly understand the seller's needs and interests and recognize how these things will influence the price and terms of a deal. It is the intermediary's responsibility to help the seller understand their negotiating position and the alternatives available so that a deal can be structured that satisfies the seller both economically and emotionally.

Negotiations should take place at a neutral site, away from both the seller's and buyer's places of business. This helps in minimizing disruptions and assists in maintaining a degree of confidentiality. Ideally, a separate room should be available where the respective negotiating teams can caucus to discuss issues that arise during the course of the negotiations. Depending on the stage and complexity of the negotiations, it may not be necessary for all of the seller's advisors to be physically present. However, the seller and key advisors should be aware of when negotiations are taking place beforehand so that they can be available by phone if necessary.

Prior to entering into negotiations, the seller should establish parameters regarding price range and deal structure, and should ensure that the buyer is prepared to consider the same general parameters. Rarely can a meaningful deal be negotiated where one or both parties take an extreme position with respect to value expectations. While effective negotiation and deal structuring can be used to bridge an expectations gap between the buyer and seller, there is a limit to what usually can be accomplished.

Prior to entering into negotiations, it is essential that the seller's negotiating team, and in particular those individuals who will be directly involved in the negotiations, be as knowledgeable as possible about each prospective buyer. The better informed the seller's negotiating team, the stronger their negotiating position. Research and information are fundamental to effective negotiation.

The seller and their intermediary should have conducted preliminary research on each buyer prior to the initial contact, and should have been gathering additional information during the preliminary due diligence stage. This includes information in respect of each buyer's:

- underlying needs and motivation, the reasons for its interest in the company and its desire to transact;
- readily available alternatives to a purchase of the company that would serve to achieve the buyer's objectives;
- decision-making and approval process in the transaction;

- business strategy and market position;
- financial position and the resources it has available to consummate a transaction;
- likely sources of synergies, quantified to the extent possible; and
- acquisition and divestiture transactions that it has consummated in the past several years, including the reasons for those transactions, the terms of those deals and the implied valuation multiples.

In addition, the negotiating team must be well informed as to the seller's needs and interests and the operations of the company, including its risks, opportunities, current and prospective industry conditions and other factors that a buyer is likely to raise during the course of the negotiations as validation for its verbal or written proposals. A strong knowledge base allows the seller's negotiating representatives to be more effective in addressing the concerns and issues a buyer may have about the company and also in challenging facts or assumptions put forth by the buyer that are inaccurate, incomplete or inconsistent.

(ii) Negotiating Strategies and Tactics

Negotiating Principles

In the course of negotiations, it sometimes is easy to lose track of the ultimate goal – to complete a transaction that provides the best value to the business owner. It is helpful to keep in mind key guiding principles that should govern the negotiating strategies and tactics used by the seller and their negotiating team, which can help in achieving the seller's objectives. In the context of selling a privately held company, there are three over-riding, inter-related principles to keep in mind:

- credibility is fundamental to maintaining a negotiating position;
- negotiating strength is a function of alternatives; and
- both the price and the terms of the deal are important.

Credibility is fundamental to maintaining a negotiating position

Underlying any negotiation is the fact that the buyer and seller each desire to advance their respective interests. However, the manner in which each party tries to achieve its goals will influence whether or not those goals will be realized.

Where the seller misleads a buyer, either knowingly or unknowingly, credibility is lost, and their negotiating position is compromised. Buyers will conduct detailed due diligence prior to executing a binding purchase agreement. As such, they inevitably will detect materially false or incorrect information put forth by the seller prior to deal closing. Such findings will cause the buyer to doubt the seller's credibility, which will increase the buyer's perception of risk and hence decrease the price it is willing to pay (or otherwise alter the terms of the deal in its favour). In some cases, the buyer will walk away from the negotiations altogether, preferring not to deal with a seller who it perceives is dishonest. This is particularly the case where the buyer anticipates entering into a management contract with the seller following the transaction.

The seller's credibility can also be compromised where the information provided is internally inconsistent. For example, the seller might initially represent that the company's operations are running near capacity, but later provide the buyer with aggressive growth projections while indicating that no significant capital investment is required to support this growth. Internal consistency is fundamental to maintaining credibility, therefore the seller must ensure that the information provided, whether verbal or written, is internally consistent.

While the risks of providing misleading or inconsistent information are self-evident, more commonly the seller will lose credibility due to their overly optimistic projections for the company. For example, where the seller presents near-term forecasts that are not met during the period up to closing, the buyer will have reason to question the credibility of the seller's longer-term forecasts. Similarly, when the seller overstates the company's competitive advantages, the buyer's due diligence inevitably will expose this overstatement, thereby compromising the seller's credibility.

It often is difficult for the seller to temper their enthusiasm for their company, because the seller often is so focused on the business that it may impair their ability to objectively assess both its strengths and weaknesses. Further, during the sale process, the seller is actively trying to augment the buyers' perceived value of their company. While enthusiasm and good salesmanship are important to realizing value enhancement, the seller must be cautious not to "over-sell", and ensure that a balanced assessment of the company's weaknesses and threats, as well as its strengths and opportunities, is offered.

Finally, credibility can be damaged where the seller attempts to change a key aspect of the deal after general agreement on that point has been reached. For example, if the seller originally indicated a willingness to remain with the company for up to two years following the transaction, and later decided to change this time to six months, absent clear and reasonable justification, the buyer would have good cause to be suspect of the reasons for this change, and to question whether the outlook for the company had diminished since discussions between the parties began.

Negotiating strength is a function of alternatives

There is a direct correlation between the seller's negotiating strength and the number of alternatives that are available with respect to a given course of action. Where the seller has two or more buyers willing to enter into a deal on equally attractive price and terms, it allows the seller to lever one buyer against the other in the negotiations. However, the seller's negotiating position is weakened where the next best alternative represents a considerably less favourable deal.

The seller may be handsomely rewarded where they are prepared to be flexible with respect to the structure and terms of a transaction that would be acceptable. Flexibility can serve to increase the number and quality of alternatives available to the seller. The ability to be flexible often originates from the efforts undertaken when preparing the company for sale in terms of financial and operational structuring, as well as income tax and estate planning for the business owner (see Stage 2).

Securing two (or preferably more) attractive offers for the company is dependent upon the ability of the seller and their intermediary to create an effective auction. As discussed in Section II, in order to create an effective auction, it is important to build momentum throughout the sale process. Sometimes this requires slowing down some buyers who are progressing too quickly, while encouraging more tardy prospects to speed up. This ensures that each prospective buyer is at approximately the same stage of the negotiation process. Influencing the timing of prospective buyers must be done tactfully to ensure that legitimate enthusiastic prospects do not become frustrated and lose interest. Therefore, it is important that stalling tactics not be seen as such. On the other hand, attempting to rush a buyer through the process might cause them to question why the seller is so anxious. Creating an effective auction is an essential art in successfully negotiating the sale of a privately held company.

Both the price and the terms of the deal are important

Too often sellers focus narrowly on getting the highest price for their company while not adequately considering the terms of the deal. Again, the highest price may not represent the best value to the business owner. Deal structuring, as discussed in Stage 6, is of fundamental importance in helping to guide the seller through the negotiations.

When evaluating a buyer's offer, the seller should carefully consider the terms of the proposal, including how much will be paid, the form(s) of consideration to be used, the timing of payment and the conditions that must be satisfied to receive payment. An effective negotiator can use deal structuring creatively to help both the seller and buyer realize their respective objectives.

The seller should remember that there are always three parties involved when negotiating the sale of a privately held company: the seller; the buyer; and the government. To the extent that the seller and buyer can work together to reduce the overall tax burden, both parties can benefit. The Canada Revenue Agency generally allows a fair degree of latitude in terms of transaction structuring among parties dealing at arm's length with one another.

The ability for the seller to be flexible as to the terms of a deal is dictated in part by their personal situation. Where the seller requires most of the purchase price to be paid in cash on closing in order to meet personal lifestyle needs or financial commitments, they cannot be as flexible as a seller who is able to offer buyers the opportunity to defer a large portion of the purchase price, subject of course to satisfactory conditions. It is important for the seller to understand their level of flexibility at the outset of the sale process to avoid the need to make a fundamental change at a later stage in the negotiations, thereby impairing their credibility.

Flexibility requires the seller to consider value from a broad perspective. Meaningful compromises on the seller's part can lead to a better deal overall. For example, owners of privately held Canadian companies normally want to sell shares due to the related tax benefits of such a transaction structure. However, some buyers insist on purchasing the net assets of a company in order to avoid undisclosed liabilities or to maximize their own tax advantages. Where the seller compromises by agreeing to sell the net assets of their company, they are in a good position to negotiate a higher price that compensates for the increased tax burden, thereby potentially increasing the after-tax proceeds received.

Specific Negotiating Strategies and Tactics

There are numerous strategies and tactics that may help in negotiating a good deal. Some of these are discussed below. When considering specific negotiating strategies and tactics, the seller and their negotiating representatives should recognize the buyer's natural advantage of self-knowledge in terms of its synergy expectations, internal valuation model and the maximum price it is willing to pay. However, if an effective auction is created, the seller has the advantage of dealing with multiple buyers and reviewing competing bids. The negotiating strategies and tactics adopted by the seller and their negotiating representatives will depend on their assessment of the perceived negotiating position of the seller relative to that of the buyer.

Building deal momentum

As discussed in Section II, the momentum of a deal begins with the search for buyers and builds throughout the effective auction, peaking during the negotiations stage. Escalating momentum leading up to and during the negotiation stage is essential to creating a competitive bidding environment among buyers. This leads to the development of attractive alternative proposals and increases the likelihood of securing a letter of intent that offers enhanced value to the business owner.

Given its importance, the seller and their intermediary should employ tactics that will help to build the momentum of the deal throughout the sale process. This includes regular discussions and correspondence with prospective buyers to retain their interest and to keep the possible acquisition a priority item from their standpoint. Controlling the flow of information to prospective buyers and the timing of discussions helps in aligning their level of preparedness to participate in a competitive bidding process. In this regard, the seller and their intermediary must be cognizant not to lose momentum with buyers that represent strong front-runners in favour of one or two buyers that are much farther behind. The seller and their intermediary must strike a balance between increasing the number of prospective buyers in the competitive bidding process and maintaining momentum with a lesser number of highly qualified prospects.

Talking price

At some point in the negotiations (and often at an early stage), the buyer will ask the intermediary how much the seller wants for the company. Rather than stating a fixed price, the intermediary should develop a position on price based on the components of value. For example, the intermediary should address the prospective cash flows, rates of return and financial position of the company in order to establish the basis for pricing (see Stage 3). Where advantageous and appropriate, reference should be made to independent valuation indicators, such as the observed multiples paid in recent merger and acquisition transactions involving similar companies.

It also is important for the intermediary to communicate that the terms of a deal are just as important as the price that is paid, in order to ease the buyer's concerns about being caught up in an auction process where price is the only variable considered by the seller.

Disclosing alternatives

The seller's negotiating representatives often are tempted to demonstrate that there are strong competitive bids for the company so as to convince a prospective buyer that it must be prepared to pay a premium. The direct use of this tactic can backfire as some buyers will refuse to participate in auctions. Consequently, alluding to alternatives should be done less blatantly in order to reduce concerns among buyers about getting drawn into an auction. In this regard, it is important for the intermediary to mention to the buyer that the terms of the deal are just as important as the price.

Generally, specific details regarding competing offers should not be shared with other buyers. However, selective information can be conveyed indirectly. For example, the intermediary might state to a particular buyer that the proposals received from other bidders reflect higher valuation multiples, without disclosing that the terms of those other bids are not as favourable (e.g., payment is made over time as opposed to cash on closing).

The existence of alternatives for the seller also can be conveyed through, for example, describing the sale process or mentioning the number of confidential information memorandums that have been sent out. However, before taking an overly confident tone, it is important for the intermediary to reflect on the number and quality of alternatives available so as to avoid having to later revise their negotiating posture in the event certain anticipated alternatives do not materialize.

Posture and style

The posture and style adopted by the seller's negotiating representatives are important as body language and non-verbal signals speak volumes to experienced negotiators. Extreme posturing generally should be avoided, as it creates an atmosphere of non-cooperation.

An effective approach to negotiating the sale of a privately held company is where the buyer and seller work together toward a common goal rather than viewing the negotiations as a win-lose situation. A tactful negotiator pays close attention to what is said, and what is not said, when gathering insights into the underlying interests behind the other party's stated positions.

Alternate negotiating styles can also be very effective in some cases, when used carefully and selectively. For example, if a buyer is consistently taking extreme positions on deal terms and conditions, the intermediary may be effective in militating against some of those positions with a more aggressive negotiating style and tone. An aggressive style and tone is more effective when it stands in contrast to a moderate style and tone that was used throughout most of the negotiations.

Making concessions

Negotiations involve making compromises. The seller should understand at the outset of the negotiations what points will readily be conceded, what compromises will be more difficult to make and what they are not willing to sacrifice.

Where the seller makes a meaningful concession, they should expect the buyer to offer something meaningful in return. In particular, where the seller reluctantly concedes on an issue that was identified as important, the buyer should make a significant concession as well. Regardless of the compromises or concessions made during the negotiations, it is important for the seller to remember that, in the end, it is the whole deal package that matters and not just selective terms.

Summary — negotiation principles, strategies and tactics

The relationship between negotiation principles, strategies and tactics is summarized in Exhibit III-7-2.

Exhibit III-7-2

NEGOTIATION PRINCIPLES, STRATEGIES AND TACTICS

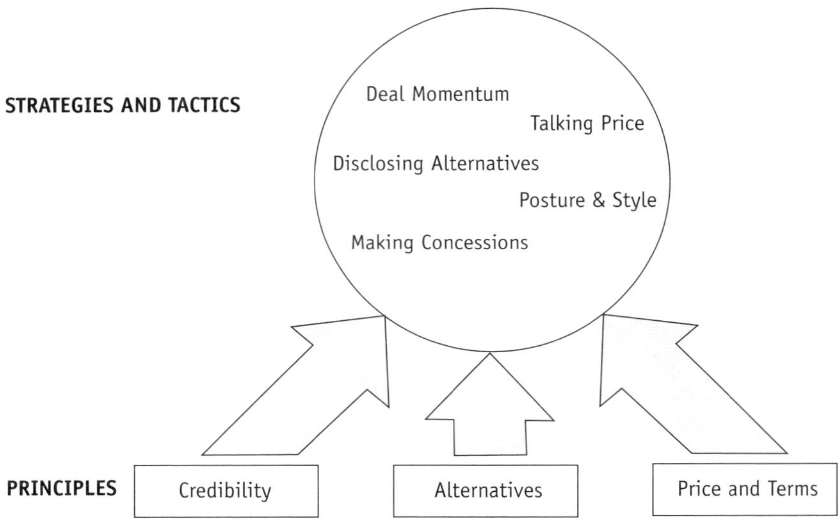

Dealing with a Single Buyer

Earlier the principle was introduced that negotiating strength is a function of alternatives, and therefore the seller should strive to have two or more competing bidders submit near concurrent offers. In some cases, however, either by desire or by necessity, the seller may deal with only a single potential buyer. While generally not ideal, there are still ways that the seller's negotiating position need not be compromised.

The single buyer scenario can be initiated either by the buyer or the seller. Buyer-initiated cases normally stem from unsolicited approaches to the business owner about the prospect of selling their company. As discussed in Section II, buyers sometimes use this tactic in order to avoid an auction and to negotiate a lower purchase price. In buyer-initiated situations, it is important for the seller to convey that viable alternatives still exist. First of all, the seller can choose not to transact. Further, the seller can reiterate to the buyer that the unsolicited approach has caused them to consider exposing the company for sale in the open market. In this regard, the seller may engage an intermediary for the purpose of dealing with the single buyer. This often causes the buyer to believe that the seller is preparing the company for sale in the open market, and may cause the buyer to offer a better deal in order to pre-empt that process. By managing a buyer-initiated single buyer scenario appropriately, the seller's negotiating position should not be unduly compromised.

A more difficult situation arises where the seller initiates a single buyer scenario. This sometimes occurs where the company is so specialized that only one logical buyer exists, or where the company is dependent on a particular buyer and would risk losing that relationship in the event that the company were sold to a third party. Even in such cases, the seller and their team of advisors should think creatively about potential buyers from other industries that might be interested in diversifying or obtaining the market platform, technology, customer base, or other intangible assets that the company has to offer.

The main issue in a seller-initiated single buyer scenario is whether or not the buyer knows or suspects that it is the only one. If not, the seller can still create the appearance of an auction. If the buyer knows or suspects that it is the only one, the seller can use various tactics to offset the risks of having to settle on a lesser deal, such as:

- assessing the viability of alternatives to selling the company, such as finding an operator to run the company or a capital injection from a third party investor. If these options are available, they should be conveyed to the buyer;
- describing the process that is being followed to market the company to a broader audience; and
- slowing the process down to allow time to search for other prospective buyers.

As a general comment, the seller's objective should be to get the single buyer to a point where it wants to do a deal because it views the acquisition as making good strategic and financial sense, and not because the company can be acquired at a bargain price. This will cause the buyer to be less price sensitive, and more focused on the incremental value that will be created through the acquisition.

Walking Away from and Restarting Negotiations

Sometimes there comes a point where the seller and the buyer conclude they are so far apart on certain key issues that even deal structuring cannot bridge the difference. The question arises as to who should walk away from the negotiations and how.

In some cases, the seller and buyer mutually agree to end the negotiations. However, before agreeing to do so, the seller should clearly understand the buyer's best offer and to get it in writing, if possible. This serves as a valuable baseline when negotiating with other prospective buyers. Further, if and when negotiations recommence, the buyer's stated position from earlier can be used as a starting point for the new talks.

The seller should always learn as much as possible about why a buyer is prepared to walk away from the negotiations. These issues can then be discussed among the seller and their team of advisors. If the buyer states that the seller's expectations are not reasonable, this information may be used to adjust the seller's negotiating strategy.

Even when terminating negotiations, it is important to keep the lines of communication open. This allows buyers to feel free to contact the seller should they later change their stated position. It also is a good idea to convey to those buyers who walked away any significant changes or developments in the company or the industry that subsequently occur, as such information may cause the buyer to reconsider its position. For example, if several weeks after the termination of negotiations the company wins a significant customer contract, this fact should be communicated to the buyer. Such changes in circumstances may save face for the buyer's negotiating team and allow them to put forward a new offer or at least reconsider their previous position. Further, where a letter of intent has been received from another buyer, it often is worthwhile conveying that fact to a buyer who left the bargaining table in case they did so under the assumption that the company would not receive any other offers.

(iii) The Letter of Intent

The importance of the LOI frequently is underestimated. An inadequate LOI often results in the failure of a deal because the expectations of the buyer and seller are not reasonably well established prior to negotiating the purchase agreement. Negotiating the LOI should coincide with the peak of deal momentum and represent the key point in the seller's value enhancement realization efforts. Once the buyer and seller have agreed in principle on the terms of the deal, the seller's focus shifts to crystallizing the value set out in the LOI.

As discussed earlier in this stage, the seller's negotiating strength derives from the number and quality of alternatives available. Therefore, to maximize value enhancement realization, the seller and their intermediary should ideally create a competitive bidding environment to secure multiple offers. Creating a competitive bidding environment necessitates that the seller must influence buyers to submit their respective offers around the same time frame, normally within a period of two weeks or less. In this regard, the seller and their intermediary may have to speed up some buyers while slowing down others. Caution must be exercised to ensure that buyers do not feel they are being rushed, or that they are kept waiting for an unreasonably long period of time.

When multiple offers are received, they can be used to aid in negotiations with various buyers using the strategies and tactics previously discussed. When negotiating the offers, the seller should seek to have buyers resubmit their LOIs once better terms and conditions have been agreed to. The submission and resubmission of LOIs from various buyers is an iterative process that the seller should carefully strategize to achieve value enhancement realization.

The buyer (or its representative) normally prepares the LOI at a point where the buyer and seller are satisfied that there is a general understanding on the price and terms of a deal. The contents of the LOI normally provide the framework for further discussions between the buyer and the seller. While the LOI does not bind the parties to transact, it generally is binding with respect to certain things such as the:

- confidentiality of the offer, and the requirement that the buyer and seller jointly agree on any announcement regarding their discussions or the proposed transaction; and
- period of time granted to the buyer to allow it to perform detailed due diligence and to negotiate a purchase agreement with the seller on an exclusive basis.

When preparing an LOI, a buyer will strive to keep its proposal rather vague. From the buyer's standpoint, a vague LOI allows it greater flexibility when negotiating the purchase agreement. For this reason, the seller should object to an LOI that does not adequately address important aspects of the deal. While it is true that an LOI is non-binding and the terms of the transaction remain open to negotiation, it is more difficult for a buyer to do so where it must specifically change certain terms of the deal without adequate justification. Any terms of the deal that are not covered in the LOI and anything addressed in the LOI in an ambiguous way are subject to negotiation after the LOI has been agreed to. At that point, the seller's negotiating position may be diminished, as discussed below.

It is critical that the seller obtain a comprehensive LOI that clearly addresses all the important aspects of the deal. This helps to prevent the buyer from opening negotiations following its detailed due diligence based on terms that were ambiguous or not addressed at all. In addition, the seller must be confident that all material risks and issues facing their company have been disclosed to the buyer and adequately addressed prior to the execution of the LOI. This will help to prevent the buyer from attempting to renegotiate the terms of the LOI based on "new information".

Typically, a buyer will balk at the seller's request to set specific terms in an LOI, on the basis that it does not have the information necessary to agree to them until its detailed due diligence has been completed. The seller can circumvent this tactic by allowing the buyer to predicate the terms of the LOI on certain assumptions about the company, provided that the seller is satisfied the buyer will be able to confirm the legitimacy of those assumptions during its detailed due diligence investigation.

Buyers normally look to the seller to counter-sign the LOI to establish agreement on the proposed terms of the deal, thereby granting the buyer a period of exclusivity to close the transaction. Buyers typically demand an exclusivity period because they do not want to expend a substantial amount of time, money and other resources where it is not reasonably likely that a transaction will occur. In addition, the exclusivity period normally protects the buyer from developing a firm proposal, only to have the seller negotiate a better deal with another buyer.

Importantly, the seller must carefully consider the implications when granting exclusivity to a particular buyer. Signing an LOI marks a threshold point in the sale process in that the seller's negotiating position usually will diminish thereafter because the competitive bidding process ends, or at a minimum, goes on hold. It often is difficult for the seller to go back to another buyer if exclusive negotiations subsequently fail in circumstances where the seller placed that other buyer "on hold" during the exclusivity period. The other buyer usually will deduce that something caused the exclusive negotiations to derail. This perception, along with a loss in momentum from being put on hold, can serve to weaken the seller's negotiating position. For this reason, and given the time, cost and risk of enduring a buyer's detailed due diligence investigation, the seller should be relatively confident that the transaction will close with the buyer who is granted exclusivity. The seller also should have a relatively high level of confidence that the terms and conditions of the purchase agreement will be substantially the same as those set out in the agreed LOI.

To summarize, prior to signing an LOI and granting exclusivity to a particular buyer, a seller should be satisfied that:

- the LOI is sufficiently detailed with respect to the purchase price, terms of payment, forms of consideration, terms of the management contract and non-competition agreement, and other key conditions and assumptions; and
- there are no significant issues that the buyer will uncover during its detailed due diligence investigation that it could use to justify a change to its proposal or a reduction in price.

Usual Contents of an LOI

While the contents of an LOI can vary substantially, the seller should be satisfied that at least the following key points are sufficiently addressed:

- the offer price or price range. It generally is preferable for the LOI to specify the purchase price in dollar terms and to state how, when and under what conditions that price will be paid. An LOI containing a statements such as "the purchase price will be established as a multiple of 5x normalized EBITDA for the past 12 months" is dangerous from the standpoint of the seller, because it requires an interpretation of what adjustments should be made to determine "normalized EBITDA";
- whether the offer is for the shares or net assets of the company. Where the offer is for the net assets of the company, the seller should obtain a list of assets to be acquired and liabilities to be assumed by the buyer. In addition, the seller should obtain an indication of how the aggregate purchase price will be allocated to the various asset classes acquired, as such allocation can have a material impact on the tax consequences to the seller (see Stage 6);

- the forms and terms of payment, including the amount of cash paid on closing, hold-back amounts, seller take-backs, and so on. If an earnout or similar arrangement is contemplated, then the basis of determining the amount and timing of payments thereunder should be specified;
- the salient provisions of any management contract, including estimated duration and basis of compensation (including salary, performance incentives and employment benefits);
- whether the offer is subject to financing, regulatory approval or other conditions;
- the length of time the buyer is granted to conduct its detailed due diligence and to negotiate the terms of the purchase agreement with the seller on an exclusive basis;
- significant balance sheet requirements, such as minimum working capital, net worth and debt levels;
- significant income statement or cash flow requirements, such as minimum levels of EBITDA and capital expenditures;
- the treatment of "stub-period earnings", being the income generated by the company between the date of the LOI and the time that the deal is closed (specifically whether stub-period earnings accrue to the benefit of the seller or the buyer). Generally, stub-period earnings considerations are a function of any minimum net worth requirements for the company;
- any significant or unusual representations and warranties that the seller will be asked to agree to; and
- the significant terms of a non-competition and non-solicitation agreement that the seller and possibly certain key employees will be asked to enter into.

Buyer Deposits

An issue that sometimes arises is whether the buyer should provide a deposit upon the seller's agreement to the LOI. From the seller's standpoint, a deposit against the purchase price provides some comfort that the buyer is serious about consummating a transaction and that it will not try to materially change the terms of the LOI without adequate justification. The seller also might argue that a deposit from the buyer is necessary to compensate the seller for the risks associated with revealing highly sensitive information where a transaction is not assured, and to compensate the seller for the opportunity cost of forgoing a possible transaction with another prospective buyer.

Not surprisingly, buyers are reluctant to provide deposits with an LOI, due to the risk from their perspective that a major issue will be discovered during the course of their detailed due diligence investigation, and that the deposit will not be recovered. Where a buyer does agree to provide a deposit, there must be a clear written understanding as to the terms of the deposit and the circumstances under which the buyer can recover it.

Expressions of Interest

As discussed in Section II, some intermediaries prefer to follow a formal auction process when selling a privately held company, although that path is not as common as an informal auction. Pursuant to a formal auction, buyers normally are requested to provide an "expression of interest" or similar document at an early stage of the sale process, based on a limited amount of information provided by the seller. The expression of interest provides the seller with an indication as to the buyer's initial view as to the price and terms of a deal. The seller then selects the buyers that have submitted the most attractive expressions of interest and restricts further discussions to those buyers.

While expressions of interest are similar to LOIs in that they are non-binding, they tend to be more vague than LOIs with respect to the terms of the deal and other pertinent factors because of the limited information that buyers have at this point on which to base their initial proposals. Further, it tends to be more difficult for the seller to demand that buyers provide greater detail in an expression of interest because of the limited information provided. Hence, the seller must beware that some buyers may purposefully inflate their value indications in an expression of interest so that they can "stay in the game", knowing (or expecting) that they will subsequently uncover information that will justify the retraction of their initial position.

Summary

Effective negotiations are fundamental to realizing value enhancement in the sale of a privately held company. The seller should strive to secure a comprehensive LOI that offers the best value combination in respect of the stated purchase price, the economic terms of the deal and the intangible aspects of the deal. This objective is more readily attained where a competitive bidding environment is created, and where the seller can be somewhat flexible with respect to the terms of the deal.

When preparing for negotiations, the seller and their advisors should agree on who will be directly involved in the negotiations and what should and should not be said. It is critical for the negotiating team to gather information that will help them better understand the needs, interests and negotiating position of the buyer and the seller.

Various strategies and tactics can be used when negotiating the price and terms of a deal. The strategies and tactics deployed should be considered in light of the principles of effective negotiation, which include: credibility is fundamental to maintaining a negotiating position; negotiating strength is a function of alternatives; and both the price and the terms of the deal are important.

The LOI is a key document that frequently does not get the degree of emphasis that it should. The negotiation of the LOI should coincide with the peak of deal momentum and should be used to maximize value enhancement realization. While the LOI is non-binding, once agreed to by the seller, it normally grants the buyer a period of exclusivity to complete its detailed due diligence investigation and negotiate the binding purchase agreement. The seller's negotiation position may be diminished after they afford exclusivity to a particular buyer. Therefore, prior to agreeing to an LOI, the seller must be comfortable that it sufficiently addresses all significant aspects of the deal. Furthermore, it is important that the seller be reasonably confident that the buyer will not uncover any previously undisclosed risks or issues facing the company in its detailed due diligence investigation that will cause the buyer to reconsider its proposal. When the seller agrees to an LOI, they should feel confident that it offers the best value attainable and that a purchase agreement will be struck with that buyer substantially on the terms set out therein.

SECTION III

Stage 8 | Closing

Introduction

Once the terms of a letter of intent (LOI) are agreed to between the seller and the buyer, the deal moves to the closing stage. As discussed in the previous stage, once the seller has granted exclusivity to the buyer (subject to certain agreed conditions in the LOI), the seller's negotiating position may diminish. This is because the competitive bidding process ends once the LOI is signed. If the buyer that was granted exclusivity does not ultimately consummate a transaction, the seller's negotiating position may be compromised where they must re-ignite discussions with another buyer.

During the closing stage, the seller's focus shifts from creating value enhancement to crystallizing the value enhancement realized throughout the sale process up to the LOI. The key to achieving this is for the seller to maintain their negotiating position once the competitive bidding process has ended and the buyer is granted a period of exclusivity.

Throughout the sale process, and including the closing stage, the seller should maintain a "business as usual" attitude, subject to any constraints imposed by the buyer. While it may be difficult for the seller to do so amidst all of the excitement and distractions of closing the deal, it is important that the seller operate their company in the normal course in order to sustain its value. The closing stage of the private company sale process normally takes between two to four months. Where the financial or operating results of the business are allowed to deteriorate during that period, it may provide justification for the buyer to re-negotiate the deal. Further, in the event that a deal is not struck with the imminent buyer, the financial and operational strength of the company will come into play when negotiations are re-ignited with other prospective buyers. Therefore, from the seller's perspective, it is preferable to reduce the time requirements of the closing stage where possible.

The closing stage of the private company sale process begins with the buyer conducting its detailed due diligence investigation on the company to satisfy itself that the offer set out in the LOI remains acceptable in light of all the known facts. Much of the buyer's detailed due diligence often is conducted in a "data room" located away from the seller's premises, in order to expedite the process and minimize disruptions within the company. The detailed due diligence period normally lasts between 30 and 90 days, as agreed to in the LOI. Concurrent with that process, and possibly extending for some time thereafter, the buyer and seller negotiate the purchase agreement and related agreements, such as the management contract and the non-competition agreement. Final closing normally takes place at an attorney's office, normally around 30 days following the date of the purchase agreement. After closing, there may be adjustments to the purchase price where an audit of the company's accounts uncovers a material discrepancy against the balance sheet targets or other defined performance measures that were agreed to at closing.

The closing stage of the private company sale process within the context of the *Value Enhancement Framework™* is depicted in Exhibit III-8-1.

Exhibit III-8-1

THE CLOSING STAGE WITHIN
THE *VALUE ENHANCEMENT FRAMEWORK*™

(i) Detailed Due Diligence

Detailed due diligence refers to the process of inquiry, inspection, review and analysis that the buyer undertakes in order to confirm the assumptions that it made about the company's cash flows, risks, growth prospects and synergy opportunities. The buyer will attempt to satisfy itself that the price and terms offered in the LOI remain justified, based on its more thorough understanding of the company. The seller should feel confident that the buyer's detailed due diligence simply will serve to confirm its facts and assumptions about the company, rather than providing material new information that would form the basis for re-opening negotiations.

The degree to which a buyer conducts its detailed due diligence may vary considerably in terms of the nature and the extent of the information that it believes is necessary to review. The depth of the buyer's detailed due diligence is influenced by the type of buyer (e.g., whether it is a strategic buyer, a financial buyer or other buyer – see Stage 4), its knowledge of the industry, its internal approval process and other factors.

The buyer's detailed due diligence normally consists of a comprehensive financial and operational review of the company and it usually involves a broader team of representatives than those that negotiated the deal on behalf of the buyer. This may include the buyer's:

- financial staff, who will review details of the company's assets, liabilities, revenues and expenses. These individuals often will develop comprehensive forecasting models in respect of the company's cash flows and the buyer's synergy expectations;
- in-house legal counsel, who will review the company's incorporation documents, minute books, contracts, tax assessments, leases and other documentation. These individuals normally are directly involved in drafting the purchase agreement and related agreements;
- operational personnel, including those with expertise in facilities management, information technology, engineering and other areas. These individuals will inspect and evaluate such things as the company's machinery and equipment, technology, software and R&D initiatives;
- marketing personnel, who will review the sales and marketing aspects of the company, such as its customer programs, sales channels, pricing policies, advertising commitments and related matters; and
- external consultants and advisors who assist the buyer's internal staff in conducting their detailed due diligence activities. This often includes accounting firms, external legal counsel and industry consultants.

It is important for the seller to thoroughly prepare for the buyer's detailed due diligence investigation by having the books and records of the company in proper order and to ensure that any disruptions caused by the process are minimal. To this end, much of the buyer's detailed due diligence may be conducted at an off-site location, such as a data room set up at the intermediary's offices, in order to avoid having the buyer's representatives present at the company's offices, thereby causing disruptions and potential concerns among the company's employees, customers and suppliers.

The business owner and company management should expect they will have to make a considerable time commitment to satisfy the buyer's due diligence requests. However, it is important to ensure that management's time (including that of the business owner) is not monopolized during the detailed due diligence investigation, thereby resulting in lost business opportunities.

Staging the Buyer's Detailed Due Diligence

The seller should control the flow of information to the buyer and control the buyer's access to the company's employees, customers and suppliers. During its detailed due diligence investigation, the buyer will have access to highly sensitive information about the company's operations, financial matters and business strategies. This may be of concern for the seller should the transaction not close, particularly where the buyer is a direct competitor, customer or supplier to the company. To militate against this risk, the detailed due diligence process may be done in stages, whereby the most sensitive information and investigative procedures are left until just prior to the final closing. This may include: access to information concerning customer-specific pricing strategies, details of proprietary software or technology and the buyer's access to the company's employees and customers.

With respect to accessing employees, customers and other parties, the seller should contact these individuals beforehand to make them aware of the nature and reason for the buyer's forthcoming call, and to ease any initial concerns they may have regarding the sale of the company. In some cases, the buyer's contact with certain parties, such as customers and suppliers, can be disguised as an independent "satisfaction survey" or similar type of program where the buyer and seller agree on such an approach.

Prior to granting a buyer access to the company's most sensitive information, the seller may ask the buyer for an affirmation statement. In an affirmation statement, the buyer confirms in writing to the seller that it has not found anything in its investigation to date that would cause it to change the terms of its LOI. If the buyer is unable or unwilling to issue such a statement when required, the seller is afforded the right to discontinue exclusive negotiations with that buyer. While an affirmation statement is non-binding, it provides the seller with some comfort that the basic terms of the deal will not be altered.

Not surprisingly, buyers are reluctant to agree to an affirmation statement requirement as it risks compromising their negotiating position. However, the seller might be able to negotiate for such a provision where, because of the nature of the buyer (e.g., a direct competitor) or the business itself (e.g., dependent on proprietary technological secrets), the company would be at greater risk in the event that the transaction does not close. The seller may also be able to negotiate for an affirmation statement where they have a strong negotiating position or where the buyer has requested a lengthy exclusivity period.

Once agreed to, the requirement for an affirmation statement and the timing thereof should be set out in the LOI.

The Exclusivity Time Period

The time period for conducting detailed due diligence and negotiating the purchase agreement on an exclusive basis is agreed to in the LOI, but the time period may be extended by mutual agreement between the buyer and the seller. That said, it is advisable for the seller to restrict the exclusivity period to a relatively short time frame because:

- most LOIs require the seller to operate the company "in the ordinary course" and preclude it from any major undertakings during the exclusivity period. A longer exclusivity period may result in missed opportunities because of these restrictions on business activities;
- a shorter exclusivity period will focus the buyer's attention on gathering the information it perceives as critical to the purchase decision, rather than getting mired with minor details that can become sticking points in the final negotiations;
- there is greater risk of an adverse change in business, industry and economic conditions with the passage of time. While these things may also give rise to upside potential for the seller, they usually are more concerned with the consequences of a material adverse development; and
- in the event that the buyer and seller discontinue their efforts toward closing, it is easier for the seller to re-ignite discussions with other prospects after a shorter passage of time.

(ii) The Purchase Agreement

During the course of the buyer's detailed due diligence investigation, and possibly for some time thereafter, the seller, buyer and their respective representatives will negotiate the terms of the purchase agreement. Related agreements are negotiated concurrently, such as the management contract (discussed in Stage 6), non-competition agreement (discussed below) and other agreements, as required. Legal counsel acting on behalf of the buyer usually drafts these agreements, which represent the legally binding contracts between the seller and buyer.

The purchase agreement is a comprehensive document (or set of documents) that addresses all aspects of the deal as negotiated between the parties. The seller and their lawyer, intermediary and other advisors (as appropriate) should carefully review the purchase agreement to ensure that it properly reflects the agreed terms of the deal and that it does not contain items not previously agreed to.

An unambiguous purchase agreement, that fully and clearly captures all agreed points of the transaction, will help to avoid costly legal disputes that can arise due to differing interpretations of matters that are not addressed or that are unclear. However, it is advisable to include a dispute resolution clause in the purchase agreement to ensure that disagreements can be settled expeditiously and in a more cost-effective manner than the traditional legal route. Mediation and/or binding arbitration sometimes are effective alternatives.

Ideally, the purchase agreement should reflect the price, terms and conditions set out in the agreed LOI. However, negotiation of the purchase agreement may be influenced by the buyer's findings in its detailed due diligence and by any material changes affecting the company, the industry or general economic conditions since the LOI was agreed to. The perception of the seller and the buyer as to their respective negotiating position and alternatives during the closing stage also influences the terms of the purchase agreement. Again, it is important for the seller to maintain alternatives available as far as is possible, but this does not mean entering into negotiations with another buyer, contrary to the terms of the LOI. Rather, the seller should be respectful of other buyers by tactfully informing them that other proposals are currently being entertained. In this way a window is left open should the seller wish to re-ignite discussions with those parties following the exclusivity period.

Throughout the closing stage, the seller should maintain a "business as usual" approach to the operations of their company. This will reduce the likelihood of inattention causing the company's operating results to decline, thereby opening the deal to re-negotiation. Sustaining the value of the company will reinforce the seller's negotiating position since the buyer is more likely to sense that the seller has viable alternatives in the event that the deal does not close. In some cases, focusing on the operations of the company may create an opportunity for the seller to negotiate an even better deal than was set out in the LOI. This may be the case where the company secures a significant new contract during the closing stage, the impact of which had not been factored into the LOI.

Representations and Warranties

The seller and their team of advisors should pay particular attention to the representations and warranties set out in the purchase agreement. Representations and warranties are assurances that the seller and the buyer provide to each other and that could give rise to substantial liability in the event that they are breached. Representations and warranties commonly made by the seller include:

- that the seller owns the shares of the company and that there are no restrictions on their disposition;
- there are no liabilities, contingencies, commitments, obligations, or legal claims against the company other than what has been disclosed to the buyer; and
- the company has no environmental liabilities other than those disclosed to the buyer.

The seller normally requires representations and warranties of the buyer in respect of liabilities that arise after the transaction is completed. In this regard, the seller should be satisfied that the buyer has the financial resources to fulfill its commitments, if necessary.

An important distinction must be made in the level of assurance granted by the seller with respect to representations and warranties, that is, whether they are made on a "best of knowledge" or "absolute knowledge" basis. When made on a best of knowledge basis, it is incumbent upon the buyer to demonstrate that the seller knew about a particular issue in order for a breach of the seller's warranty or representation to be enforced. Conversely, where the seller offers absolute assurance, there is liability for a breach regardless of whether they knew of the matter at the time. Therefore, the risk that the seller undertakes in offering absolute assurance may be considerably greater.

In some cases, the buyer will insist that a portion of the purchase price be placed in escrow for a period of time to ensure that the seller can compensate the buyer (at least in part) where the seller's representations and warranties are breached. It is important for the seller to recognize that, depending on the terms of the purchase agreement, their liability may extend beyond any escrow amounts, and may have dire personal consequences.

In the end, the seller should view representations and warranties, including whether they are granted on a best of knowledge or an absolute knowledge basis, as an integral component of the overall deal. The seller should be satisfied that the prospective rewards of the deal offset the risks that are involved.

Purchase Price Adjustments

There are three time frames where adjustments to the stated purchase price may arise, and which should be addressed when negotiating the purchase agreement. They are:

- between the date that the LOI is agreed to and the date of the purchase agreement;
- between the date of the purchase agreement and the final closing date of the transaction; and
- following the closing date of the transaction.

Purchase price adjustments commonly arise because specified performance targets were either under-achieved or over-achieved. This often includes balance sheet targets in respect of the company's net working capital and/or net worth requirements (see Stage 3). For example, if the purchase agreement required the company's net worth to be no less than $5 million at the closing date and a subsequent audit revealed that its net worth actually was $4.8 million, the purchase price would be reduced by $200,000 (likely by virtue of a reduction to the hold-back amount paid to the seller). Purchase price adjustments may also be required where the buyer discovers previously undisclosed liabilities against the company or where the buyer is unable to realize on certain assets (such as accounts receivable) within an agreed period following the closing date.

It is important that the purchase agreement clearly specify the conditions giving rise to a purchase price adjustment and that it be specific on how such adjustments are to be quantified. In this regard, the seller should strive to ensure that the purchase agreement allows for an upward adjustment where agreed targets are exceeded and that the tax consequences of adjustments are considered. It also is important to ensure that adjustments are not double-counted by virtue of how multiple targets are defined. These issues were discussed in Stage 3.

Other reasons for purchase price adjustments relate to conversion rates for shares or currency. For example, where the seller agrees to a share exchange with a public company buyer, the value of the deal will depend on the buyer's share price at the closing date of the transaction. Given fluctuations that may occur in the buyer's share price after the date of the purchase agreement (which would specify the number of shares tentatively to be issued to the seller), the buyer and seller should agree on the adjusting calculation for the number of shares issued in the event that the buyer's share price falls outside of an acceptable range at the closing date. For example, assume that the purchase agreement indicates a price of $10 million for the company to be satisfied through the issuance of 400,000 shares of the buyer's company based on their trading price of $25 per share at the date of the purchase agreement. If at the closing date of the transaction, the buyer's share price had fallen to $20, the seller should expect to receive 500,000 shares in order to preserve the $10 million purchase price. Similarly, where the seller accepts a deal denominated in U.S. dollars or some other foreign currency, adjustments should be made where foreign exchange conversion rates fall outside of an acceptable range.

Why Deals Fail to Close

Common reasons that buyers and sellers do not come to terms on the purchase agreement after agreeing to an LOI include:

- entering into detailed negotiations with vastly different expectations because the terms of the deal as set out in the LOI were too vague. This reinforces the importance for the seller to obtain a comprehensive LOI that clearly addresses all of the significant terms and conditions of the offer;
- where the buyer's detailed due diligence uncovers one or more previously unidentified issues that negatively impacts its view of the company or the risks involved in a transaction. Sometimes the discoveries are such that the buyer is not willing to consummate a transaction under any terms. This reinforces the importance for the seller to ensure that all material issues, risks and weaknesses facing the company are adequately disclosed and addressed prior to the execution of the LOI;
- a material change in the company between the time the LOI is agreed to and the time the purchase agreement is negotiated. For example, the loss of a major customer or severe product quality issues might cause the buyer to reconsider its offer. This reinforces the importance that the seller adopt a business as usual attitude during the closing stage; and
- external circumstances beyond the control of the buyer and seller, such as extreme social, political and economic developments that cause the buyer to place its major investment decisions on hold pending the outcome of these conditions. This reinforces the importance that the seller strive for a

relatively short exclusivity and closing period, to reduce the possibility that such events will occur.

The common reasons for deals failing to close after the LOI is agreed to, and what the seller can do to prevent those things from happening, are summarized in Exhibit III-8-2.

Exhibit III-8-2

COMMON REASONS FOR DEALS FAILING TO CLOSE

Reason for Deal Failure	Possible Remedy
Unclear understanding prior to detailed negotiations	Obtain an unambiguous, comprehensive LOI
New issues uncovered in the buyer's detailed due diligence	Address all issues, risks and weaknesses prior to the LOI
Material adverse change in the company's operations	Adopt a "business as usual" attitude in the closing stage
External circumstances beyond the seller's control	Negotiate a relatively short exclusivity time period

Non-competition Agreements

Most buyers will insist that the seller enter into a non-competition agreement concurrent with the closing of the transaction, regardless of whether they were actively involved in the company prior to the sale. The provisions of the non-competition agreement can have a significant influence on the intangible aspects of value received by the seller. Non-competition agreements normally are tied into management contracts for active shareholders, which were discussed in Stage 6.

The contents of the non-competition agreement revolve around three main parameters, being the:

- scope of the prohibited activities. The seller normally is prohibited from working with a competitor to the company for a period of time in any capacity, including as an employee, owner or consultant. Further, the seller normally is prohibited from having a material financial interest in a competitor. It is important that the scope of the prohibited activities be clearly defined to avoid disagreements should the seller seek work following the

transaction in a related type of business, such as a supplier or customer to the company or in a related industry. In some cases, in order to avoid any doubt, the non-competition agreement specifies the companies that the seller is not permitted to be involved with following the transaction;
- duration of the non-competition agreement. A period of one to five years is not uncommon. The time period normally begins following the closing of the transaction and takes into account the period of any post-transaction management contract; and
- geographic area to which the restrictions apply, which may range anywhere from a local or regional basis to Canada-wide or worldwide. The geographic element of the non-competition agreement normally takes into account the nature of the company, the type of goods and services being sold and the location of the company's customer base.

Prior to entering into a non-competition agreement, the seller should carefully reflect on what they plan to do following the sale of their company. Where the seller anticipates actively pursuing other business opportunities within the same or related industry, they must ensure that nothing in the non-competition agreement would disrupt those intentions. In order to avoid any misunderstandings later in the sale process, if a fairly unrestrictive non-competition agreement is desired, the seller should disclose this at a relatively early stage in the discussions with prospective buyers.

In some cases, a portion of the purchase price is allocated specifically to the non-competition agreement on the basis that it causes the non-competition agreement to be more easily enforced. The seller and their income tax advisor must consider the tax consequences of such an arrangement. If not properly structured, payments received under a non-competition agreement may be taxed as ordinary income to the seller. As noted in Stage 6, it is advisable for the seller to obtain expert income tax advice to ensure a tax-efficient deal structure.

In some cases, the buyer will ask that the seller enter into a separate non-solicitation agreement, whereby the seller is prohibited from soliciting the company's customers and employees for a period of time following the transaction. While a separate non-solicitation agreement may seem redundant, it provides the buyer with an alternative legal mechanism in the event that certain provisions of the non-competition agreement prove unenforceable.

(iii) Final Closing

The final closing of the transaction normally takes place at an attorney's office, usually within about 30 days of the purchase agreement being finalized. At that time, share certificates and the cash amount due on closing are transferred (as applicable) and the sale of the company is complete.

In some cases, the buyer and seller engage in last-minute negotiations on items that either had not been included in the purchase agreement or where the buyer or seller want to change one or more provisions included therein. In unusual circumstances, these last minute negotiations may delay, or even prevent, the closing of the deal. It generally is advisable for the seller to avoid last minute negotiations where possible. It also is advisable that the closing be completed without undue delay, in order to reduce the possibility of factors arising that could lead to re-negotiation or affect the closing. For example, the purchase agreement normally specifies that closing may be affected by a material adverse change, such as an extreme and unusual economic, political or social event, the risk of which increases with the passage of time.

Post-closing Audit

A post-closing audit of the company's accounts normally begins shortly after the closing date of the transaction. The purpose of the audit, which normally is conducted by the buyer's external accountants, is to verify the accuracy and completeness of the assets, liabilities and balance sheet targets (and other agreed performance targets) of the company as of the closing date. Where excesses or deficiencies are uncovered, there may be an adjustment to the purchase price in accordance with the terms of the purchase agreement.

The seller should feel reasonably confident that no technical accounting issues will arise in the post-closing audit that will result in an unexpected reduction to the purchase price. Therefore, it usually is advisable for the seller to requisition an audit (or at least a review) of their company's financial statements prior to the time that their company is exposed for sale in the open market. It also is important for the seller to be aware of the terms of the post-closing audit. For example, for the purpose of the post-closing audit, the buyer might insist that the company's financial accounting policies be aligned with its own or that the company's financial statements be prepared in accordance with U.S. accounting standards rather than Canadian standards. Depending on the accounting policies adopted by the company, provisions such as these can result in substantial purchase price adjustments. This reinforces the importance for the seller to have a competent financial advisor review the purchase agreement before it is finalized.

Summary

During the closing stage of the private company sale process, the seller's focus shifts from creating value enhancement to crystallizing the value that has been created from the planning phase through to the LOI. To be effective, the seller must maintain their negotiating position in circumstances where the competitive bidding process has ended and the buyer is granted a period of exclusivity. The seller's negotiating position can be maintained where they keep alternatives available and sustain the value of their company throughout the closing stage. These things serve to reduce the likelihood that a buyer will try to re-negotiate the deal and to facilitate re-igniting discussions with other prospective buyers in the event that a deal with the imminent buyer does not close.

Following an agreed LOI, the buyer will undertake its detailed due diligence investigation in order to satisfy itself that the terms of the proposed deal are satisfactory in light of all the known facts. The seller should maintain a "business as usual" attitude in the closing stage and strive to keep the buyer's exclusivity period relatively short in order to decrease the likelihood of adverse changes occurring during that time. Further, the seller should feel reasonably assured that the LOI clearly addresses all significant aspects of the deal and that there are no material issues, weaknesses or risks faced by the company which were not disclosed to the buyer prior to the LOI.

The purchase agreement represents the binding contract between the buyer and seller. The seller and their team of advisors should ensure that the purchase agreement fully documents all aspects of the deal and that the seller is not being burdened with unforeseen risks through the representations and warranties being sought by the buyer. It also is important that the purchase agreement clearly set out the basis for any purchase price adjustments arising from such things as balance sheet targets, fluctuating share prices and foreign exchange rates. Concurrent with the purchase agreement, the buyer and seller will finalize other agreements, including the management contract and non-competition agreement. The non-competition agreement will detail the seller's restrictions as to the scope, time period and geographic area in which they are prohibited from engaging in competitive activities. Non-competition agreements, non-solicitation agreements and management contracts should be carefully reviewed, as these things can have a material impact on both the economic terms of the deal and the intangible aspects of value.

The final closing of the transaction normally takes place within a few weeks following the date of the purchase agreement. Ideally, there should be no last-minute changes or re-negotiations. A post-closing audit is conducted in the ensuing weeks or months, which may give rise to purchase price adjustments in respect of the company's assets, liabilities, balance sheet targets and other agreed performance measures at the closing date. At this point, the sale process is complete and the seller can begin to enjoy the value that has been realized.

Value Enhancement Planning and Execution

Section IV

SECTION IV

Value Enhancement Planning and Execution

Introduction

The sale of a privately held company is a time-consuming and complex process. Ideally, business owners should plan for the sale at least one to three years before their company is exposed to the open market. During that time, the business owner should be considering when to sell their company, preparing for the sale and obtaining an estimate of the company's equity value and the price that a buyer might be willing to pay. Thereafter, it generally takes about six months to a year (or longer) to execute the sale of the company from the time that the search for buyers begins, through the stages of preliminary due diligence, deal structuring and negotiations, to closing.

While this book has discussed the private company sale process as a series of stages and components, it is important to recognize that these stages and components overlap. Therefore, each must be considered in the context of the whole and with the end objective of securing a deal that offers the best value to the business owner. The seller and their intermediary should set the foundation for deal momentum in the planning phase and build momentum throughout the execution phase of the private company sale process. Ideally, deal momentum will peak upon the signing of the LOI, and remain at that level through to closing.

The ability to create and realize value enhancement in the private company sale process is a function of adequate planning and effective execution. The foundation for value enhancement creation is set in the planning phase. This includes selecting a time to sell that coincides with favourable personal and business conditions, structuring the affairs of the company to increase its attractiveness to buyers, and identifying and undertaking initiatives that increase the intrinsic and strategic equity value of the company. Value enhancement is realized in the execution phase by attracting a sufficient number of qualified prospective buyers to create the platform for an effective auction and then controlling the flow of information to increase the perceived value of the company among buyers. Each proposal should be evaluated based on its risk-reward parameters and tax-efficiency to the seller, and a comprehensive letter of intent (LOI) that offers the best value to the business owner should be secured. The seller's negotiating position must be maintained in the closing stage to crystallize the value enhancement that has been created throughout the sale process.

Value ultimately is in the eyes of the business owner. It not only incorporates the stated purchase price, but also the terms of the deal, which influence both the economic and intangible aspects of value that are unique to every business owner. In this regard, it is important for the business owner to recognize that the stated purchase price and the terms of the deal are inter-related, and they cannot be viewed in isolation when evaluating offers that are received for the purchase of their company.

Business owners and their team of advisors can make common mistakes when selling a privately held company which can result in compromising the value that might otherwise be realized upon the sale. Some of these common mistakes are discussed in this Section.

The Private Company Sale Process and Deal Momentum

Two concepts that were introduced early in this book are briefly discussed again here in order to reinforce their importance to the overall objective of value enhancement. These concepts are: the integration of the stages and components of the private company sale process; and deal momentum.

The private company sale process was introduced in Section I. While the process has been discussed in this book as a series of stages and components, it is important to recognize that those stages and components do overlap and they cannot be viewed in isolation. This concept is illustrated in Exhibit IV-1.

Exhibit IV-1

THE PRIVATE COMPANY SALE PROCESS:
AN INTEGRATED VIEWPOINT

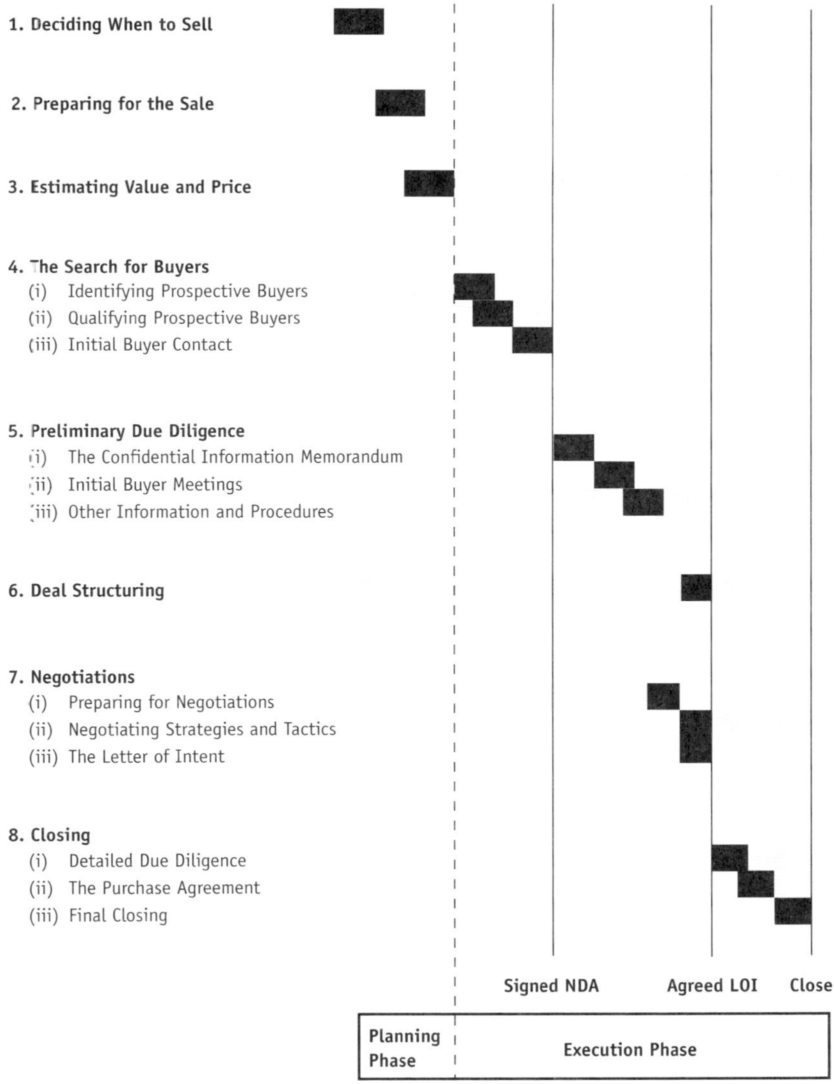

As evidenced in Exhibit IV-1, there is considerable overlap in several stages of the sale process. For example, while estimating value and price is formally addressed as part of the planning phase, the underlying principles and processes of that stage extend from deciding when to sell through to the closing of the deal. Similarly, while the deal structuring stage is concurrent with negotiations, deal structuring considerations should commence in the planning phase, and they extend through to closing. Preparing for negotiations commences when prospective buyers are first being identified, qualified and contacted. Finally, negotiating strategies and tactics are not only used when negotiating the LOI, but also when negotiating the purchase agreement and closing the deal.

Section II introduced the concept of building momentum in the private company sale process. The extent to which value enhancement can be achieved is governed by the ability of the seller and their team of advisors to create a strong foundation for value enhancement in the planning phase and to build upon that foundation in the execution phase. Ideally, the momentum for value enhancement should peak at the signing of the LOI (in the negotiations stage) and remain at that level through to closing, in order to crystallize the value enhancement generated throughout the sale process. This concept is illustrated in Exhibit IV-2.

Exhibit IV-2

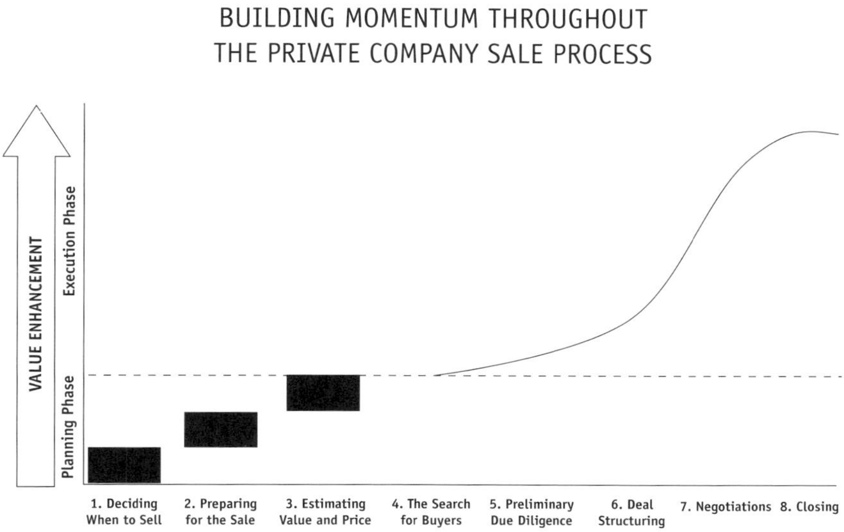

Summary of the *Value Enhancement Framework™*

As explained in previous Sections, value enhancement is achieved through a combination of adequate planning and effective execution. This section reviews the key points to value enhancement in each stage of the private company sale process, which were discussed throughout this book and are summarized in the *Value Enhancement Framework™* in Exhibit IV-3.

Exhibit IV-3

THE *VALUE ENHANCEMENT FRAMEWORK*™

The Planning Phase

Stage 1 — Deciding when to sell

The first stage in the planning phase of the private company sale process is for the business owner to decide when to sell their company. Value enhancement opportunities are created where the timing of the sale coincides with favourable conditions in terms of the owner's personal situation, economic and industry conditions and the company's recent and prospective operating performance.

The business owner should consider their own personal interests, financial position, general health and life goals in an overall context when deciding whether and when to sell their company. Where the owner is willing to remain with the company for a period of time following the sale, this will serve to diminish the concerns that some buyers may have regarding the ability to effectively transition the company.

Prices paid for privately held companies tend to be higher when economic and industry conditions are favourable. Because a greater number of buyers will have an interest and the ability to consummate a transaction during a favourable business climate, this will lead to greater liquidity in the market and consequently greater value enhancement opportunities for business owners. Prices paid for companies during a period of industry consolidation can be particularly attractive due to the competitive bidding environment that is created.

Companies able to demonstrate strong historical and prospective operating and financial performance also tend to be more saleable and fetch higher prices. Strong recent performance normally gives buyers greater comfort about the company's ability to achieve future results.

Stage 2 — Preparing for the sale

Once the decision to sell has been made, the business owner should begin preparing for the sale. Value enhancement opportunities reside in the ability of the owner and their team of advisors to structure the affairs of the company to increase its attractiveness to buyers. Preparing for the sale also involves income tax and estate planning for the business owner and engaging transaction advisors.

Structuring the operational and financial affairs of the company includes the removal of redundant assets, ensuring that contracts and records of the company are in proper order, hiring, replacing and terminating managers and employees as required, and undertaking initiatives that will make the operations appear orderly and efficient. Importantly, business owners should focus on structuring initiatives that will cause buyers to perceive that their company has a sustainable competitive advantage, while being conscious of the costs to implement such initiatives. A sustainable competitive advantage may come from the company's products and services, its technology, customer base, internal processes or other areas where the company can distinguish itself as offering something to a buyer that cannot be easily replicated. Further, business owners should consider undertaking initiatives that offer buyers flexibility when integrating the company with their existing operations so as to raise their perceived ability to readily achieve post-acquisition synergies.

Personal income tax and estate planning initiatives should be designed to facilitate the transition of ownership and to afford the business owner flexibility in structuring a deal with prospective buyers on a tax-efficient basis. Personal income tax and estate planning for the owner and their family need not wait until the company is being prepared for sale. Conversely, such initiatives should be undertaken whether or not the owner has decided to sell their company, in order to react to issues and take advantage of opportunities that might arise unexpectedly.

Finally, the business owner should engage a lawyer, tax advisor, intermediary and other advisors to assist them in preparing for and eventually executing the sale of their company. It is important that the advisors who are retained be knowledgeable and experienced in the sale of privately held Canadian companies, and that they have a reputation for providing business owners with well-considered, objective advice. The business owner should appoint one advisor, usually the intermediary, to co-ordinate the efforts among the team of advisors and to champion the sale process.

Stage 3 — Estimating value and price

When preparing for the sale, and sometimes in deciding when to sell, business owners want to know the value of their company and the price that it might fetch in the open market. While these things cannot be answered with certainty, an independent valuation can lead to value enhancement opportunities by helping the business owner to identify and undertake initiatives to increase the intrinsic and strategic equity value of the company prior to the time that it is actively marketed for sale. These things relate to initiatives that positively influence the prospective discretionary cash flows of the company, the rates of return (or valuation multiples) applied thereto and the company's financial position.

Buyers of privately held companies are most interested in the amount of discretionary cash flow that a company will generate in the future. Discretionary cash flow is calculated as the company's revenues less cash operating costs, cash income taxes, capital expenditure requirements and incremental working capital requirements. Accordingly, all of these variables must be taken into account when determining whether or not to undertake an initiative in an effort to increase the equity value of the company.

The rates of return and valuation multiples applied to the cash flows are a function of the perceived risk levels, growth opportunities and debt capacity of the company. To the extent that the business owner can undertake initiatives to improve on these variables prior to sale, the equity value of the company can be increased. However, it is important to note that rates of return (or valuation multiples) and the cash flows to which they are applied are inter-related. As such, cash flow and rates of return must be considered in tandem.

The financial position of the company refers to its assets and liabilities. Financial liabilities (including interest-bearing debt and equivalent amounts) are deducted from the company's enterprise value to determine its equity value, being the value of its overlying shares or underlying net assets, which is of primary interest to the business owner. Further adjustments to enterprise value may be required where there is an excessive or deficient amount of net operating assets or where redundant assets exist. The company's equity value can be increased through effective asset and liability management in the years prior to the sale.

The Execution Phase

Stage 4 — The search for buyers

With the commencement of the execution phase, the business owner transitions from being an operator of the company (either passively or actively) to a seller. The key to value enhancement in the execution phase is to build the momentum of the deal. This is achieved by creating an effective auction for the company. The platform for creating an effective auction is established by attracting a sufficient number of qualified buyers who have the interest and the ability to complete a transaction on terms satisfactory to the seller.

In terms of identifying prospective buyers, the seller should consider a full spectrum of possibilities. Prospective buyers may exist among direct competitors, customers, suppliers, related industry groups, financial buyers and possibly even company management and third party individuals. When identifying prospective buyers, the seller should consider what the company has to offer in terms of its intangible assets (e.g., its customer base and proprietary technology) and how buyers are likely to perceive the potential to achieve a competitive advantage through buying the company.

Preliminary research is important to determine which of the identified buyers represent qualified prospects. The seller should assess each buyer's interests and motivations, as well as the types and quantum of synergies each buyer might perceive to be attainable through an acquisition. This allows the seller to rank prospective buyers and to modify the approach taken with each.

Initial contact with prospective buyers is best done directly, such as by telephone. A well-scripted initial dialogue is more likely to secure a prospective buyer's interest than a generic e-mail message. Further, direct contact by the intermediary may provide a base of information that can prove invaluable in subsequent discussions and negotiations with that buyer. The acquisition profile should be designed to highlight the attractive elements of the acquisition opportunity, while not revealing the identity of the company until the buyer has agreed to execute a non-disclosure agreement (NDA).

Stage 5 — Preliminary due diligence

Buyers who execute a satisfactory NDA are invited to conduct preliminary due diligence on the company. The key to value enhancement in the preliminary due diligence stage is for the seller to control the flow of information to increase the perceived value of their company among buyers. This is done through the confidential information memorandum, initial buyer meetings and the manner in which information is conveyed.

The confidential information memorandum normally is the first document that a buyer receives containing non-public information about the company. Therefore, it is important that the content and presentation of the confidential information memorandum be well thought out so as to effectively convey the attractive elements of the company. Caution should be used so as not to divulge highly sensitive information too early, in the event that a particular buyer is not interested in proceeding further.

The seller should establish the protocol for initial meetings with prospective buyers beforehand so that the focus of such meetings remains on determining whether there is a fit between the buyer and the company, as opposed to discussing the price and terms of a deal at this point. The seller should use the initial meetings to portray the company's strengths and opportunities, as well as to discuss the company's weaknesses and risks. These latter things are important in order to manage the concerns that a buyer may have about the company and to ensure that such issues do not come to light only after an LOI has been agreed to.

The seller should control the flow of other preliminary due diligence information and procedures so as to create a "give-and-take" atmosphere with the buyer. This allows the seller to gather important information on each buyer's interests and motivations, which will become important during the negotiations.

Stage 6 — Deal structuring

The structure of the deal is fundamental to the value received by the seller. The realization of value enhancement rests in evaluating each proposal based on its risk-reward parameters and tax-efficiency to the seller. Offers should be compared on a cash-equivalent basis, taking into account the risk of whether the proceeds will be realized and the timing thereof. Deal structuring involves whether the shares or the net assets of the company are sold, the forms and terms of payment and the terms of the management contract.

Sellers generally prefer to sell the shares of their company due to the income tax advantages available to them in doing so. Buyers tend to prefer to buy assets due to the advantages to them in terms of taxation and the avoidance of undisclosed liabilities. Therefore, buyers often are willing to pay a higher price for the underlying net assets of a privately held company as opposed to its overlying shares. When assessing whether to sell the shares or the net assets of their company, the seller should consider the after-tax proceeds that would be generated based on each alternative. In addition, when assessing an offer for the net assets, the seller should consider the specific assets being acquired and the specific liabilities the buyer will assume in order to assess the equity value implied by the offer.

The forms and terms of payment can include cash on closing, hold-backs, vendor take-backs, share exchanges, earnouts and similar types of arrangements. Any amounts not received in the form of cash on closing are subject to risk. The seller should be satisfied that the rewards, in terms of a potentially higher purchase price, are sufficient in light of the risks that are assumed by agreeing to accept some or all of the purchase price in the form of non-cash consideration. The seller and their team of advisors also should carefully consider the tax implications of accepting non-cash forms of consideration and the availability of tax planning opportunities.

The management contract establishes the roles and responsibilities of the seller for a period of time following the transaction. The seller should reflect on the parameters of suitable post-transaction arrangements during the planning phase of the sale process. The terms of the management contract play into the intangible aspects of the value realized by the business owner, as well as the economic value received for the company where a portion of the purchase price effectively is embedded in post-transaction remuneration levels.

Stage 7 — Negotiations

In spite of all the financial analysis that may be conducted to estimate the value of a privately held company, the price and terms agreed to between the buyer and seller are determined through negotiation. The key to value enhancement in the negotiations stage is to secure a comprehensive LOI that offers the best value to the business owner. Value is a function of the stated purchase price, the economic terms of the deal and the intangible aspects of the deal. Securing a favourable LOI is facilitated by creating a competitive bidding environment and in the seller remaining flexible regarding the terms of the deal.

Preparation for negotiations is essential in order to understand the interests and motivations of each buyer and the negotiating position of the buyer and seller. Research and information are fundamental to effective negotiations. It also is important for the seller and their team of advisors to agree at the outset who will be directly involved in the negotiations and what will, and will not, be said.

The negotiating strategies and tactics that are used by the seller's negotiating representatives should be determined in reference to the perceived relative negotiating positions of the buyer and the seller. Negotiating position is a function of the number and quality of alternatives available to each of the buyer and the seller and the need and desire of each party to transact. It is important for the seller to maintain their credibility throughout the negotiations and to focus on both the terms of the deal as well as the price to ensure that value enhancement is realized.

Negotiating the LOI represents the height of the seller's negotiating leverage in the effective auction. It is of fundamental importance that the seller strives to secure a comprehensive, unambiguous LOI that clearly addresses all of the major aspects of the proposed deal. While buyers normally will resist submitting a detailed proposal at this stage, the seller should recognize that any aspects of the deal not clearly set out in the LOI are subject to negotiation once the buyer has been granted a period of exclusivity. At this point, the seller's negotiating position may be diminished.

Stage 8 — Closing

Following an agreed LOI, the seller's focus shifts from building value enhancement to crystallizing the value that has been created throughout the sale process. The key in this regard is for the seller to maintain their negotiating position through the closing stage when the competitive bidding process has ended and one buyer is granted exclusivity to finalize the deal with the seller. It is preferable for the seller to negotiate a relatively short exclusivity period where possible, in order to reduce the likelihood of developments that adversely affect the company, its industry or the economy.

During its detailed due diligence investigation, the buyer will perform a comprehensive review of the company's operations and financial results in order to satisfy itself that the offer as set out in the LOI remains acceptable. The seller should be reasonably certain that the buyer will not uncover any negative surprises that would provide it with justification to re-negotiate the deal.

The purchase agreement represents the binding contract between the buyer and seller. The seller and their team of advisors should ensure that the purchase agreement accurately reflects all aspects of the transaction that are agreed to. The seller must carefully consider the provisions dealing with representations and warranties and purchase price adjustments, as these may materially impact the value received for the company.

The final closing of the transaction normally takes place at an attorney's office within a few weeks following the signing of the purchase agreement. From the seller's perspective, it is advisable to avoid last-minute negotiations that could materially affect the deal. In this regard, it is important that the seller adopts a "business as usual" attitude in order to avoid a situation where inattention causes the company's operating results to decline, thereby affording the buyer justification to re-negotiate the deal. Further, the seller should sustain the value of their company in the event that negotiations must be re-opened with another buyer. Following the closing date, a final audit is conducted to verify the financial accounts of the company, which may result in an adjustment to the purchase price. The seller should be satisfied that adverse accounting issues are unlikely to arise.

Common Mistakes When Selling a Privately Held Company

In the course of selling their privately held company, business owners and their advisors sometimes do certain things, or fail to do certain things, that cause them to miss out on opportunities for value enhancement creation and realization. Some of the more common mistakes that are made at each stage of the private company sale process and how they might be avoided are set out in Exhibit IV-4.

Exhibit IV-4

COMMON MISTAKES MADE WHEN SELLING A PRIVATELY HELD COMPANY AND POSSIBLE RESOLUTIONS

Common Mistakes	Possible Resolution
Stage 1 — Deciding When to Sell	
Waiting until retirement before beginning the sale process. Buyers often are wary about the ability to effect a smooth transition where the business owner who was actively involved in the company is not prepared to enter into a meaningful management contract following the sale. This can result in the buyer offering a substantially reduced purchase price, less attractive terms of the deal, and possibly withdrawing its offer altogether. Alternatively, the business owner may have to defer their personal goals and compromise the intangible aspects of value where an onerous management contract is entered into.	The business owner should remove themself from the company gradually in the years prior to the sale and also ensure that the company has a management team in place that can effect a smooth transition.

Common Mistakes	Possible Resolution
Missing out on an industry consolidation opportunity. When an industry is going through a period of consolidation, business owners sometimes believe that they will fetch a higher premium for their company the longer they wait. However, valuation multiples often decline near the end of the consolidation period.	Business owners should keep themselves abreast of transactions occurring in their industry and keep their personal and company affairs up to date so that they can react to opportunities that may arise unexpectedly.
Delaying the sale of the company in an effort to realize one more year of growth. This can prove detrimental where expected growth does not materialize or, alternatively, adverse developments in the company, the industry or the economy cause the timing of the sale to be less favourable than previously was the case.	Business owners should understand the basic components of business valuation and reflect on the underlying drivers of their company's equity value when considering the timing of a sale.
Stage 2 — Preparing for the Sale	
Decreasing spending on important operational initiatives in the years prior to sale. Business owners sometimes cut expenses that are believed to have no immediate payback, such as advertising and R&D, to inflate cash flows and earnings in the years prior to sale. Buyers usually detect such things in the course of their due diligence and adjust the price and terms of their offer accordingly.	Business owners should focus on doing those things that will cause buyers to perceive their company as an attractive investment opportunity with a sustainable competitive advantage. However, expenses that truly are discretionary in nature and not essential to the operations of the company should be curtailed.

Common Mistakes	Possible Resolution
Missing out on income tax and estate planning opportunities by not undertaking such initiatives on a regular basis. This situation is particularly acute where the company must be sold quickly due to a sudden change in circumstances (such as failing health) or an unsolicited offer.	Business owners should regularly review their personal affairs and be proactive in income tax and estate planning.
Not retaining competent, objective advisors. Business owners sometimes are reluctant to retain advisors to assist them when preparing for and selling their company for such reasons as the costs involved, confidentiality issues, and the belief that they can manage the process better themselves.	Business owners should find and retain competent, experienced advisors to assist them in preparing for and executing the sale of their company, with a view that such advisors should effectively "pay for themselves" through the value enhancement initiatives they bring to the private company sale process. One advisor, normally the intermediary, should be appointed to coordinate efforts among the business owner's team of advisors.
Stage 3 — Estimating Value and Price	
Failing to understand the underlying determinants of economic value. This causes business owners to have unrealistic price expectations and hence failing to capitalize on an offer that would afford the business owner good value for their company.	Business owners should obtain an independent valuation and consider the initiatives that will increase the company's intrinsic and strategic equity value prior to the time it is exposed for sale in the open market.
Failing to recognize the relationship between cash flow and risk. This causes business owners to undertake initiatives prior to sale that may offer good growth potential, but fundamentally changes the risk profile of the company.	Business owners should consider cash flows and risks in tandem when making decisions that impact the equity value of their company.

Common Mistakes	Possible Resolution
Focusing only on the income statement. This can lead to adverse purchase price adjustments when balance sheet targets are not achieved. Further, business owners sometimes fail to realize that most sophisticated buyers take into account working capital and capital expenditure requirements when determining the value of a company.	Business owners should monitor and manage the assets and liabilities of their company to increase its equity value prior to the time it is exposed for sale in the open market.
Stage 4 — The Search for Buyers	
Restricting the search to only one or a few buyers. This diminishes the ability of the seller to create an effective auction.	Sellers should think broadly about what their company has to offer in terms of its intangible attributes and the types of buyers that would perceive an opportunity to realize a sustainable competitive advantage through an acquisition.
Conducting insufficient preliminary research. This causes the seller to be unable to determine which buyers represent qualified prospects and how they should be approached.	Adequate preliminary research should be done to help the seller in attracting a larger number of qualified prospects and to avoid spending a lot of time and resources on buyers that are unlikely to consummate a transaction on reasonable terms.
Soliciting prospective buyers in a way that does not capture their initial interest. For example, sending out web broadcasts or generic faxes, which often are ignored by qualified prospects.	The intermediary should initiate direct contact with prospective buyers and tailor the message to highlight features of the company that may be of particular interest to each.

Common Mistakes	Possible Resolution
Stage 5 — Preliminary Due Diligence	
Disclosing highly sensitive information at an early stage in the sale process. This can be harmful to the company where a particular buyer is a competitor, customer, or supplier and does not proceed with a transaction.	The seller should disclose information to buyers gradually and in summary form where details can be verified by a buyer during its detailed due diligence investigation.
Failing to address the company's weaknesses and threats up front. This can prove detrimental when a buyer detects these things following the agreed LOI.	The seller should candidly address the weaknesses and threats facing their company, with an emphasis on how these things are being managed and how they may represent opportunities for the buyer.
Allowing the preliminary due diligence process to become a one-way street. This happens when information is not gathered on the buyer's interests, motivations, synergies and so on.	The seller should control the flow of information and create a "give and take" atmosphere with prospective buyers. This serves to increase the perceived value of the company among prospective buyers and provides the seller with a base of information that can be used in the negotiations.
Stage 6 — Deal Structuring	
Over-emphasizing the stated purchase price. This is a lack of recognition that the terms of the deal are just as important (and perhaps more important) than the price that ultimately may be paid.	The seller should consider when, how and under what conditions the purchase price will be paid, and should recognize that any portion of the purchase price not received in the form of cash on closing is subject to the risk of non-realization. The prospective rewards to the seller must offset the risks.
Failing to recognize the income tax implications of an offer. This can significantly erode the amount of proceeds retained by the seller.	The seller should engage competent professional tax advisors as required to assess the tax implications of the deal and to investigate tax planning opportunities that may be available.

Common Mistakes	Possible Resolution
Demanding a remuneration level in the management contract based on ego satisfaction. This reduces the price paid for the equity of the company, which may result in a less tax-efficient transaction.	The seller should consider remuneration levels and other provisions of the management contract in the context of the overall deal structure.
Stage 7 — Negotiations	
Allowing too many individuals to be directly involved in the negotiations. This results in confusion and inconsistency, thereby eroding the seller's negotiating position.	The intermediary ideally should directly conduct negotiations. Other members of the seller's advisory team should provide the intermediary with input and advice.
Dealing with a single buyer prior to the LOI. This is harmful to the seller where the buyer believes that the seller has no other viable alternatives, thereby negating the seller's ability to develop a competitive bidding environment for the company.	Where a single buyer scenario does exist, the seller should contemplate other alternatives that may be available, such as finding an equity investor, an operator for the company or deferring the sale until a later date.
Executing an LOI that is ambiguous or not comprehensive. Any aspects of the deal that are not clearly addressed in the LOI are subject to negotiation afterwards, at a time when the seller's negotiating position may be diminished.	The seller should strive to have all the important aspects of the deal clearly documented in the LOI.
Stage 8 — Closing	
Allowing a lengthy exclusivity period. This increases the likelihood of an adverse change affecting the company, the industry or the economy in general.	The seller should negotiate a relatively short exclusivity period and obtain an affirmation statement from the buyer where possible.

Common Mistakes	Possible Resolution
Failing to maintain a strong negotiating position when negotiating the purchase agreement. This can result in the buyer negatively changing the price or terms of the deal compared to what was set out in the LOI.	The seller's negotiating position can be maintained where viable options remain available, such as retaining some degree of flexibility as to changes in the terms of the deal (within reason) or being able to readily re-ignite discussions with another buyer.
Ceasing to focus on the operations of the company throughout the closing period. This can lead to weaker financial and operating results and a weaker outlook for the company, which may cause the buyer to re-negotiate the deal prior to closing.	The seller should adopt a "business as usual" attitude in operating the company through the closing stage, to ensure that their negotiating position is not compromised.

Conclusion

The sale of a privately held company is one of the most significant monetary and emotional events in a business owner's lifetime. The *Value Enhancement Framework™* is designed to help guide business owners through what can be a very daunting process. It emphasizes that value, and value enhancement, are achieved through a combination of adequate planning and effective execution. The seller and their team of advisors should consider how value enhancement can be created and realized in each stage of the private company sale process.

While this book has addressed the stages and components normally involved in the private company sale process, and the initiatives for creating and realizing value enhancement, every situation is unique. Therefore, the business owner and their team of advisors should be flexible and should adapt the process and their decisions as necessary in order to react to issues and opportunities as they arise.

In the end, the business owner must be satisfied that they are receiving the best value for what their company has to offer, given the stated purchase price, the economic terms of the deal and intangible aspects of the deal that affect the owner's personal value system. Value is in the eye of the beholder. However, by understanding how economic value is established and how value enhancement can be created and realized through the sale process, business owners are in a better position to sell their privately held company on terms that help them to achieve their ultimate financial and personal goals.